For Lucile Coleman —
with best wishes
and memories of a
good evening at
Staten Island —

Van Allen Bradley

THE NEW
GOLD IN YOUR ATTIC

THE NEW
GOLD IN YOUR ATTIC

by

Van Allen Bradley

ℱ

FLEET PRESS CORPORATION
New York

PREFACE

Although *Gold in Your Attic* has been out of print for several years, there has been a steady demand for it from followers of the syndicated newspaper column "Gold in Your Attic" and from collectors, librarians, and booksellers. Most of the time, when copies were offered for sale they were at a premium; we even paid $12 a year or so ago to obtain a mint copy for a friend and found it something of a shock to realize that our own book about rare books had become a collector's item.

The first edition of *Gold in Your Attic* appeared in 1958, and although there were some revisions incorporated in the second printing, this new and revised edition is the first in which every individual listing has been reviewed and, where necessary, revised to bring it into line with the current book market. The task of revision has been under way for several years. It has been a tedious and detailed process, carried down to late in the summer of 1967 in order to provide the most up-to-date information possible. There have been vast changes in the rare book market in the period of almost a decade since *Gold in Your Attic* first appeared. Major sales of a great number of important libraries, especially literary collections and collections of historical Americana, have taken place both in America and abroad over the last decade. They have lifted price levels not only of individual titles but of related books in their general fields. In this new edition we have undertaken not only to record the upward price swings as reflected in the catalogues of rare book dealers but to supply relevant information from the auction market as well. This information (usually with the date of the auction record) is incorporated in the Price Index and Guide along with catalogue prices. The presentation is purposely informal and follows no strict bibliographical style. A further explanation of the method used in this compilation will be found in the Prefatory Notes to the Price Index and Guide.

We have also included much other new information in the revisions. In the first edition of *Gold in Your Attic* there were few inclusions of such bibliographical details as illustrations and binding. In revising the individual entries, we have tried, wherever possible, to include this information as an aid to identification. In a great many entries we have also provided further designations as to editions, printings, etc., and have clarified certain confusing points.

A final word on interpretation and use of the Price Guide and Index: In general, we have listed prices and price ranges *at retail* for books in *fine condition*. This means, of course, that in the case of modern books, where a dust jacket should normally be present, the top price figures are valid only for copies with jackets. Condition is always extremely important in determining the price level at which a book should sell.

Many of the entries reflect a range of prices from a number of sources, both at the retail level and/or at the auction level (which is essentially a "wholesale" market). For this reason, and to avoid an unnecessarily complicated and technical job of typesetting and editing, we have not keyed the individual entries to specific dealers or specific auction sales (except in the notations of auction sale dates). A listing of certain of the dealers whose catalogues we have drawn upon is included in the Prefatory Notes to the Price Index and Guide.

Van Allen Bradley

Barrington, Illinois
January 1968

CONTENTS

A PRIMER FOR BOOK HUNTERS

What about those old books in your attic? The chances are that most of them are worthless. On the other hand, they could be worth a small fortune. Consider the Maine woman who ran across a copy of Edgar Allan Poe's *Tamerlane* a few years ago. It was the rare 1827 first edition, paperbound, of which only 500 copies were printed —a book for which collectors have paid up to $20,000.

Literally hundreds of valuable books are buried away across the country in old book shelves, boxes, trunks, and other half-forgotten hiding places. For many of them, the law of supply and demand has established fabulous prices. Depending upon condition, scarcity and demand, certain old books are worth hundreds, even thousands of dollars. . . .

*　　　*　　　*

IT WAS ON SUCH A NOTE in November, 1957, that I began to write a weekly column of comment on old and rare books, entitled "Gold in Your Attic," for the *Chicago Daily News.*

The response from newspaper readers—an army of them, obviously hungry for "inside" information about the "mysterious" old book trade and eager for clues as to the values of their literary treasures—was immediate, and astonishing in its volume. Literally hundreds of letters poured in, not only from readers in the immediate circulation area of the *Daily News* but from every section of the country.

The idea for "Gold in Your Attic" had been many years a-borning. As long as I can remember, I have been a collector of books. And when the course of my newspaper writing led me gradually into the literary field, first as a reviewer and book columnist and then as the Literary Editor of a large metropolitan daily newspaper, the impulse to collect the books of my favorite authors and the books that deal with my special fields of interest grew even stronger.

No one can collect books for long—especially an impecunious newspaperman—without becoming aware of the phenomenon of *scarcity* of certain books in the old book stores, and of how that phenomenon, in concert with another phenomenon known as *demand,* forces the prices of desirable books higher and higher. In my case, the study of these phenomena of the rare book trade held a certain fascination; gradually it evolved from the status of a hobby to that of an avocational specialty. It has demanded, now that I reflect upon it, incredibly many more hours than I would have ever believed possible when it all began—as well as unconscionable amounts of energy and cash.

But it has all been a species of rare delight. In the course of it, I have somehow managed to accumulate, in addition to the books I wanted as a collector, a very large and very expensive bibliographical reference library; a tremendous stock of American and foreign bookseller catalogues, which have afforded me unending hours of absorbing study; and a formidable cross-reference file of bibliography and book-price information. I have further enjoyed an ever-changing and adventurous experience in the pursuit of elusive books in the great auction houses, in the towering, dusty stacks of rare and second-hand book stores from Boston to Biscayne Bay, from Deadwood to Acapulco, from Seminole to Syracuse, and in the attics and basements of innumerable friends, relatives, bare acquaintances, and perfect strangers.

It has also been my great good fortune to have numbered among my friends and counselors some of the greatest figures in the antiquarian book trade and some of the greatest collectors. From them I have been privileged to learn at first hand something about the inner workings of the rare book business. For their patience and tolerance in answering my innumerable questions, I am especially indebted to such rare friends and bookish companions as John Carter, the distinguished London bookman who is a member of the auction house of Sotheby & Company; Ralph Newman of Chicago's Abraham Lincoln Book Shop; Wright Howes of Chicago, the foremost authority on Americana; the late and lamented Ben Abramson, a bookman of the old school, and others prominent in the world of rare books.

Over the years of these antiquarian adventurings, one thing that always impressed me was the fact that to the average book lover the old book business is pretty much a mystery. He looks at his prized possessions and vaguely wonders from time to time about their value. But seldom has he had the time or the know-how to make his own inquiries into the very complex fields of bibliographical research and the study of book prices that occupy the antiquarian bookseller.

It was primarily for this type of book owner—the general reader and lover of good literature and of interesting and absorbing books in any number of fields—that "Gold in Your Attic" was developed. The kind of general and representative information that has been passed along in this weekly column is available to anyone who will take the trouble to dig it out through personal endeavor and the study of a multitude of widely scattered reference works, but there are few who can or will make the effort.

That there existed a real need among the general public for this kind of information became even more apparent to me early in 1958, when General Features Corporation acquired the syndication rights to "Gold in Your Attic" and began its nationwide distribution. As in the case of the *Daily News* readers, the response of readers of other newspapers was an avalanche of mail.

The limitations of newspaper space, as well as the inexorable pressures of time upon myself and those who assist in handling the column correspondence, have made it impossible for me to write a personal reply to all the many thousands of readers who have written in. However, all their letters have been read and the inquiries evaluated. This book, which includes excerpts from the first year's columns, plus a great amount of other information on rare books and their prices, is an effort to answer as many of those reader questions as possible.

*　　　　*　　　　*

What kinds of books are valuable?

Any book that is important is potentially valuable. Its value probably will depend on how many copies of it are available and how many people want it. In other words, there are three influences that determine a book's value—importance, supply, and demand.

The kinds of books that are potentially valuable include the whole range of printed materials—from a paperbound guide for emigrants of the gold rush period to the poems of Edna St. Vincent Millay on Japan vellum.

In the main, however, there are two dominant categories of valuable books on the American collector's market today—Americana and the first editions of important books or of important authors.

What is Americana?

It is the historical literature of the American scene—in the hemisphere sense—anything that deals with the history, exploration and development of the New World. The term, Americana, as Wright Howes has pointed out, is loosely used for what is really "U. S.-iana" (and Mr. Howes in 1954 published a bibliographical checklist of Americana under the title "U. S.-iana" to get his point across). It is literally true, as he suggests, that modern collectors of Americana are interested almost wholly in the United States scene and not in Canada, Mexico, or the other Americas.

Specifically, any book published up to about 1875 in any of the following fields is typical Americana, and is potentially valuable: State, county and local history; adventure, travel and explorations; Indians and Indian captivities; almanacs; Indian laws and treaties; territorial laws; overland narratives; travel, atlases and view books; Utah and the Mormons; the Old Northwest; the Middle West; the Far West; state laws and constitutions; the Confederacy; railroads and canals; Davy Crockett; Daniel Boone; Mike

Fink; Andrew Jackson; the Black Hills gold rush; the California gold rush; Colorado and the mines; the Kansas gold rush; Oklahoma and oil; Texas and cattle; the Great Plains and the Rockies; sporting and hunting; the Northwest Coast; the fur trade; the Dakotas; Arizona; California; Oregon; Indian fighting on the Western frontier; outlaws and badmen; government documents; Alabama; Florida; Georgia; Louisiana; Mississippi; etc.

What is a first edition?

A first edition, in the book-collecting sense, is the first appearance of a work between book covers. (For a fuller explanation, please turn to the section of this book entitled "Brief Dictionary for Book Hunters.")

How can one tell a first edition from another edition?

There is no absolute answer. A general rule of thumb is that a book probably is a first edition if the date on the title page agrees with the copyright date (on the reverse of the title page). This is not always true, however. Some books are published without a dated title page. In the case of undated books, it is necessary to pursue the question of which edition is the first by looking up the book in the catalogue of a large library. The librarian usually can help you by referring you either to a bibliography of the author concerned or to some general reference work in the field of rare books such as Jacob Blanck's multi-volume *Bibliography of American Literature* or Merle Johnson's *American First Editions*.

In some instances, identifying a first edition can be tricky, as in the case of identically dated books of variant issue. The variations that occur in some books cause book collectors to break a first edition down into various issues or states. Take a well-known case in point: Henry Wadsworth Longfellow's *The Song of Hiawatha* was published in Boston in 1855. However, not every copy dated 1855 is a true first edition. The valuable *first issue* of the first edition bears advertisements that are dated "November, 1855." This is the "point" that determines whether this book is worth a top price or something less. Other points in other books might be a missing letter in a word, where the type broke down in printing; a misspelled word; differences in binding cloth; the insertion of an errata slip; differences in the end papers, etc. The Blanck and Johnson books are helpful in identifying points.

Many modern book publishers have adopted the practice of indicating a "first edition" on the reverse of the title page. Sometimes a publisher similarly will identify a book as a "second printing" or a "second edition," etc. But there is no standard practice in this respect, and every book therefore constitutes something of a challenge to the book hunter.

Why do collectors want first editions?

This is a hard one to answer, but the first printed form of a favorite author's work is usually the form most desired by an admirer. As a consequence, first editions are generally more valuable than later editions, especially in the creative fields of poetry, fiction and the drama. Likewise, it is almost always true that the first edition of any great or monumental book in any field of human endeavor— medicine, the arts, science, agriculture, history, discovery, etc.—is the most valuable edition. And because a first edition printing order tends to be somewhat limited in size, every important book bears with it the prospect of eventually becoming a collector's item.

Who are some of the important authors whose works are valuable in the first edition?

Among the older authors whose first editions are generally sought after are Washington Irving, James Fenimore Cooper, Herman Melville, Edgar Allan Poe, Ralph Waldo Emerson, Henry Wadsworth Longfellow, Nathaniel Hawthorne, and Oliver Wendell Holmes. Among the late 19th century authors, the firsts of Bret Harte, Mark Twain, Lafcadio Hearn, and Stephen Crane all command good prices. Among the moderns, Ernest Hemingway, William Faulkner, John Steinbeck, and Eugene O'Neill are currently in favor.

Recently one of New York City's top specialists in rare first editions advertised his willingness to "pay good prices" for first editions, inscribed copies and association copies, letters and manuscripts of the following authors: Henry Adams, Stephen Vincent Benet, Willa Cather, Samuel Langhorne Clemens (Mark Twain), Winston Churchill, Baron Corvo (Fr. Wolfe), Stephen Crane, Emily Dickinson, Norman Douglas, A. Conan Doyle, T. S. Eliot, William Faulkner, F. Scott Fitzgerald, Robert Frost, Eric Gill, Lafcadio Hearn, Ernest Hemingway, Dard Hunter, James Joyce, D. H. Lawrence, T. E. Lawrence, Sinclair Lewis, Somerset Maugham, Herman Melville, Edna St. Vincent Millay, Eugene O'Neill, Ezra Pound, Carl Sandburg, Bernard Shaw, John Steinbeck, Dylan Thomas, Henry David Thoreau, Walt Whitman, Woodrow Wilson, Thomas Wolfe, Virginia Woolf, Elinor Wylie, and William Butler Yeats.

Are all books marked "First Edition" valuable?

Of course not. As a general rule, it is the great books in the various fields of human endeavor, the enduring and the permanent books that are in demand; and it is principally the important works of the important authors in the creative fields that become collector's items. You must therefore study books as books, as contributions to the field of human knowledge and human experience, as well as physical objects, before you can begin to assess their value in monetary terms.

How can I determine the value of my old books?

The first step in determining a book's value is to determine what you have. Find out if the book is a first edition or just another old book. Find out if it has any basic importance at all. It may be that the question of edition is not too important. In some fields—Americana, for example—a second, third, fourth, or fifth edition may have value. Consult the index included in this book. If your book is not listed there, try the reference book *American Book-Prices Current* at your public library. This is an annual series that reports on the sales of books at auction (see AUCTION in "Brief Dictionary for Book Hunters" elsewhere in this volume). Except for the higher priced rarities, the auction prices, largely made by dealers, are "wholesale" prices. (Read the items carefully, however, since auction prices may vary widely because of differences in the condition of books offered for sale.) If your book is in good condition, it should be worth half again or twice as much as the prices quoted in the auction lists. If, after studying the available price records you still are in doubt as to your book's value, the best thing to do is to confer with a reputable rare book dealer. He should be willing to pay you from one third to half its retail value if he has an immediate prospect of sale; on books he buys for stock he probably will offer 20 to 30 per cent, which is considered fair in view of the nature of the market.

Where can I find an honest book dealer?

The overwhelming majority of rare book dealers are reputable and honest businessmen operating under high professional standards. Stay away from the junk shops and cheaper second-hand stores, where books are often bought by the pound. Few of the dealers in this category know anything or care anything about rare books. Your best bet is to get in touch with a bookseller who is a member of the Antiquarian Booksellers Association of America.

This association of bookmen is a nonprofit organization established in 1949 to maintain high standards in the rare book field and to stimulate book collecting by private collectors and public institutions. Write to the ABAA offices at 630 Fifth Avenue, New York, New York 10020, for a complete list of members. Enclose a stamped, self-addressed envelope.

Shall I take my book collection to a dealer?

This is not advised unless he invites you to do so. The bookseller may be a specialist in another field and totally disinterested. Send him a description of what you have and ask if he wants to see it. Again, enclose a stamped, self-addressed envelope.

Do you mean a list of my books?

No. A bookseller has neither the time nor the inclination to examine a long list of books. Instead, investigate carefully what you have, and select only the most likely items to describe.

What do you mean by describe? How do you do it?

Write out a detailed and correct description of each book. Use the following form (a recommendation of the ABAA):

AUTHOR:
TITLE:
SIZE (give size of pages in inches):
BINDING (full leather, half leather, cloth, paper cover):
PUBLISHER AND PLACE WHERE PUBLISHED:
DATE (if no date on title, give copyright date on reverse of title):
NUMBER OF PAGES AND ILLUSTRATIONS (plain or colored):
CONDITION (inside and out; state if stains and tears are present):

As the ABAA adds in its instructions, "The bookseller can then decide whether the book is worth anything to him and if so will ask to see it. It can be sent by insured parcel post (book rate) or Railway Express prepaid, and he will return it the same way if you do not come to an agreement. If the books to be sold are numerous and important enough to justify the expense, the bookseller will travel to see them. Before he can decide to do this, he must have a general description of the contents of the library (for example: Americana, theology, or old novels, etc.), a detailed description of the more important titles, and the approximate number of volumes. Valuable books must be seen before an appraisal can be given; pages have to be counted, illustrations and plates carefully checked.

It is obvious that a valuation cannot be given over the telephone."

What if I want to sell my book at retail instead of taking a dealer's "wholesale" price?

Then you must seek out your own buyer. Getting in touch with book collectors should not be too difficult, but it will require some time and an expenditure of effort on your part. To start, inquire among the clubs and organizations that cater to the particular field of interest represented by your book. The officers of these clubs may know of collectors within their ranks who will be interested in what you have. Further, they may know of publications that cater to their members, and an advertisement in such a publication could make a sale for you. Hunt out the interests of private buyers in *Who's Who* and other references. Ask your librarian for directories of college and public libraries, special collections, museums, historical societies, and other institutional buyers. The American Book Collector, 1822 School Street, Chicago, Illinois, 60657, sometimes has a collector's list for sale at $1. Collectors also advertise for books in this magazine and in Hobbies, 1006 South Michigan Avenue, Chicago 60605; Antique Trader, Box 327, Kewanee, Illinois, 61443, and Collectors News, Box 156, Grundy Center, Iowa, 50638.

Caution: Before you attempt to sell your book to a private collector, be sure on two points: 1) Know what you have and ask a fair price; 2) Be absolutely scrupulous in your description of the book's condition.

How can I describe my book's condition?

Before we go into that, take a tip from the Antiquarian

Booksellers Association's bulletin on the importance of condition:

"Even in a book of exceptional rarity and importance, the state of both the book and the binding, whether cloth, paper cover or contemporary leather, is important to its value. Any collector prefers a fine copy to a battered one, and a rebound copy finds little favor, except in rare cases, since *fine original* condition is the collector's choice. A loosened group of pages is a defect, but a more serious one is a missing page. A leaf should never be torn out of a book. Any deficiency reduces the value of a book or even may make it worthless. Music books, children's books, navigation books, cook books—all material which by its very nature would have been much handled—can obviously seldom be found in really fine state. Old pamphlets in paper covers may be of value if they contain source material."

All right, condition is important, I see.
But how do I describe my books?

Just state in the simplest, plainest terms what, if anything, is wrong with your book. If it is fresh and clean and apparently as good as when first issued, describe it as "fresh and clean and apparently as good as when first issued." (The dealer will understand, although he would describe it in his catalogue as "Mint.") If it is very fine but not perfect, just say, "Very Fine." (The bookseller's equivalent would be simply, "Fine.") If it is very good but not quite very fine, describe it as "Very Good." (The bookseller uses "Very Good" also.) If it is simply good, say it is "Good." (That is the bookseller's term also.) If it is somewhat soiled but still useful and presentable, describe it as "Fair." (The bookseller's term is also "Fair.")

If there are serious defects in your book, be very plain and specific: Describe them as "Title page missing," "Thirteen pages missing, pages 26 through 38," "Covers missing," "Half of spine missing," etc. Don't leave the bookseller in doubt.

All right. But back to my question of selling at retail. Are there any magazines that cater to collectors in which I might advertise?

Yes. All four of the publications mentioned two pages back will accept your advertising, as will many other specialized hobby publications. *Caution:* In advertising or writing to collectors, describe your books with the same degree of scrupulous accuracy you use in dealing with booksellers. Remember that there are federal laws against using the mails to defraud.

Let's be specific. What is my grandmother's old Bible worth?

I'll let the Antiquarian Booksellers Association speak on this subject:

"It should be borne in mind that the *Bible* is the most frequently reprinted book of the Western world, and by its nature the one book most carefully treasured by its owners. In many households it was the only book. Therefore as a text it is not scarce. Many editions, even of the later 15th century, during the first 50 years of printing, are comparatively common and worth very little. Rare and important editions are easily recognized by experts: the *Gutenberg Bible,* circa 1450-1455, generally considered to be the first printed book; the *Mentelin Bible* of 1460, in German; the first *Bible* in each language; the first polyglot; the first authorized *(King James)* version; the first *Indian Bible,* etc. Then there are oddities such as the *Breeches Bible,* the *Vinegar Bible,* the *wicked Bible,* which command special prices for some misprint or curious phrase in the text.

"Although of sentimental value, it is fairly safe to say of all the rest that they are valueless in the commercial market, and by this is meant anything in excess of $10.00. An exception to this might be if the *Bible* belonged to a distinguished or important family and has extensive family records written in it."

Many hundreds of readers have written to "Gold in Your Attic" about old *Bibles,* despite repeated statements that I have published which say essentially what the ABAA says in its bulletin. For those who wish to pursue the subject further, I recommend a reading of Edwin A. R. Rumball-Petre's *Rare Bibles* (New York, 1938; revised, 1954), which contains a descriptive checklist of all the important *Bibles* of the world.

What about my old copy of the Ulster County Gazette *of January 4, 1800?*

There are few old newspapers of value. Those that are important have been reprinted often in facsimile, and it is difficult to distinguish between an original and a copy. If you believe you have a rarity and want to check further, take it to a specialist dealer who knows old newspapers. Or write to the Periodical Division of the Library of Congress, Washington, D. C. 20402, for its bulletin on the phony reprints that have fooled so many, among them the *Ulster County Gazette,* the wallpaper editions of the *Vicksburg Gazette,* and the *New York Herald* reporting Lincoln's assassination, etc.

I have a price guide to old books that was published

some years ago. Is it dependable today?

It can be helpful as a general guide, but it cannot be depended upon unless it is kept in continuous revision. The book market is always changing. Generally, the tendency is for important books to climb steadily in value. However, in certain fields, particularly literary first editions, the fickle taste of the public is often inclined to let an author down, whereupon his books begin to decline in value. An example is Kipling, whose prices have been down for some years now because he is much less popular than he once was. Another is James Branch Cabell, whose *Jurgen* once commanded as much as $150 in the first edition, signed. A fine copy in the original dust jacket, is worth about half that today. William Faulkner, Ernest Hemingway, Willa Cather, and William Butler Yeats are authors whose first editions have risen sharply in value in recent years. Time alone will tell whether their prices will go higher and higher—or whether public taste will let them down. In the field of historical Americana, however, the tendency of books to decline in value is negligible; almost invariably they continue to move upward.

BRIEF DICTIONARY FOR
BOOK HUNTERS

ADVANCE COPY: A first edition copy, usually the first from the presses and therefore a first issue, released by a publisher in advance of the scheduled publication date. These are usually copies sent out for advance reading to specialists, from whom comment is solicited; to booksellers and to reviewers. They are sometimes specially bound, or they may be left unbound and wrapped in plain wrappers or a dust wrapper.

AMERICANA: Any book dealing historically with the American scene. The term may be applied in bookseller usage to maps, broadsides, pamphlets, prints, and other printed materials, as well as to books.

ANONYMOUS: A book published without the name of the author being given. An example: James Fenimore Cooper's two-volume, *The Spy: A Tale of the Neutral Ground,* published in 1821. Instead of carrying Cooper's byline, the title page merely stated that the book was "By the Author of *Precaution.*"

ASSOCIATION COPY: Any book which bears an identifiable relationship to the author, or to some famous person, through the inclusion of a signature, a photograph or letter (laid in), or other tangible evidence. Collectors pay premium prices for items in this category.

AUCTION PRICES: The prices realized by books sold at auction. The larger auction centers for books are New York and London. In general, the prices realized are indicative of wholesale or bookseller values, since these auctions are largely attended by booksellers or representatives of collectors. They do not therefore provide a very accurate gauge of retail book values, unless the interpreter is a bookseller or has a knowledge of the book trade. The major American sales are recorded, and the prices (over $5) are published annually in *American Book-Prices Current,* edited by Edward Lazare. There are also cumulative five-year volumes in the Lazare series.

AUTOGRAPHED COPY: A book signed by the author.

BACKSTRIP: The spine of a book, or the part that is visible when it is lined up with other books on a shelf. The term "back" is also used to indicate the backstrip or spine. Often the strip is made of some material other than the rest of the binding, as for example in a board-bound book with a cloth backstrip.

BIBLIOGRAPHY: A systematically arranged listing of books (usually in alphabetical order) about a special field of interest or about an author. A bibliography of an author includes all his published works. (For detailed information on bibliographical practice, see Ronald McKerrow's *An Introduction to Bibliography.*)

BIBLIOPHILE: A lover of books.

BIBLIOPHOBE: A hater of books. This may refer to the wife of a book collector.

BINDING: The cover of a book.

BINDER'S TITLE: The makeshift title, or title chosen for convenience, applied by a bookbinder and imprinted on the cover of a collection of material issued without an overall title or without a title page and specially bound.

BLIND STAMPING: The ornamental impressions or toolings on a binding which have not been colored or gilded.

BOOKPLATE: A printed slip pasted to an end paper or flyleaf of a book by an owner to indicate ownership. Unless the bookplate is that of a well-known personage, it generally downgrades the value of a book. Ideally, a bookplate should never be affixed permanently to a book but merely tipped in with rubber cement, so that it can be removed, if necessary, without a trace of damage.

BUCKRAM: A type of coarse linen used as a binding cloth. It is more expensive and more durable than ordinary book cloth.

CALENDERED PAPER: Specially treated paper with a hard, slick finish.

CALFBOUND: Bound with leather made from calf skin. Many old books still survive with original calf and sheep skin bindings, although with age the tendency of leather bindings is to deteriorate unless specially treated to prevent this.

CASE: A book's cover.

COLLATE: To check a book page by page, leaf by leaf, to see that flyleaves, printed pages, plates, etc., are all present in proper sequence as known and recorded by bibliographers. In the case of extremely rare and expensive books, the collation is especially important, since even the absence of a required blank page or flyleaf can materially reduce the price a collector will pay for the book.

COLOPHON: A final notice, usually at the back of a book, in which is given the name of the printer or publisher, the date and place of publication, and sometimes, in the case of a limited edition, the size of the edition or the number of copies printed. Few modern books are published with a colophon, since most of the information is generally carried on the title page.

COLOR PLATES: Colored illustrations included in a book. Originally the color plates were hand-colored, but the term is now applied loosely to mechanically processed color illustrations.

COMPILER (abbreviated "comp."): One who compiles a book or brings its contents together from various sources, usually with the addition of an introduction or notes.

CONDITION: The physical state of a book, especially with regard to its preservation. This is the single most important influence affecting a book's price, aside from rarity or scarcity. A thorough study of Part III of this book will afford numerous illustrations of the manner in which condition affects prices. Reputable booksellers describe their books accurately as to condition.

CONTEMPORARY BINDING: A book binding which, while not necessarily the original binding in which the book was issued, dates, or apparently dates, from the same period in which the book was published.

COPYRIGHT PAGE: In most books, the back, or verso, of the title page. In addition to the copyright date, the copyright page may carry other important information relating to the book, including the date of publication, the name of the author, the name of the printer, the number of copies printed, etc.

CORNERS: The fore-edge extremities, top and bottom, of a book cover. Sometimes the corners are protected, either in the original binding or later, with cloth, paper, metal or leather pieces covering them.

COVERS BOUND IN: Used to describe the process of re-binding a book and preserving the original binding by including it, usually at the end, as evidence of the book's authenticity. The process is resorted to only when the covers have begun to deteriorate or are in danger of being destroyed. A book with original covers intact is usually more valuable than one that has been rebound in this manner.

CUT: Illustration, or the engraving itself, from which the illustration is printed.

DAMPSTAINED: Pages or covers stained or discolored by dampness or excess humidity. Such damage is usually not as serious as waterstaining. (See: FOXED.)

DECKLE EDGE: Rough, irregular fore-edge and top and bottom edge of a leaf, usually occurring in hand-made paper but sometimes produced in machine-made papers.

DENTELLE: Lace-like design on the binding of a book, usually executed near the edges of the covers. An inner dentelle is on the inside page.

DESIDERATA: List of wanted books submitted to a bookseller by a librarian or collector.

DOUBLURE: A term used in fine binding for a leather panel glued to the inside of a book's cover. Usually used together with a facing silk or cloth end leaf.

DUODECIMO: A book size, sometimes written "12mo." or "twelvemo," indicating a book printed on paper folded into 12 leaves.

DUST WRAPPER (also dust jacket): Protective cover, usually printed or pictorial paper, issued with the book by its publisher. A mint copy of a book should have a mint dust wrapper, if one is issued, to have the highest value.

ED.: Abbreviation for "edition" or for "editor."

EDITION: The whole number of books ordered by a publisher to be printed at one time.

8VO.: Abbreviation for the octavo book size, eight leaves folded, about 6 by 9 inches.

ELEPHANT FOLIO: Large book size, about 14 by 20 inches, sometimes used in art books. (Audubon's *The Birds of America* was an elephant folio set.)

END PAPER: The double leaf—blank, printed or decorated —at the beginning and the end of a book. The outside half of each end paper is pasted to the inside cover of the book.

ERRATA SLIP: A printed slip listing the errors in a book that have been discovered after printing. Usually pasted in or tipped in but sometimes laid in.

EX-LIBRARY COPY: A discard from a library, usually bearing a library stamp or other such indication. Such books are generally worthless as collector's items because they are worn or damaged.

EXTRA-ILLUSTRATED: Said of a book which has been expanded by its owner with the pasting in or tipping in of extra illustrations from sources outside the book. Sometimes the book is rebound to care for the expansion. Usually such copies are less valuable than before, unless the work has been done by the author himself or some famous person.

FACSIMILE: An exact copy or duplication of a book.

FIRST EDITION (abbreviated "1st ed."): The first printing or first issue of a book. A first edition, however, may have several "issues"—first, second, third, etc.—but the first issue is usually the most valuable. Further, the issues of an edition may by divided into "states." To be more explicit—a separate issue of an edition is one in which the type has been changed in some manner. A separate state of an issue is a condition of the issue in which there may be other noticeable changes; for example: a breaking down of type, which shows up in the printed page; a change in the binding of the book; the insertion of an errata slip, etc. Book collectors are inclined to much hair-splitting over the fine points of edition, issue and state, and it is their demands that make one book more valuable than another.

FLYLEAF: The blank leaf (or leaves) between the end papers and the printing at the beginning and the end of a book.

FOLDING MAP (and folding plate): A large map or illustration for a book printed on a sheet larger than the book page and folded into the book to protect it. Books with the plate or plates missing or torn are considerably less valuable than books with the folding matter intact.

FORE-EDGE PAINTING: An art form, executed in water color on the front edge of a book with the leaves bent back to expose a greater area of the edges than is shown when the book is closed in normal position. After the painting is completed, the book is closed and a heavy coat of gilt applied to conceal the painting. After drying, the leaves may be riffled or flexed to expose the painting. Some collectors go in for fore-edge paintings, which achieved their greatest popularity in the first part of the 19th century, but fore-edge painting is rarely ever practiced any more.

FORMAT: The general makeup of a book as to size, binding, paper, stock, typography, etc.

4TO.: Abbreviation for the quarto book size, about 9 by 12 inches.

FOXED: Said of a book's pages when they are spotted, stained, browned, yellowed, molded, or otherwise discolored or damaged—because of the rusting of iron in the paper as a result of dampness, because of the growth of bacteria in the paper, or because of chemical stains originating in the chemical impurities in paper. Experts on the rehabilitation of books can sometimes remove the foxing by washing and bleaching the pages, but the process is tedious and therefore expensive. Foxing is common in books 100 or more years old. A foxed book is less desirable than one that has survived with bright, clean pages. Foxing in a modern book is inexcusable and will downgrade its value.

GILT EDGE (and gilt top): Fore-edges or top edges of books

to which gilt, or gold, has been applied.

HALF-BOUND (half cloth, half leather, etc.): Said of a book in which the covers are bound in one material (cloth, paper or boards, etc.) and the spine in another (leather or cloth).

HALF TITLE: A leaf appearing in some books in advance of the title page and carrying only the title (or a shortened form of it). Sometimes referred to as the "bastard title."

HEADBAND: A reinforcing strip of fabric glued to the spine or backstrip of a book at the top edge of the leaves. A footband is a similar strip at the bottom of the spine.

HINGE: The flexible point in a leather, cloth or paper binding where the covers of a book and the backstrip meet. The terms "hinges cracking" or "hinges weak" are commonly encountered in booksellers' catalogues.

IN PRINT: Said of a book still in stock with the publisher and available from him at regular prices.

INSCRIBED COPY: A book especially inscribed to a particular person by the author and named in the inscription. Same as a "presentation copy."

JAPAN VELLUM: A type of high quality, heavy-weight, slick-surfaced rice paper, resembling vellum. Used principally in expensive limited editions.

JOINTS: Same as "hinges," which see.

LABEL: Printed paper, cloth or leather slip glued to the spine of a book or to the cover and containing the name of the book, name of the author and, in some cases, other information.

LAID IN: Said of any extraneous material—a letter, an

autographed slip, an errata slip, a photograph, a section of manuscript, etc.—placed in a book but not attached to it.

LARGE PAPER COPY: A book printed from the same type as the regular edition but on paper of extra large size with larger margins. Most large paper copies are printed on higher grade paper than that used in the regular edition.

LEVANT: A common term for Levant morocco, a bookbinding leather made from Levantine goat skins.

LIMITED EDITION: An edition consisting of a certain specified number of copies and no more. A limited edition may or may not be a first edition. In some cases, limited editions are numbered and signed by the author.

MINT: A bookseller term used to describe a book that is in flawless or immaculate condition, just as issued by the publisher. Mint copies are the most desirable from a collector's standpoint. If a dust wrapper is issued with the book, it must accompany the mint copy and be in mint condition itself for the book to be classified as mint.

MOROCCO: A leather made from goat skins tanned with sumac. It was first introduced into the European book trade from Morocco, hence its name. In the modern book trade, there is much reference made to morocco leather that is not actually morocco.

NO DATE (abbreviated "n. d."): Notation made by a bookseller to indicate that a book contains no date on its title page. The date sometimes may appear elsewhere in the book, or it may be known to the bookseller, in which case it is indicated in his catalogue in parentheses.

Example: "No place (Milwaukee), 1879."

NO PLACE (abbreviated "n. p."): Notation made by a bookseller to indicate that the book contains no place of publication on its title page. If the bookseller knows the place of publication, he will so state in parentheses. Example: "No place (Milwaukee), 1879."

OCTAVO: A book size, about 6 by 9 inches, achieved by printing eight leaves (16 pages on a sheet of paper).

ORIGINAL CLOTH (or binding): As issued by the publisher.

OUT OF PRINT (abbreviated "o. p."): Said of a book when the publisher's stocks are completely depleted and no other copies are available through him. A desired book's price begins to rise when it goes out of print.

PAPERBOUND: Said of a book or pamphlet whose covers are of paper or cardboard. Referred to in bookseller catalogues as "wrappers," "pictorial wrappers," etc.

PART: A part of a book published separately from the rest, usually in paper covers, in advance of book publication. Many of the novels of Charles Dickens and other 19th century novelists appeared first in parts. The original parts are the most desirable form, in the view of collectors. They are difficult to find in good condition, because of their fragile form, and therefore expensive.

PASTEBOARD: A bookbinding board made of sheets of paper pasted together.

POINT: An identifying characteristic by which one determines the edition, issue or state of a book. It can be any one of numerous variations that occur in the publication of a book—a typographical error, damage to a line of type, etc.

PP.: Abbreviation for "pages."

PRESENTATION COPY: Same as "inscribed copy," which see.

PSEUDONYM: The pen-name or assumed name of an author. Example: Mark Twain was the pseudonym of Samuel Langhorne Clemens.

QUARTO: A book size, about 9 by 12 inches, achieved by folding printed sheets into four leaves to make eight pages.

RARE: Said of books which are extremely scarce and hard to find. Most booksellers agree that a book is not really rare unless there are only a few copies known to exist outside of libraries and known collections. Rarity itself does not make a book valuable, however; it is the combination of scarcity and demand that creates talked-about prices.

REBACKED: Said of a book from which the original back-strip or spine has been removed and a new back substituted. A rebacked book is less valuable than a book with original spine.

REBOUND: Said of a book in which the original binding has been replaced.

RECASED: Said of a book which has had its covers replaced by a new case or binding but which has not been renewed, as in rebinding.

RUBBED: Said of a binding which shows evidence of wear or rubbing.

SCARCE: As used by booksellers, this means a book not easy to find but not necessarily in the rare category. An out-of-print book tends within a few years to become scarce if there is much demand for it.

SCOUT: A book speculator who scouts out scarce and rare books, buys them if he finds them underpriced and then resells them to a book dealer or to a collector. In the larger cities, there are scouts who make a comfortable living through such operations.

SCUFFED: Said of a leatherbound book which is gouged, rubbed, or otherwise worn.

SEWED: A term used to describe a method of binding in which a book or pamphlet is stitched together with thread. Usually bound with paper covers or wrappers.

SIGNATURE: A section of a book—8, 12, 16 or 32 pages.

SLIP CASE: A protective case for a book, made of cardboard or pasteboard, covered with paper, cloth or leather, and especially made to fit a specific book.

SPINE: Same as "backstrip," which see.

STARTED: Said of a signature which has become loose or sprung. A book with signature started should be taken to a bookbinder for tightening.

STITCHED: Sewed but lacking a separate cover.

TITLE PAGE (or title): The page at the front of a book which contains the title of the book, the author's byline, the place of publication, the date of publication and other pertinent information. Sometimes a part of this information may be lacking, in which case reference to bibliographical works is required.

12MO. (or twelvemo): Same as "duodecimo," which see.

UNCUT: A term meaning that the edges of the leaves of a book are not trimmed.

UNOPENED: Used to indicate that the untrimmed fore-edges of a book's leaves have not been cut apart. (It is a terrible thing so say, but an unopened book is more valuable in the collector's market than one that has been opened.)

VELLUM: The skin of calves, lambs or young goats, prepared for writing, printing or bookbinding.

VERSO: The reverse of a book page; a left-hand page.

WATERSTAINED: Stained or discolored by water. More difficult to remedy than dampstaining, because water damage often shrinks a page or a binding.

WRAPPERS: The paper covers of a book or a pamphlet. (See: PAPERBOUND.) Books in wrappers often attain great rarity because of their fragile nature. A book originally appearing in wrappers is usually much less valuable if it has been rebound in cloth or leather. (See: COVERS BOUND IN.)

A LIBRARY FOR BOOK HUNTERS

ON MY DESK as I write this there lies a catalogue of reference books about books that contains 1,356 entries. Each of these bibliographies and reference works contains information that would at one time or other be of practical assistance to the working bookman, be he librarian, bookseller, or collector.

It is obviously impossible and impracticable for the book hunter to assemble such a large library of working tools. There are, however, certain basic books that I have found to be indispensable in my own collecting and in my writing about old and rare books. The list of these is appended here, along with a supplemental list for those who are interested.

Basic List:

ADAMS, Ramon F. *Six-Guns and Saddle Leather.* University of Oklahoma Press, Norman, Okla., 1954. A bibliography of books and pamphlets about Western outlaws and gunmen. Contains 1,132 items with critical descriptions. Illustrated with title pages.

BENNETT, Whitman. *A Practical Guide to American Book Collecting (1666-1940).* Bennett Book Studios, Inc., New York, no date (1941). A chronological arrangement of notable American books. Especially valuable for its detailed descriptions of first edition "points."

BLANCK, Jacob S. *Bibliography of American Literature*. Vols. 1, 2, 3, and 4. Yale University Press, New Haven, Conn., 1955-57-59-63. The first four volumes of the most exhaustive bibliographical reference work ever attempted in the field of American literature. A superb reference series.

CARTER, John. *ABC for Book-Collectors*. Alfred A. Knopf, New York, no date. An alphabetic dictionary for book collectors, containing a vast amount of information on little-known phases of the endeavor. By Britain's foremost authority.

CARTER, John. *Taste and Technique in Book-Collecting*. R. R. Bowker Company, New York, 1948.

CARTER, John. *Books and Book-Collectors*. World Publishing Company, Cleveland, no date (1957).

DE RICCI, Seymour. *The Book Collector's Guide*. Philadelphia, 1921. A handbook of American and British bibliography. Useful for reference, despite the fact that the prices are out of date and unreliable.

DOBIE, J. Frank. *Guide to Life and Literature of the Southwest*. Southern Methodist University Press, Dallas, 1952. Revised edition of an excellent critical guidebook.

FULLERTON, B. M. *Selective Bibliography of American Literature, 1775-1900*. Dial Press, New York, 1936. Covers representative works of the most important authors. Helpful on first edition "points."

HARWELL, Richard Barksdale. *Cornerstones of Confederate Collecting*. University of Virginia Press, Charlottesville, 1953. 2d, revised, edition. A thin but indispensable volume with much information on a little known field.

HEARD, J. Norman. *Bookman's Guide to Americana.* Scarecrow Press, Metuchen, N. J., 1967. A price list, including the cheapest books, based on catalogue listings. (Beginning to be out of date now on many items.)

HENDERSON, Robert W. *Early American Sports.* A. S. Barnes & Company, New York, 1953. Excellent bibliography, containing much hard-to-find information.

HOWES, Wright. *U. S.-iana (1650-1950).* R. R. Bowker Company, New York, 1963. The most useful single work of bibliographical information in the Americana field. Classifies 11,620 separate items into five broad price ranges but offers no specific price information. (This is the enlarged edition of Howes' pioneering Americana list, first published in 1954. Both editions are out of print.)

JOHNSON, Merle. *American First Editions.* Revised and enlarged by Jacob Blanck. New York, no date (1947). A basic work on the identification of important editions.

MUMEY, Nolie. *A Study of Rare Books.* Clason Publishing Company, Denver, 1930. Profusely illustrated with colophons, printers' devices and title pages of European and American books. Instructive for beginner or veteran.

QUINN, Arthur Hobson (editor). *The Literature of the American People.* Appleton-Century-Crofts, Inc., New York, no date (1951). An historical and critical survey, including hard-to-find-information on many obscure American books and authors.

SPILLER, Robert E. and others. *Literary History of the United States.* Revised one-volume edition. Mac-

millan Company, New York, 1953. A superb basic
guidebook.

WEMYSS, Stanley. *The General Guide to Rare Americana*. New Enlarged Edition. Philadelphia, 1952.
Bibliographical and price information on some of the
rarer books in the field. (Prices are out of date, but the
book has material not found easily elsewhere.)

WRIGHT, Lyle. H. *American Fiction, 1774-1850*, and
American Fiction, 1851-1875. Huntington Library,
San Marino, Calif., 1957. An excellent bibliograph-
ical series.

Supplemental List:

ADAMS, Bess Porter. *About Books and Children*.
Henry Holt and Company, New York, no date (1953).
A history of children's literature.

BOUTELL, H. S. *First Editions of To-day and How to
Tell Them*. Revised edition. J. B. Lippincott Company, Philadelphia, 1939.

HART, James D. *The Popular Book: A History of
America's Literary Taste*. Oxford University Press,
New York, 1950.

HACKETT, Alice Payne. *Sixty Years of Best Sellers,
1895-1955*. R. R. Bowker Company, New York, 1955.

MOTT, Frank Luther. *Golden Multitudes: The Story
of Best Sellers in the United States*. Macmillan Company, New York, 1947.

ROSKIE, Philip M. *The Bookman's Bible*. Roskie &
Wallace Bookstore, Oakland, Calif., 1957. A coded
guide, useful to book dealers and experienced collectors, covering books in English, 1850 to 1899.

STERN, Madeleine B. *Imprints on History*. Indiana
University Press, Bloomington, Ind., 1956. About
American book publishing.

FORTY-TWO FABULOUS AMERICAN
BOOKS AND HOW TO
RECOGNIZE THEM

IN THE FOLLOWING SECTION, selected from the syndicated newspaper column, "Gold in Your Attic," are brief descriptions of forty-two fabulous American books and pamphlets in the category of collector's items. They range from such masterpieces of American fiction as *The Scarlet Letter* and *Moby-Dick* to such mundane subjects as the weather in Florida and the behavior of the stomach's gastric juice. All are books wanted by collectors. All are within the range of possible discovery by the book hunter. In a number of cases, the title pages of these books are reproduced in a section of illustrations following the summaries. Additional price information and aids to identification are to be found in the alphabetized index and price guide beginning on page 108.

1. Moby-Dick
by Herman Melville

Herman Melville's classic whaling adventure *Moby-Dick* affords a good example of how scarcity operates to

MOBY-DICK

OR,

THE WHALE.

BY

HERMAN MELVILLE.

AUTHOR OF

"TYPEE," "OMOO," "REDBURN," "MARDI," "WHITE-JACKET."

———~~~~———

NEW YORK:
HARPER & BROTHERS, PUBLISHERS.
LONDON: RICHARD BENTLEY.

1851

make a desirable book an expensive and sought-after collector's item.

It was first published in London as *The Whale* in 1851 and made its appearance in New York about a month later. Because most of the copies of this first American edition were destroyed in a fire at the publishing house, surviving copies are scarce and worth $1,000 and up if in fine condition. The title page reads:

MOBY-DICK or The Whale. By Herman Melville. Author of *Typee, Omoo, Redburn, Mardi, White-Jacket.* New York: Harper & Brothers, Publishers. London: Richard Bentley. 1851.

The principal distinguishing points among the desirable first editions include the following: The scarcest issues are in red cloth binding with orange end papers. Other bindings in order of relative scarcity are blue, green, black, gray, and brown. There are several kinds of end papers, with plain white the least desirable.

Typical current retail prices of the first American edition as shown in bookseller catalogues range from $750 to $1,050, with worn copies going for less. A very fine copy sold at auction for $2,500 in 1967.

Moby-Dick was slow to be recognized by Americans as the masterpiece it is, but since the turn of the century it has grown steadily in stature. It is an essentially tragic narrative of man's struggle against nature, in which the onetime cabin-boy pits his whaling captain hero against the monstrous great white whale.

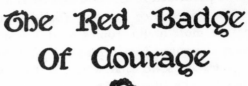

The Red Badge Of Courage

An Episode of the American Civil War

By

Stephen Crane

New York
D. Appleton and Company
1895

2. The Red Badge of Courage
by Stephen Crane

The case of the broken type on page 225 of the scarce first edition of Stephen Crane's great Civil War novel *The Red Badge of Courage* illustrates the importance of identifying "points" in determining book values.

In the first copies issued, the last line of type on page 225 contains perfect type. A mint copy in dust wrapper is worth $350 to $400 today, possibly more.

While the first edition was being printed, the line of type in question became damaged and was then corrected. The copies with damaged type are second issue copies and are worth around $50 on the collector's market. Copies of the third issue, with the line corrected but containing an imperfect, slanting "d," are worth about $25.

It is easy to recognize the title page of this valuable book, which reads:

THE RED BADGE OF COURAGE. An Episode of the American Civil War. By Stephen Crane. New York. D. Appleton and Company. 1895.

The lettering is black. The surrounding ornaments, all red, are a plumed helmet and 17 small fleurs-de-lis. In format, the book is smaller than the average current novel, and it is bound in light tan buckram. The end papers are gray. There are four pages of book advertisements at the rear.

THE

SCARLET LETTER.

A ROMANCE

BY

NATHANIEL HAWTHORNE

BOSTON:
TICKNOR, REED, AND FIELDS
M DCCC L

3. The Scarlet Letter
by Nathaniel Hawthorne

Whatever happened to the 4,000 copies (one authority says 2,500) of the first edition of Nathaniel Hawthorne's *The Scarlet Letter?* If you have one in nice condition, it may be worth $150 or more. In 1962 a fine copy brought $300 at auction.

The great New England novelist was filled with trepidation when he turned in the first draft of Hester Prynne's story. "It is either very good or very bad, I don't know which," he told his publisher.

Ten days after its publication on March 16, 1850, the first edition had disappeared. A second edition in the same year sold out before publication. It became the first American novel to earn a place among the masterpieces of world literature.

The title page reads:

THE SCARLET LETTER; A Romance. By Nathaniel Hawthorne. Boston: Ticknor, Reed, and Fields. 1850.

You can tell the first edition from the second (also dated 1850) by the reading "reduplicate" for "repudiate" in line 20, page 21. There are four pages of advertisements at the front of this 322-page book.

Mc Teague

A Story of San Francisco

By FRANK NORRIS

AUTHOR OF "MORAN OF THE LADY LETTY"

NEW YORK
DOUBLEDAY & McCLURE CO.
1899

4. McTeague
by Frank Norris

Any important or influential book is a potential collector's item, and Frank Norris' San Francisco novel, *McTeague,* is an example of this principle. A first edition in fine condition is worth $150 to $200.

The Chicago-born Norris was a leader of the naturalistic school of fiction around the turn of the century. *McTeague* is the story of a dentist whose life became ruled by greed. Because it influenced the author's contemporaries, it is a fictional landmark in America, and thus a desired item in the first edition.

The title page reads:

McTEAGUE. A Story of San Francisco. By Frank Norris. Author of *Moran of the Lady Letty.* New York. Doubleday & McClure Co. 1899.

A positive first edition point: The last word on page 106 is "moment."

Sister Carrie

By
Theodore Dreiser

NEW YORK
Doubleday, Page & Co.
1900

5. Sister Carrie
by Theodore Dreiser

Among the giants of American fiction, the late Theodore Dreiser, for all his naturalistic crudeness, holds a firm place. Nearly 60 years after publication, his first novel, *Sister Carrie*, still is sought by collectors.

A fine copy of the first edition is worth up to $250 today.

The title page, in which the type is enclosed in a double-ruled frame, reads:

SISTER CARRIE. By Theodore Dreiser, New York. Doubleday, Page & Co. 1900.

A wreath design separates the author's name and the place of publication. The book is bound in red buckram. There is a black border around the front cover.

6. Ben-Hur
by Lew Wallace

Although ordinary copies of the first edition of Lew Wallace's *Ben-Hur* have been listed recently in booksellers' catalogues for as low as $18.50, a really fine copy in the decorated light blue binding is worth up to $150 on the collector's market.

The title page of the first issue of this famous tale, the most successful novel ever written about the life of Christ, reads as follows:

BEN-HUR. A Tale of the Christ. By Lew Wallace. Author of *The Fair God.* (Quotation from Count de

FANSHAWE,

A TALE.

"Wilt thou go on with me?"—SOUTHEY.

—◦◦●◦◦—

BOSTON:
MARSH & CAPEN, 362 WASHINGTON STREET.

PRESS OF PUTNAM AND HUNT.
1828.

Gabalis.) New York. Harper & Brothers, Franklin Square. 1880.

Later 1880 issues do not contain the date on the title page. The first issue is distinguished by the six-word quotation, "To the Wife of My Youth," changed in later issues with the addition of the words, "Who Still Abides With Me."

7. Fanshawe
by Nathaniel Hawthorne

Don't let anybody tell you all the valuable rare books are already on dealers' shelves.

Early in 1958 a news item reported the discovery of a rare first edition of Nathaniel Hawthorne's *Fanshawe* among the books about to be discarded by a North Carolina library.

A rare book dealer made the discovery and arranged for the sale of it for the library in March at New York's Parke-Bernet auction galleries. The $2,600 sale price set a new record for *Fanshawe,* topping its last appearance for sale by $800.

The book is important because it was Hawthorne's first, published while he was a student at Bowdoin College. Its title page reads, in part:

FANSHAWE, A Tale. "Wilt thou go on with me?"— Southey. Boston . . . . 1828.

It is a rare book today because Hawthorne paid for its publication and could afford only a few. In addition, he later destroyed a number because he was ashamed of them.

UNCLE TOM'S CABIN

OR,

LIFE AMONG THE LOWLY.

BY

HARRIET BEECHER STOWE

VOL. I

BOSTON:
JOHN P. JEWETT & COMPANY.
CLEVELAND, OHIO
JEWETT, PROCTOR & WORTHINGTON
1852

8. Uncle Tom's Cabin
by Harriet Beecher Stowe

Although its literary merit is questionable, there is no doubt about the importance of Harriet Beecher Stowe's *Uncle Tom's Cabin.*

As a young woman in Cincinnati, Mrs. Stowe was deeply impressed by the slave evil just across the Ohio River. Her sensational fictional attack on it appeared in two volumes in 1852 and helped to set the stage for the Civil War. Its title page—on which there must be no indication of the number of thousands printed—reads, in part:

> *UNCLE TOM'S CABIN;* Or, *Life Among the Lowly.* By Harriet Beecher Stowe. Vol. I. Boston: . . . . Cleveland . . . . 1852.

There are several first edition bindings. The rarest, buff paper covers, is worth $1,000 and up. The second issue cloth binding was plum-colored. The bottom of the spine reads "J. P. Jewett & Co." There was also a gift binding in several colors of cloth, gold decorated. These cloth copies are worth $400 to $600 in fine condition, possibly more.

9. The Wonderful Wizard of Oz
by L. Frank Baum

Never mind what the librarians say when they try to explain the barring of *The Wonderful Wizard of Oz* from their children's reading rooms. The L. Frank Baum classic of fantasy is here to stay.

One evidence of its enduring merit is the value book collectors put on the first edition, which exists in several states or variations. The least desirable of these states is listed by book dealers today at $175, and a first state copy brought $825 at auction a few years ago.

You can identify the first edition by its hand-lettered title page, which reads:

THE WONDERFUL WIZARD OF OZ. By L. Frank Baum with Pictures by W. W. Denslow. Geo. M. Hill Co. Chicago. New York. 1900.

The valuable first issue has an 11-line colophon (instead of 13 lines) on the back pasted-down end paper.

The author was an interesting character. He manufactured an axle grease, raised poultry, sold crockery, edited a paper, acted and wrote plays before he wrote out his Oz tale on old envelopes, wrapping paper, and other scraps. His first book was *The Book of the Hamburgs* (1886), which are a breed of chickens. In all, he wrote some sixty books, using his own name and seven pen names.

10. Little Women
by Louisa M. Alcott

As the well known collector, C. Waller Barrett, notes in *Bibliophile in the Nursery* (Cleveland, 1957) a "rather ordinary copy" of Louisa M. Alcott's *Little Women* in the first edition brought $750 at auction not long ago.

A very fine copy of this classic of childhood should do even better.

Little Women was published in two volumes in 1868-69. The title page of the first volume reads as follows:

ALICE'S

ADVENTURES IN WONDERLAND.

BY

LEWIS CARROLL.

WITH FORTY-TWO ILLUSTRATIONS

BY

JOHN TENNIEL.

NEW YORK

D. APPLETON AND CO., 445, BROADWAY.

1866.

LITTLE WOMEN or, *Meg, Jo, Beth and Amy.* By
Louisa M. Alcott. Illustrated by May Alcott. Boston.
Roberts Brothers. 1868.

A further clue: The first edition, Part I, does not contain the announcement of *Little Women, Part Second*
at the bottom of the last page of text. Also, the backstrip,
or spine, of the first volume does not bear the words *Part
One,* although the backstrip of the second volume is
labeled *Part Two.*

Still another clue to the first edition: The ads at the
back of the first book contain a notice of the price—$1.25.

11. Alice's Adventures in Wonderland
by Lewis Carroll

There are two valuable first editions of Lewis Carroll's
Alice in Wonderland, the most famous being the first London edition of 1865, suppressed because the illustrator,
John Tenniel, disliked the printing of his plates. Only 48
copies are supposed to exist, and they are worth $5,000 or
upward. The second London edition appeared in 1866.

More within the range of discovery by American readers
is the first American edition, consisting of sheets (pages)
of the London "first" with an American title page. It is
dated 1866 and bound in red cloth. If we subtract the 48
rare London copies from the 2,000 sets of sheets originally
printed, there are then supposed to be left 1,952 copies
of the American "first." Its title page reads:

ALICE'S ADVENTURES IN WONDERLAND. By
Lewis Carroll. With Forty-Two Illustrations by John
Tenniel. New York. D. Appleton and Co., 445 Broad-
way. 1866.

THE

LUCK OF ROARING CAMP,

AND

OTHER SKETCHES.

BY

FRANCIS BRET HARTE.

BOSTON:
FIELDS, OSGOOD, & CO.
1870.

A perfect copy should command $500 today. Copies less than fine have been offered recently at $350 and $300. Worn copies have been offered at $150 and $175.

12. The Luck of Roaring Camp
by Bret Harte

Bret Harte's classic collection of short stories, *The Luck of Roaring Camp,* is another example of how a really important book is always in demand and, if scarce, will command good prices.

Harte was a master of romantic realism and local color, and his tales about the West are landmarks of American literature.

The title page of this sought-after work reads:

THE LUCK OF ROARING CAMP, and Other Sketches. By Francis Bret Harte. Boston: Fields, Osgood & Co. 1870.

An important point: The first issue of the first edition (and therefore the most valuable) does not include the story, "Brown of Calaveras," which was added in a second printing in the same year.

A first issue is worth $150 to $200 in fine condition. A good copy is worth around $100. Other copies have been advertised recently as follows: Worn and faded, $75 and $45; back frayed, hinges repaired, $25.

THE

PROSE ROMANCES OF EDGAR A. POE,

AUTHOR OF "THE GOLD-BUG," "ARTHUR GORDON PYM," "TALES
OF THE GROTESQUE AND ARABESQUE,"
ETC. ETC. ETC.

UNIFORM SERIAL EDITION.

EACH NUMBER COMPLETE IN ITSELF.

No. I.

CONTAINING THE

MURDERS IN THE RUE MORGUE.

AND THE

MAN THAT WAS USED UP.

PHILADELPHIA:
PUBLISHED BY WILLIAM H. GRAHAM.
NO. 98 CHESTNUT STREET.
1843.

Price 12½ cents.

13. The Murders in the Rue Morgue
by Edgar Allan Poe

The most astonishing rise in book values in modern times—from 12½ cents a copy to $25,000 a copy in little more than 80 years—was registered by Edgar Allan Poe's *The Murders in the Rue Morgue.*

Poe was a gifted, hard-drinking man who died at 40, leaving behind an extraordinary record of creativeness. He invented the modern detective story, and his short story "The Murders in the Rue Morgue" is the granddaddy of them all.

First published in Graham's Lady's and Gentleman's Magazine in 1841, it made its first separate appearance in a 40-page, paper-covered book in 1843. The title page of the book as published reads:

> *The Prose Romances of Edgar A. Poe . . .* , Uniform Serial Edition . . . . No. 1. *Containing the MURDERS IN THE RUE MORGUE and the MAN THAT WAS USED UP.* Philadelphia . . . . 1843.

When this seventh of Poe's books appeared, it was sold in Philadelphia bookstores for 12½ cents a copy and had only a mild success. This "No. 1" of a planned series of reprints was the only number to appear.

Fewer than half a dozen copies of this first edition are known to exist, although there is always a possibility another will turn up. The rarest copies contain only the cover title *The Murders in the Rue Morgue* and were salesmen's samples, which were never published, according to Hervey Allen, Poe's biographer.

The late Charles P. Everitt, a famous bookseller, tells in his book *The Adventures of a Treasure Hunter* of selling for $25,000 a copy that was discovered in a pile of bookstore junk in 1926. The purchaser was the industrialist Owen D. Young. The book now rests in the New York Public Library.

14. The Old Swimmin'-Hole
by James Whitcomb Riley

As literature goes, the work of James Whitcomb Riley, the Hoosier poet, has very little standing with the critics. But the American people loved him. Proof that his writing endures is the scarcity of the first edition of his first book of poems and the price it brings today.

Riley used the pen name of "Benj. F. Johnson" for this first book, which was published in a first edition of only 1,000 copies. It contained 50 pages, bound in printed wrappers, or covers. It sold for 50 cents.

The full title, place of publication, and date of this scarce item follow:

THE OLD SWIMMIN'-HOLE, AND 'LEVEN MORE POEMS. By Benj. F. Johnson, of Boone. James Whitcomb Riley. Indianapolis, Ind. George C. Hitt & Co. 1883.

Fine copies in the original dust jacket retail in the $200-$300 range. Other copies have brought $210 and $140 at auction in recent years. Still others have been catalogued by dealers at $150 and $175.

The first edition should not be confused with a facsimile issued in 1909 as a banquet souvenir by the Indiana Society of Chicago. The facsimile can be identified by the missing "W" in the name "William" on page 41.

15. Leaves of Grass
by Walt Whitman

In 1955, on the centennial of the publication on July 4, 1855, of *Leaves of Grass*, the Library of Congress described the Walt Whitman classic as "the most controversial book of the 19th century."

Controversy and the fact that this modest 94-page collection of poems is a landmark of literature have combined to make it one of the most sought after of American first editions. It has commanded prices up to $3,700 at auction. It currently sells for $650 (for a worn copy) and up, depending on condition.

The *Leaves* first is not difficult to identify, although its four known issues have confused collectors. The title page of the first edition, first issue, reads simply:

LEAVES OF GRASS. Brooklyn, New York: 1855.

There is no author's name on the page. Opposite on plain paper is a steel engraved frontispiece portrait of the bearded poet in slouch hat, open-necked shirt, and trousers. There is no identification beneath the portrait. On the reverse side of the title page the copyright notice bears the name "Walter Whitman."

Here are other tips on identifying this rarity: The binding is dark green cloth with an elaborately designed title sprouting fine roots and leaves. The title and border bands on the cover are stamped in gold leaf, and all the edges of the leaves are gilded. The end leaves are gilded. The end

SNOW-BOUND.

A WINTER IDYL.

BY

JOHN GREENLEAF WHITTIER.

BOSTON:
TICKNOR AND FIELDS.
1866.

papers are marbled. Line 20, page 23, reads "abode" for "adobe."

Some first issue copies were in paper covers or wrappers, some pink, some green. There are at least three of these known to exist.

Second issue copies have plain end papers. Regardless of variations in the edition, any of the first edition copies is extremely valuable. There were said to be 1,000 printed, but this figure is uncertain.

16. Snow-bound
   by John Greenleaf Whittier

Literary fashions come and go, but the enduring charm and universal appeal of John Greenleaf Whittier's New England classic *Snow-bound,* still keep it high on the list of literary collector's items.

Snow-bound was written in Whittier's maturity, at the close of a vigorous career in the abolitionist movement. In it, the poet recaptured the memories of a happy childhood.

A fine copy of the first edition commands $200 and up. The title page reads:

SNOW-BOUND. A Winter Idyl. By John Greenleaf Whittier. Boston: Ticknor and Fields. 1866.

The binding is green, blue or terra-cotta cloth. A few copies in white cloth are second issue copies, less valuable than the first. All first edition copies have the number "52" at the foot of the last page of text.

POEMS

BY

WILLIAM CULLEN BRYANT.

—

CAMBRIDGE :

PRINTED BY HILLIARD AND METCALF.

1821.

17. Poems
by William Cullen Bryant

William Cullen Bryant's *Poems,* a little book of only 44 pages, is worth up to $1,000 in the rare book market today because it established its 27-year-old author as the first American to have produced poetry worthy of a place in world literature.

Bryant's great work included "Thanatopsis," his most famous poem, written when he was a mere seventeen. It also contained the celebrated "To a Waterfowl." The title page reads:

> *POEMS.* By William Cullen Bryant. Cambridge: Printed by Hilliard and Metcalfe. 1821.

Poems was issued in brown printed boards, as well as in printed brown paper covers. The leaves should be uncut. The last copy I saw catalogued was chipped and defective and was listed at $600. A similar copy was sold at auction to a dealer not so long ago for $575 and another for $450.

A Little Book

OF

WESTERN VERSE

BY.

EUGENE FIELD

CHICAGO

MDCCCLXXXIX

18. A Little Book of Western Verse
by Eugene Field

Because it contains, among other poems, his immortal "Little Boy Blue," there is a price tag of up to $100 on the 250-copy limited edition of Eugene Field's *A Little Book of Western Verse*.

Field won his fame on the *Chicago Daily News* as the first of the newspaper columnists. He published this book in 1889 in a first edition of two issues—one a limited, oversized book on deckle-edged "large paper" and the other a smaller-sized trade edition (worth up to $25 if fine).

The title page reads:

A LITTLE BOOK OF WESTERN VERSE. By Eugene Field Chicago MDCCCLXXXIX.

The limited edition appears infrequently. It is printed on handmade paper and bound in blue-gray boards with a white cloth spine, bearing a gold-stamped black leather label. There is a list of 114 subscribers at the back.

WALDEN;

OR,

LIFE IN THE WOODS.

BY HENRY D. THOREAU,

AUTHOR OF "A WEEK ON THE CONCORD AND MERRIMACK RIVERS."

I do not propose to write an ode to dejection, but to brag as lustily as chanticleer in the
morning, standing on his roost, if only to wake my neighbors up. — Page 92.

BOSTON:

TICKNOR AND FIELDS.

M DCCC LIV

19. Walden
by Henry D. Thoreau

Money meant very little to Henry David Thoreau, an occasional house painter, mason, surveyor and carpenter who worked only when he had to do so in order to satisfy his modest needs as a bachelor.

He would therefore be quite surprised if he came back to life today and discovered that book collectors will pay $200 to $500, possibly more, for fine first edition copies of his classic *Walden*, the most famous nature book ever written by an American.

This much-sought rarity is Thoreau's account of two years spent in a lonely hut on Walden Pond (1845-1847). The title page reads, in part:

WALDEN; or, *Life in The Woods.* By Henry D. Thoreau. Author of *A Week on the Concord and Merrimack Rivers,* Boston: Ticknor and Fields. MDCCC-LIV.

The binding is cloth, in dark brown and other colors, with gold lettering on the spine. Advertisements at the back of the book are dated variously, from April to October, 1854. No priority of issue has been established.

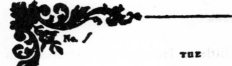

No. 1   Price $1.

THE

BIRDS OF AMERICA,

FROM

DRAWINGS MADE IN THE UNITED STATES

AND THEIR TERRITORIES.

BY JOHN JAMES AUDUBON, F. R. SS. L. & E.

Fellow of the Linnean and Zoological Societies of London, Member of the Lyceum of New York, of the
Natural History Society of Paris, the Wernerian Natural History Society of Edinburgh, Honorary
Member of the Society of Natural History of Manchester, and of the Royal Scottish
Academy of Painting, Sculpture and Architecture, Member of the American
Philosophical Society of the Academy of Natural Sciences at Philadelphia,
of the Natural History Societies of Boston, of Charleston in South
Carolina, the Quebec Literary and Historical Society,
the Ornithological Society of London, the Society
Imperiale de Botanique Universelle de Paris,
&c. &c.

NEW YORK:
J. J. AUDUBON, 86 WHITE STREET.

PHILADELPHIA:
A. B. CHEVALIER, 2 DOCK STREET.

COPYRIGHT SECURED.

20. The Birds of America
by John James Audubon

While it is hardly likely that a set of the original London hand-colored plates of Audubon's classic "The Birds of America" in "double elephant" folio size (39½ by 29½ inches) is lying around unnoticed, the first American edition is within the range of possibilities.

There were fewer than 200 copies of the original sets, which are worth up to $10,000 if complete.

The first American edition was published in seven octavo volumes of text and 500 plates in 1840-1844, as well as in unbound parts, which are the rarest and most valuable state.

The title, appearing on the paper covers, reads:

> THE BIRDS OF AMERICA, from Drawings Made in the United States and Their Territories. By John James Audubon, F. R. SS. L & E . . . . New York: J. J. Audubon . . . Philadelphia: J. B. Chevalier . . . .

The seven-volume set sells for $1,000 or more if in good condition. There were two different sets offered for auction in 1963, and they realized $750 and $850, respectively.

Even later editions, such as George R. Lockwood's New York edition of about 1870, currently command $600 or more.

21. Flower and Fruit Prints of the 18th and Early 19th Centuries
by Gordon Dunthorne

That a book need not always be old to be extremely valuable is well illustrated by Gordon Dunthorne's *Flower and Fruit Prints of the 18th and Early 19th Centuries,* privately published in 1948.

In the first dozen years after publication, it sold at book auctions for a minimum of $40, with the top price recorded at $105. Since 1950 the minimum auction record has been $75, and the price trend is steadily upward. Booksellers currently ask $250 to $350 a copy.

The title page of this scarce modern collector's item reads:

> *FLOWER AND FRUIT PRINTS OF THE 18th AND EARLY 19th CENTURIES. Their History, Makers and Uses, With a Catalogue Raisonne of the Works in Which They Are Found.* By Gordon Dunthorne, M. A. (Oxon). Published by the Author, Washington, D. C. 1948.

Handsomely bound and contained in a protective slip case, it had a printing of 2,500 copies, of which 750 contained a folding color plate listing subscribers. (The latter copies are worth a little more than those without the plate.)

22. Western Scenery
by Otto Onken and William Wells

If in your book hunting you run across an old lithographic picture book called *Western Scenery*, take a second look. It might be the rare Cincinnati work published by Otto Onken in 1851.

There are few known copies of this much-sought book. The Chicago Historical Society has an incomplete copy. A bookseller recently listed a "pristine" copy at $1,500. Less than perfect copies should be worth from $300 to $600 to Americana collectors.

The publisher and illustrator, Otto Onken, was a lithographer, about whom little is known. His book contains 19 full-page lithographic views of Midwestern scenes, along with a text by William Wells. There are 52 pages, not counting the printed wrappers. Some copies are bound in boards and calf.

It is easy to recognize the title page, which is ornamented and bears drawings of the St. Louis and Louisville courthouses, the Kentucky and Indiana state houses and the Ohio Lunatic Asylum.

The title page reads as follows:

WESTERN SCENERY; or Land and River, Hill and Dale, In the Mississippi Valley. Superbly Lithographed From Original Sketches. Literary Department by William Wells. Cincinnati, O. Published by the Lithographic Establishment of Otto Onken. 1851.

The Mississippi Valley scenes portrayed in the book range from Ohio to Memphis, Vicksburg, and New Orleans.

CENTENNIAL, 1876.

———

THE

SENTIMENTAL

SONG BOOK.

———

BY JULIA A. MOORE.

———

GRAND RAPIDS, MICH:
C. M. LOOMI BOOK AND JOB PRINTER,
1876.

23. The Sentimental Song Book
by Julia A. Moore

The collector's item is almost always a book of some merit, literary or otherwise. But the strangest case of all, perhaps, is the absolutely terrible work of Julia A. Moore, the "sweet singer of Michigan."

Miss Moore, who fancied herself a poet, flourished in the 1870's and published some of the worst verse ever written in America. It was so incredibly bad that collectors prize it. Stephen Leacock seriously called her in one of his essays the "greatest super-comic poet who has lived since Milton."

The first edition of her *Sentimental Song Book,* of which only a few copies are known, is worth up to $100 on the collector's market. The title page reads:

> *THE SENTIMENAL SONG BOOK.* By Julia A. Moore. Grand Rapids, Mich: C. M. Loomi Book and Job Printer, 1876.

At the top of the page are the words "Centennial, 1876." The book is paper covered and has 54 pages. There also exists an 1893 reprint, which is of little value.

24. Experiments and Observations On the Gastric Juice
by William Beaumont

In general, old medical books are of little value on the book market, because the advances of medicine keep making them obsolete.

UNIFORM AND DRESS

OF THE

ARMY

OF THE

CONFEDERATE STATES

ADJUTANT AND INSPECTOR GENERAL'S OFFICE,
Richmond, September 12, 1861

The work styled the "Uniform and Dress of the Army of the Confederate States," for which a copyright has been secured by Blanton Duncan, is published by authority.

S. COOPER,
Adjutant and Inspector General.

RICHMOND:
CHAS. H. WYNNE, PRINTER, 94 MAIN STREET
LITHOGRAPHS BY E. CREHEN.
1861.

One that survives and remains an important and durable contribution to medical science is Dr. William Beaumont's pioneering report on his studies of the gastric juice. Its title page reads:

EXPERIMENTS AND OBSERVATIONS ON THE GASTRIC JUICE, and the Physiology of Digestion. By William Beaumont. Plattsburgh, 1833.

Beaumont was a United States Army surgeon, first commissioned as a surgeon's mate to the Sixth Infantry at Plattsburgh, N. Y., in 1812. His famous book was a detailed study of 238 experiments he carried out in Washington, D. C.

The book was published at Beaumont's own expense in a first edition of 1,000 copies. It is worth up to $500, possibly more, today. A copy was sold at auction for $475 in 1966.

25. Uniform and Dress of the Army of the Confederate States

One of the rarest of Confederate items is the official army uniform book published at Richmond, Va., in 1861.

Richard B. Harwell, the Chicago collector, describes it in Cornerstones of Confederate Collecting (Charlottesville, 1953), as being 13¾ by 10¾ inches, bound in boards. Its title page reads, in part:

UNIFORM AND DRESS OF THE ARMY OF THE CONFEDERATE STATES . . . . Richmond: Chas. H. Wynne, Printer, 94 Main Street . . . 1861.

There are two issues, each containing five pages plus 15 plates by Ernest Crehen and an errata slip. The text is a

THE

MODERN ART

OF

TAMING WILD HORSES.

BY J. S. RAREY.

COLUMBUS:
PRINTED BY THE STATE JOURNAL COMPANY.
1856.

general order. The first issue, which brings around $125, contains black and white lithographs.

In the second issue (same date), four of the plates are printed in color. In addition, there is a tipped-in strip showing field caps in color. The price on this issue runs up to $300.

26. The Modern Art of Taming Wild Horses
by J. S. Rarey

John Solomon Rarey was a 19th century Ohio horse trainer who won international fame with his book *The Modern Art of Taming Wild Horses,* the most important and most sought after of all early American books on horses.

Rarey announced his publication plans in the summer of 1855 with a broadside, published in Groveport, Ohio. Headed simply "Wild Horses," it stated: "I wish to announce . . . I have a system of training wild horses."

In September he obtained a copyright. Shortly thereafter he published his paperbound book, dated 1856. Thievery by book publishers was quite common in those days and despite Rarey's copyright, half a dozen publishers rushed into print immediately with pirated editions. Even these stolen editions have attained collector's value today.

The title page of Rarey's first edition reads:

THE MODERN ART OF TAMING WILD HORSES.
By J. S. Rarey. Columbus: Printed by the State Journal Company. 1856.

There are only a few known copies of this edition. The last one to appear on the market lacked the original paper covers and had been rebound. It was priced at $325. Copies in original binding should be worth $350 to $400, possibly more.

27. The Traveller's Directory and Emigrant's Guide
by Oliver G. Steele

That guidebook that Grandpa used on his way West may have a lot of cashable value.

On November 4, 1957, Brigham Young's own copy of *The Latter-Day Saints' Emigrants' Guide* (St. Louis, 1848) brought $2,016 at auction in London. Another copy, not signed by Smith, brought $1,700 at auction some years ago.

Then there is the fantastic price of $3,400 realized in 1948 for a copy of Joseph Cain's and Arieh Brower's *The Mormon Way-Bill*, another emigrants' guide, published in Salt Lake City in 1832.

It is true that such extremely valuable items are rarely met with. Yet there is always a chance you will strike gold. Any 19th century travelers' guide used by the Western pioneers has potential value. Take, for example, Oliver G. Steele's anonymous title of 1852:

THE TRAVELLER'S DIRECTORY AND EMI-GRANT'S GUIDE . . . Buffalo: 1832.

Bound in boards and bearing paper labels, this 85-page collector's item is worth $150 in good condition. Even the editions of the 1840's bring $35 or more.

28. Gazetteer of The States of Illinois and Missouri
by Lewis C. Beck

Among American books, the biggest prices are associated with two main categories—the scarcest works of highly regarded authors and the literature of place, or Americana.

Typical of the latter is Lewis C. Beck's gazetteer of Illinois and Missouri. A copy in fine condition currently sells in the $300 to $500 range at retail.

Beck was a New Yorker who piled up an astonishing list of scientific accomplishments in the last century. Famed as chemist, botanist and mineralogist, he published his gazetteer in 1823. It was a 352-page work with five plates and a large folding map. The long-winded title page reads, in part:

> *GAZETTEER of The States of Illinois and Missouri;* . . . By Lewis C. Beck, A. M. . . . Albany: Printed by Charles R. and George Webster . . . 1823.

In some copies the leaves are trimmed. The rarest have wide, untrimmed edges.

29. Arithmetick Vulgar and Decimal
by Isaac Greenwood

As the book collector uses the term, Americana is anything printed that helps to tell the story of the American past—how our ancestors came to these shores, the record of their progress, how the people lived and what they did.

THE LIFE, TIMES

AND TREACHEROUS DEATH

—OF—

JESSE JAMES.

THE ONLY CORRECT AND AUTHORIZED EDITION.

GIVING FULL PARTICULARS OF EACH AND EVERY DARK AND
DESPERATE DEED IN THE CAREER OF THIS
MOST NOTED OUTLAW OF ANY
TIME OR NATION.

The Facts and Incidents contained in this Volume, were Dictated

—TO—

FRANK TRIPLETT,

—BY—

MRS. JESSE JAMES, AND MRS. ZERELDA SAMUEL,

Wife of the Bandit. *His Mother.*

CONSEQUENTLY EVERY SECRET ACT — EVERY HITHERTO
UNKNOWN INCIDENT — EVERY CRIME AND
EVERY MOTIVE IS HEREIN
TRUTHFULLY
DISCLOSED.

TRUTH IS MORE INTERESTING THAN FICTION.

1882.

J. H. CHAMBERS & CO.,

CHICAGO, ILL. ST. LOUIS, MO. ATLANTA, GA.

Arithmetic was of special importance to the pioneer, in the schools as well as in the daily business of making a living.

A great many arithmetics of an earlier day still survive, but few are of value except as sentimental reminders of Great Grandfather's time.

There are a few, however, that are prized by collectors. One of these is Isaac Greenwood's anonymously published arithmetic of 1729, a little leatherbound classic said to be the first to be published by a native American.

The title page of this early American textbook reads as follows:

ARITHMETICK VULGAR AND DECIMAL with the Application Thereof to a Variety of Cases in Trade and Commerce. Boston: S. Kneeland and T. Green, for T. Hancock. 1729.

As rare books go, this one is in the $100 to $300 class and not too difficult to find. The last one I saw offered was priced by its owner at $225.

30. The Life, Times and Treacherous Death of Jesse James
by Frank Triplett

Any book about Western outlaws tends to become valuable—and especially so if an effort has been made to suppress it.

A case in point is Frank Triplett's exceedingly rare life of Jesse James, which has all but disappeared from the scene. The effort to suppress it is said to have been made by Gov. T. T. Crittenden of Missouri, who is criticized

LIFE, ADVENTURES

AND

CAPTURE

OF

TIBURCIO VASQUEZ.

The Great California Bandit and Murderer.

By Maj. BEN. C. TRUMAN,

Editor of Los Angeles Star.

PRINTED AT
LOS ANGELES STAR OFFICE,
1874.

severely by James' wife and mother in Triplett's account.
The long-winded title page reads, in part:

> THE LIFE, TIMES AND TREACHEROUS DEATH
> OF JESSE JAMES. The Only Correct and Authorized
> Edition . . . Dictated to Frank Triplett by Mrs. Jesse
> James . . . and Mrs. Zerelda Samuel . . . 1882. J. H.
> Chambers & Co., Chicago . . . St. Louis . . . Atlanta.

A fine copy, clothbound, is worth about $150 at retail,
and a Midwest dealer recently advertised a copy of this
rarity, apparently rebound in leather, worn, and with the
end papers slightly chipped, for $125.

31. Life, Adventures and Capture of Tiburcio Vasquez
by Ben. C. Truman

References to the exploits of Tiburcio Vasquez, the
California bandit and murderer, abound in the literature
of the Far West. There are 62 of them alone in Ramon F.
Adams' famous bibliography of Western gunmen, *Six-
Guns and Saddle Leather*. Yet the books about Vasquez
are few and hard to find.

One of the rare ones is Ben. C. Truman's paperbound,
44-page biography, published in 1874. Much sought by
collectors, it brings $100 and upward in fine condition.
The title, printed on the front cover with a portrait of
Vasquez, reads:

> LIFE, ADVENTURES AND CAPTURE OF TIBUR-
> CIO VASQUEZ, The Great California Bandit and
> Murderer. By Maj. Ben. C. Truman, Editor of Los
> Angeles Star. Printed at Los Angeles Star Office. 1874.

THE

Banditti of the Plains

— OR THE —

Cattlemen's Invasion of Wyoming in 1892

[THE CROWNING INFAMY OF THE AGES.]

By A. S. MERCER.

On the face of the first leaf following the pictorial front cover is a map showing the location of Vasquez's capture. The insides and the back of the cover carry advertisements.

32. The Banditti of the Plains
by A. S. Mercer

The Johnson County cattle war of 1892 between the entrenched cattle interests of Wyoming and the independent ranchers was responsible for Asa Mercer's *The Banditti of the Plains,* one of the most sought after of Western books.

It commands from $250 to $400 if in fine condition.

The title page of this 139-page book, bound in black cloth, reads:

THE BANDITTI OF THE PLAINS or the Cattlemen's Invasion of Wyoming in 1892 (The Crowning Infamy of the Ages.) By A. S. Mercer.

Although the title page bears no date, Mercer published it in Cheyenne in 1894. The Wyoming cattlemen reacted violently because he named names and showed how they collaborated with public officials to accuse the independents of "rustling" in order to drive them out.

They burned the author's print shop and seized and burned all the copies of the book they could find. To this day their descendants carry on a ruthless war against it. Even the copies in Wyoming libraries have been mutilated or stolen.

TRAVELS

IN

MEXICO

—AND—

CALIFORNIA:

Comprising a Journal of a Tour from Brazos Santiago,
through Central Mexico, by way of Monterey, Chihuahua, the country of the Apaches, and the River
Gila, to the Mining Districts of California.

BY A. B. CLARKE.

BOSTON:
WRIGHT & HASTY'S STEAM PRESS,
3 Water Street.
1852.

33. Travels in Mexico and California
by A. B. Clarke

Among the accounts of travelers lured to California by the gold discovery of 1849, Asa B. Clarke's *Travels in Mexico and California* is outstanding. The paperbound first edition currently brings from $250 to $400 at retail if in fine condition.

Clarke was a member of the Hampden Mining Co. group of 46 persons who left New York City in January, 1849, and made their way westward, arriving in California in July.

His book is "a journal of a tour from Brazos Santiago, through Central Mexico, by way of Monterey, Chihuahua, the country of the Apaches, and the River Gila, to the mining districts of California." Its title page reads, in part:

TRAVELS IN MEXICO AND CALIFORNIA: . . . By A. B. Clarke. Boston: . . . 1852.

Leatherbound and clothbound copies retail at $150 to $300.

34. A Journal of Captain Cook's Last Voyage
by John Ledyard

That hitherto undiscovered rarities in the book world can and do turn up where least expected is shown in the experience of Mrs. E. Y., a reader of my newspaper column, "Gold in Your Attic," living in Smithtown, Long Island, N. Y.

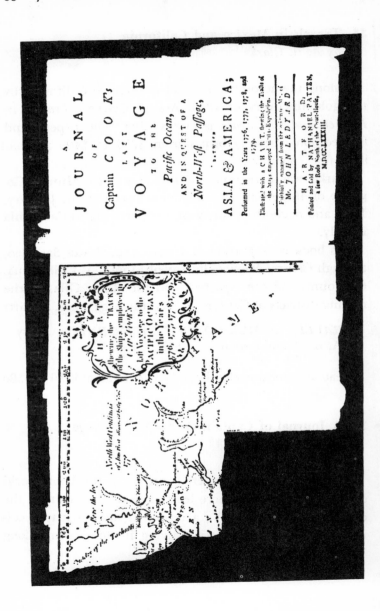

After reading about the values of old books, she began looking into her old leatherbound book of 1783 describing Captain James Cook's last voyage. It turned out to be an extremely rare item of Americana—worth $1,200 or more if in fine condition.

The title page reads, in part:

> *A JOURNAL OF CAPTAIN COOK'S LAST VOYAGE to the Pacific Ocean, etc. . . . .* Faithfully narrated from the original MS. of Mr. John Ledyard. Hartford . . . . MDCCLXXXIII.

It is important, as the Chicago rare book authority Wright Howes has noted in his *U.S.-iana,* because it is "the first American book describing the Northwest Coast."

It is unfortunate that Mrs. Y.'s copy, like most of the others found to date, was defective. In this case, the folding map was damaged, which reduced the value of the book considerably.

35. History of Oregon Territory
by H. L. W. Leonard

In view of its extreme rarity, you can just about name your own price on H. L. W. Leonard's famed *Oregon Territory*—if you are lucky enough to find one.

There are only three copies known. The last one to turn up, somewhat damaged, was sold some years back for $1,000 by Ernest J. Wessen, the Mansfield (Ohio) rare book specialist. It once sold for 25 cents.

Imprinted on the cover of this 88-page paperbound book is the following title:

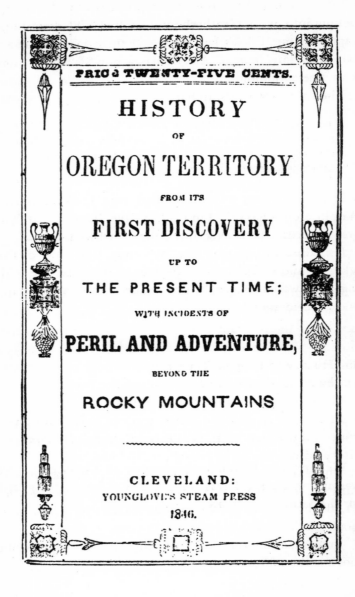

PRICE TWENTY-FIVE CENTS.

HISTORY

OF

OREGON TERRITORY

FROM ITS

FIRST DISCOVERY

UP TO

THE PRESENT TIME;

WITH INCIDENTS OF

PERIL AND ADVENTURE,

BEYOND THE

ROCKY MOUNTAINS

CLEVELAND:

YOUNGLOVE'S STEAM PRESS

1846.

HISTORY OF OREGON TERRITORY from its First Discovery Up to the Present Time; with Incidents of Peril and Adventure, Beyond the Rocky Mountains. Cleveland: Younglove's Steam Press. 1846.

It is historically important as an account of Spanish, English, and American discoveries on the northwest coast of the United States.

36. Life and Adventures of Ben Thompson
by W. M. Walton

One of the rarest of Texas collector's items is W. M. Walton's paperbound life of Ben Thompson, a notorious gambler and gunman.

Much sought by collectors of Western Americana, it retails in the $300 range—when a copy can be found.

Just as an illustration of the potential thrills of book hunting, I might point out here that a dealer unfamiliar with his wares catalogued a copy at $12 some years ago and was promptly buried under an avalanche of telegrams. The first lucky collector naturally got the prize.

The title page of this 229-page rarity reads, in part:

LIFE AND ADVENTURES OF BEN THOMPSON, the Famous Texan . . . By W. M. Walton. Austin . . . 1884.

Walton was a lifelong acquaintance of Thompson, who was at one time a Texas Ranger and at another a guard for the Santa Fe railroad.

37. Articles of an Association by the Name of the Ohio Company

At $1,700—its auction value in a New York sale late in 1958—the 12-page pamphlet that marked the birth in 1786 of the famed Ohio Company is worth $141.66 a page.

Americana collectors are usually willing to pay dearly for the "firsts" in any chosen field, and this item is a prime example. There are fewer than a dozen known copies. It is the first published work on the settlement of the Northwest Territory. Its title page reads:

ARTICLES OF AN ASSOCIATION BY THE NAME OF THE OHIO COMPANY. Printed at Worcester, Massachusetts, By Isaiah Thomas, MDCCLXXXVI.

The Ohio Company was a land company formed by Rufus Putnam of Massachusetts to acquire tracts for settlement between the Ohio River and Lake Erie. Some of the land it got free from Congress, some at 9 cents an acre. It was influential in shaping the Northwest Ordinance of 1787.

38. Florida and Texas
by B. M. Byrne

Sometimes the rare book hunter finds that a later edition of a book is more valuable than the first. Such is the case of Dr. B. M. Byrne's famous letters praising Florida's superiority over Texas as a goal for settlers.

The third edition of this 40-page paperbound rarity is

said to be possibly the first book produced in Ocala, Fla., where it appeared in 1866. A leading New York dealer in Americana offered a copy at $150 in a catalogue not so long ago. The title reads, in part:

FLORIDA AND TEXAS: A series of letters . . . setting forth many advantages that East and South Florida offer to emigrants. Ocala: Printed at the East Florida Banner Office. 1866.

Wright Howes, in his bibliographical record *U.S.-iana*, records a less expensive, undated first edition of Bryne, published at Ralston, Pa., under the title *Letters on the Climate . . . of Florida*, and an 1851 second edition, printed at Jacksonville, Fla.

39. A Brief Sketch of Colorado Territory
by J. Wetherbee, Jr.

In your treasure hunting among the books about the American West, there are certain key words to keep in mind, among them "California," "Oregon," and "Colorado." Often they are golden words to the book hunter.

I cite these state names particularly because they were centers of action and prime goals of emigrants in the 19th century. Valuable books abound among the extensive lists that deal with them.

An example is Wetherbee's extremely rare "Sketch of Colorado," a 24-page paperbound booklet dealing with the gold mines of the Rocky Mountains. It is easily recognized by the plainly printed title page, all in capital letters, which reads:

THE NEW NORTHWEST,

BY

Mrs. LINDA W. SLAUGHTER,

A PAMPHLET STATING BRIEFLY THE
ADVANTAGES OF BISMARCK
AND VICINITY.

Soil, Timber, Climate, Settlements, Business, &c., &c.

PUBLISHED BY THE BURLEIGH COUNTY
PIONEERS' ASSOCIATION.

Bismarck Tribune Print
1874.

A BRIEF SKETCH OF COLORADO TERRITORY and the Gold Mines of That Region. By J. Wetherbee, Jr., Treasurer of the Excelsior Mining Co. of Colorado. Boston: Wright & Potter, Printers, 4 Spring Lane. 1863.

There are only a few copies of this booklet in existence. If you find one in good condition it is worth $350 and up. Good hunting!

40. The New Northwest
by Mrs. Linda W. Slaughter

Nothing illustrates more aptly the thrills of the book hunter's search than a letter received some years ago from a Minneapolis college student who devoted his summer vacations to scouring the Black Hills in search of a $1,200 paperbound book.

This little brown item is Mrs. Linda W. Slaughter's "pamphlet stating briefly the advantages of Bismarck and vicinity." It is said to be the first item printed in North Dakota.

The wife of the surgeon for the military expedition from Fort Rice to the Yellowstone in 1871, Mrs. Slaughter wrote the first description of the newly opened region. The title page of her 24-page, paperbound booklet reads:

THE NEW NORTHWEST, by Mrs. Linda W. Slaughter . . . Published by the Burleigh County Pioneers' Association. Bismarck Tribune Print. 1874.

My Minnesota correspondent writes that on a summer trip in the mid-1950s he saw a copy of this Western rarity tucked away and ignored in the 50-cent bookshelves of a

THE FIFTH CAVALRY IN THE SIOUX WAR
OF 1876.

CAMPAIGNING WITH CROOK

BY
CAPT. CHARLES KING U.S.A.

MILWAUKEE, WIS.
PRINTED BY THE SENTINEL COMPANY.
1880.

junk shop in the Black Hills. He thought nothing more of it until months later when he noticed in a bookseller's broadside a reference to its estimated value as "$100 to $500 and up."

In the summer of 1957, he spent his entire vacation searching the Black Hills in vain for his "lost opportunity." To emphasize his sense of potential loss, he sent me a page from a New York bookseller's catalogue which listed Mrs. Slaughter at a cool $1,200.

The cataloguer adds: "Apparently no copy of the book has been on the market in the past half-century."

All of which has led my collegian to believe "there may be gold in them Black Hills yet!"

41. Campaigning With Crook
by Capt. Charles King

Capt. Charles King was one of the more prolific writers of the last century. His novels sold by the tens of thousands.

Why then, one may ask, are collectors willing to pay $200 and more for his little paperbound book, *Campaigning with Crook*?

The answer is that this particular book is exceedingly scarce. It is also one of the most interesting and valuable accounts of Indian warfare in Wyoming and the Dakotas in 1876.

The title page of the first edition reads as follows:

CAMPAIGNING WITH CROOK. By Capt. Charles King U. S. A. Milwaukee, Wis. Printed at the Sentinel Company. 1880.

Entered according to the act of Congress, in the year 1845,
BY WM. M. DANIELS,
In the clerk's office of the district court of Illinois.

A

CORRECT ACCOUNT

OF THE

Murder of Generals Joseph and Hyrum Smith,

AT CARTHAGE,

ON THE 27TH DAY OF JUNE, 1844;

BY WM. M. DANIELS, AN EYE WITNESS

—◦|◦—

PUBLISHED BY JOHN TAYLOR,
FOR THE PROPRIETOR:
NAUVOO, ILL.
1845

At the top of the page is a sub-title that reads: *The Fifth, Cavalry in the Sioux War of 1876.* There are 134 pages.

42. A Correct Account of The Murder of Generals Joseph and Hyrum Smith
by Wm. M. Daniels

Never throw away a book or pamphlet dealing with the early Mormon days in the American West without ascertaining its value. It could be worth hundreds of dollars.

A prime example is William M. Daniels' paperbound booklet describing the murder of the Mormon prophet Joseph Smith at Carthage, Ill., in 1844. It is worth from $1,500 to $2,000, depending on condition.

Daniels' eyewitness story is important because it is the only detailed account of the tragedy by an unprejudiced observer. The title (and cover) page of this 24-page rarity is imprinted as follows (beneath a copyright notice at top of the page):

A CORRECT ACCOUNT OF THE Murder of Generals Joseph and Hyrum Smith, at Carthage, on the 27th day of June, 1844; by Wm. M. Daniels, an eye witness. Published by John Taylor, for the proprietor: Nauvoo, Ill. 1845.

The woodcut engravings depict the murder scene, although the rarest—and most valuable—first printing copies appeared without the engravings.

A rebound copy of the second issue, with two woodcut engravings added, sold at auction for $1,100 in 1966.

A REPRESENTATIVE PRICE INDEX AND GUIDE TO VALUABLE BOOKS OF THE NEW WORLD— PREFATORY NOTES

IN THE SECTION THAT FOLLOWS, more than 2,500 of the most valuable books and pamphlets published in the New World, primarily on the North American continent, have been catalogued for the convenience of book collectors and booksellers. In compiling this index, which is based on my own private files, every effort was made to reflect the current state of the book market as of the summer of 1967. Prices from a great variety of sources were assembled, compared, and weighed against one another. Wherever possible, note was taken of the influences of condition, the auction (or wholesale) market, physical differences in the editions or issues of books concerned, etc.

Method of Listing: For the benefit of scholars, bibliographers and others who may be inclined to question the method of cataloguing, I should explain that no special effort was made to conform to orthodox bibliographical procedures. The primary objective was to prepare a list that would be useful to the layman and, incidentally, to the professional bookman. For example, anonymous books and books written under a pseudonym are in many cases listed by title or pseudonym, just as they appear on the title pages, rather than under the real name of the author. The reason for this is obvious if we take a case in point: Suppose a reader discovers a copy of Sinclair Lewis' pseudonymous book, *Hike and the Aeroplane,* by Tom Graham. If he has never heard of this item, he cannot know that Graham was really Lewis and that in fine condition it is worth $250 or more. Thus, I have listed it in the index under, "GRAHAM, Tom," as a matter of simple convenience. Likewise, it is not probable that the uninitiated book hunter will know that the anonymous *Wieland* is a novel by Charles Brockden Brown. I have listed it under *WIELAND* so that such a reader can look it up quickly without further bibliographical reference. It should be added that such a method of listing has not been followed in all cases in this index, principally because of the extraordinarily exhaustive researches such a listing would involve. However, that was the ideal envisioned in the creation of the list, and further advances toward this goal have been made in this new edition, and others will be made in the future.

An Apology for Error: It is inevitable that in such a listing as this errors of several varieties will appear—confusion as to exact bibliographical data in respect to names, titles, places of publication, dates of publication, editions, prices, etc. This is true because the information was assembled from a variety of sources, primarily the catalogues of booksellers, and in certain instances it was impossible to cross check or verify. In many cases, the errors of bibliographers and booksellers have been detected and corrected. In others, however, I must concede the possibility that I may have compounded error, and even committed new and more grievous mistakes. In such cases, I shall, of course, welcome the aid of booksellers, bibliographers, librarians, collectors and readers with a view toward correcting these errors in the future.

$25 and Up: The price range embraced in the following list was set up arbitrarily with $25 as a starting point because it is at about that point, according to my experience, that the owner of a scarce or valuable book will begin to consider selling it for cash. Such a limitation also has the virtue of keeping the listing small enough to be confined within the covers of a handy-sized single-volume reference work. There are literally tens of thousands of mildly valuable books in the range below $25. Readers who are interested in these items or in other possibly valuable books not included herein are referred to the annual volumes of *American Book-Prices Current* (for auction prices) and to other compilations, such as J. Norman Heard's *Bookman's Guide to Americana,* which are available in reference rooms of larger public libraries. In considering auction listings, it is important to note that book auctions both in America and abroad are attended largely by booksellers. The prices realized, in the majority of cases, are in effect wholesale prices. It is thus reasonable to assume that most auction prices of books represent about half the true retail value. In other words, if a book brings $5 at auction, it is reasonable to assume that the bookseller who bought it will catalogue it or sell it eventually for approximately $10. This is a rule-of-thumb assumption, however, and cannot always be depended upon to hold true. The best and surest guide to the current book market lies not in the auction records but in the current catalogues of booksellers.

Inclusions and Exclusions: In compiling this list, no attempt has been made to break down the material into classifications such as Americana, Fiction, First Editions, Art, Science, etc. This is a simple author and title index, without regard to subject classification. In general, the list is confined to books and pamphlets, although an occasional map or document has crept in. Among the items specifically excluded are written manuscripts, almost all *Bibles,* almost all McGuffey readers, almost all magazines, all newspapers, almost all collected and multi-volume works of standard authors, and almost all foreign-language books, except for a few items in the Spanish language dealing with New World subjects or published in the New World.

Bibles are a highly specialized field, discussed briefly in Part I of this book. For an authoritative guide to the valuable editions in the field, the reader is referred to Edwin A. R. Rumball-Petre's *Rare Bibles: An Introduction for Collectors and a Descriptive Checklist,* available in the larger public libraries. Actually, there are very few American *Bibles* that are worth much on the collector's market, primarily because *Bibles* are printed in huge quantities and are widely distributed.

Likewise, the McGuffey reader series was widely distributed and contains few items of real value, despite the widespread impression that these old books are priceless.

Much the same reasoning lies behind the exclusion in general of the works of standard authors published in sets or multi-volume editions. The print order for most such sets is large, and most of them are therefore worth little in the collector's market. An exception, of course, is the truly limited edition published in fine leather binding. But this again is a specialized field, beyond the aims of a general book list.

Abbreviations and Terminology: Because this book is primarily designed for the use of the interested layman, an effort has been made to avoid most of the bibliographer's jargon and to keep the abbreviations and the terminology in the listings relatively simple. "1st ed." means simply, "First Edition." (Definitions of this and other terms, such as "1st issue," "1st state," "Foxed," etc., will be found in the "Brief Dictionary for Book Hunters" at the end of Part I.) The abbreviation "pp." means "pages." In some of the listings, there appear the statements, "No place" and "No date," sometimes separately, sometimes together. They mean that the book concerned does not contain on its title page a statement as to the place of publication or the date of publication, as the case may be. In the event this information is known, it follows in parenthesis after the statement in the listing. Thus: "No place (Milwaukee), no date (1918)" or "No place, no date (1916)," etc. In the case of anonymous or pseudonymous works, the author's name, if known, is carried in parenthesis following the listing of the book (after date of publication).

Price Information: The prices given herein are as accurate as it has been possible to make them after a study of many thousands of listings. Wherever possible, they take into account the principal factor of condition. Where there is doubt about a price, this has been indicated either directly or by a listing of conflicting prices, the causes for which may or may not be indicated. In summary, it has been my aim to provide for layman, bookseller and librarian alike an up-to-date and reliable index and guide on which he can safely base his own estimates of book values.

The Basic Price Figure: In most cases, an effort has been made to provide a basic price figure applying to books in fine or first-class condition. In addition, the prices asked for defective books have been supplied, wherever possible, in order to offer a useful comparison.

In numerous instances, a wide variation is recorded in the prices shown from dealer to dealer and in the sales at auction. In most cases, such instances are accounted for by differences in condition of the books or pamphlets concerned. For example, an especially fine copy of a book in an unmarked dust jacket may command an especially high price, while one with a tattered dust jacket may be sold at a considerably lower level and one without a jacket at all still lower. (In the case of auction sales, there are admittedly some instances in which the reasons for large price variations are obscure; they may be accounted for by condition, but they also may be accounted for only by the whims of the moment or the temperature of auction room.)

The Sources: The catalogues of a great many dealers were freely consulted in the original researches for this book as well as in the work of revision. Long established dealers were favored over those less experienced or less well known. Among the more prominent dealers whose catalogues were consulted are the following: Carnegie Book Shop, 140 East 59th Street, New York, New York 10022; Philip C. Duschnes, 699 Madison Avenue, New York 10021; Edward Eberstadt & Sons, 888 Madison Avenue, New York 10021; House of Books, Ltd., 667

Madison Avenue, New York 10021; House of El Dieff, Inc., 30 East 62 Street, New York 10021; Maxwell Hunley, 9533 Santa Monica Boulevard, Beverly Hills, California; Leamington Book Shop, 623 Caroline Street, Fredericksburg, Virginia 22401; Edward Morrill & Son, Inc., 25 Kingston Street, Boston, Massachusetts 02111; Henry Schuman Rare Books, Ltd., 2211 Broadway, New York 10024; L. Weitz, Inc., 1377 Lexington Avenue, New York 10020; William P. Wreden, 405 Kipling Street, Palo Alto, California 94302; Herbert West, Box 82, Hanover, New Hampshire 03755; Zeitlin & Ver Brugge, 815 North La Cienega Boulevard, Los Angeles, California 90069; Argosy Book Stores, 116 East 59th Street, New York 10022; J. S. Canner & Company, 618 Parker Street, Boston-Roxbury, Massachusetts 02129; Peter Decker, 45 West 57th Street, New York 10019; Scribner Book Store, 597 Fifth Avenue, New York 10017; Goodspeed's Book Shop, 18 Beacon Street, Boston 02108; Lathrop C. Harper, Inc., 8 West 40th Street, New York 10018; Robert G. Hayman, R. F. D. 1, Carey, Ohio 43316; Holmes Book Company, 274 14th Street, Oakland, California 94612; T. N. Luther, 6840 Cherry Street, Kansas City, Missouri 64131; Kenneth Nebenzahl, Inc., 333 North Michigan Avenue, Chicago, Illinois 60601; Stechert-Hafner, Inc., 31 East 10th Street, New York 10003; International Bookfinders, Box 3003, Beverly Hills, California 90212, and Bernard Quaritch, Ltd., 11 Grafton Street, New Bond Street, London W. 1, England.

The catalogues of others whom I have not named here were also consulted over a period of many years and provided the private card index from which this price guide has been built. Because these dealers are so numerous, and because many of them have changed addresses or are now out of business, it has seemed impracticable to list them here.

In addition to the dealer sources, I must acknowledge a further indebtedness to two auction houses, Sotheby & Company, 34 and 35 New Bond Street, London, W. 1, England, and the Parke-Bernet Galleries, Inc., 980 Madison Avenue, New York 10021.

Finally, I should have been severely handicapped, even with the availability of all these published bookseller sources, had I not been able to consult other invaluable standard references such as the following: the annual issues of *American Book-Prices Current*, edited by Edward Lazare; *U. S.-iana; 1650-1950*, selected by Wright Howes, and *Selective Bibliography of American Literature: 1775-1900* by B. M. Fullerton. Many other volumes, too numerous to mention here, also contributed materially to this price study. Some of them are included in the compilation, A Library for Book Hunters, in Part I of this book.

VAN ALLEN BRADLEY

Revised, November, 1967.

PRICE INDEX AND GUIDE

ABEL, Henry I. *Traveller's and Emigrant's Guide to Wisconsin and Iowa.* Folding colored map and text pasted into cloth case. Philadelphia, 1838. 1st ed. $125-$150. Worn, $75.

ABERT, Lt. J. W. *A Report and Map of the Examination of New Mexico.* Senate Ex. Doc. 23. Folding map, 24 plates. 132 pp., paperbound. No place, no date (Washington, 1848). 1st ed. $200 (1966 auction).

ACCOUNT of Louisiana, (An), Being an Abstract of Documents, etc. Philadelphia, 1803. $40-$50.

ACCOUNT of a Tour of the California Missions, etc. No place (San Francisco), 1952. One of 375, Book Club of California, boxed. $35-$50.

ACKERLY, Mary Denham and Lula Eastman Jeter Parker. *"Our Kin."* No place, no date (Lynchburg, Va., 1930). $35-$50. Ex-library copy, $25.

ACTS, Resolutions and Memorials Passed at the Several Annual Sessions of the Legislative Assembly. Salt Lake, 1855. $45.

ADAMS, Amos. *A Concise Historical View of the Perils, Hardships, Difficulties and Discouragements which attended the planting, etc., of New England.* 66 pp., paperbound. Boston, 1769. 1st ed. Uncut copies, $150 and $100.

ADAMS, Andy. *The Log of the Cowboy.* 6 plates. Clothbound. Boston, 1903. 1st ed. $35-$50.

ADAMS, Charles W. *Civil War Reminiscence Interestingly Told.*
20 pp., paperbound. No place, no date (Greenfield, Ohio,
1918). $150.

ADAMS, Henry. *The Education of.* Clothbound, leather label.
Washington, 1907. 1st ed., privately published. One of 100.
$400-$600. Boston, 1918. 1st trade ed. Clothbound. $25 in
dust jacket. Lacking jacket, $10.

ADAMS, Henry. *A Letter to American Teachers of History.*
Clothbound. Washington, 1910. 1st ed. $20-$25. One of a
few copies, signed. $50.

*ADDRESS and Recommendations to the States, by the United
States in Congress Assembled.* 35 leaves. Philadelphia, 1783.
1st ed. $35.

ADDRESS to the Emigrants from Connecticut (An). 19 pp.,
sewed. Hartford, 1817. Margin chewed, affecting a few lines
of text, $45.

*ADDRESS to the Reader of the Documents Relating to the Gal-
veston Bay & Texas Land Company, Which Are Contained
in the Appendix.* 38 pp., sewed. New York, 1831. (By David
G. Burnet.) $125.

ADVENTURES of Robin Day (The). 2 vols. Clothbound. Philadelphia, 1839. (By Robert Montgomery Bird.) 1st ed. $50-$100.

*AFFECTING Narrative of the Captivity and Sufferings of Mrs.
Mary Smith, etc. (An).* 24 pp. Providence, no date (1815). 1st
ed., 1st issue, with account of Indians killing 30 persons. $150-
$250. Later issues, same date, lacking this account, $150.

AGASSIZ, Louis. *Lake Superior: Its Physical Character, Veg-
etation, and Animals, etc.* Map, 16 plates. Clothbound. Boston,
1850. 1st ed. $50-$75. Top of spine chipped, $27.50. Hinges
cracked, $35.

AGEE, G. W. *Rube Burrows King of Outlaws, and His Band of
Train Robbers.* 194 pp., paperbound. No place, no date (Cincinnati, 1890). 1st ed. $50. Chicago, no date (1890). $35.

AKEN, David. *Pioneers of the Balck Hills.* 7 full-page sketches.
151 pp., paperbound. No place, no date (Milwaukee, 1920?).
1st ed. $45-$75.

AKIN, James. *The Journal of.* (Cover title.) Edited by E. E.

Dale. 32 pp., paperbound. Norman, Okla., 1919. 1st ed. $35-$50.

ALCOTT, Louisa May. *Flower Fables*. Clothbound. Boston, 1855. 1st ed. $50. Another, $40. Inscribed by the author, $60 and $70.

ALCOTT, Louisa May. *Hospital Sketches*. Green boards or cloth. Boston, 1863. Unrecorded 1st ed., 1st printing, with ad for Wendell Phillips book at $2.50 instead of $2.25. $65. Another, clothbound, 2d printing, $25.

ALCOTT, Louisa M. *Little Men*. Clothbound. Boston, 1871. 1st Am. ed., 1st issue, with ads in front announcing *Pink and White Tyranny* as "nearly ready." $30. Worn, $7.50 and $10.

ALCOTT, Louisa May. *Little Women*. 2 vols. Clothbound. Boston, 1868-1869. 1st ed., with Vol. 1 lacking "Part One" at base of spine and with Vol. 2 having no notice of *Little Women, Part First,* on page iv. $750. Worn and stained, $85 (1964 auction). Vol. 1, alone, $500 (1965 dealer catalogue).

ALDRICH, Thomas Bailey. *The Story of a Bad Boy*. Clothbound. Boston, 1870. 1st ed., 1st issue, with page 14, line 20, reading "scattered" and page 197, line 10, reading "abroad." $475 (1960 auction). Other copies, fine, up to $250 at retail. Worn, $40. Another, backstrip repaired, $25. Another, binding stained, $125.

ALLAN, Francis D. *Lone Star Ballads*. Leatherbound. Galveston, 1874. 1st ed. $100.

ALLEN, Ethan, Esq. *Reason the Only Oracle of Man*. Bennington, Vt., 1784. 1st ed. $100-$150.

ALLEN, Lewis F. *The American Herd Book, etc.* Buffalo, 1846. 1st ed. Two blank flyleaves torn, dampstains, $40.

ALLISON, Scout (Edwin Henry). *The Surrender of Sitting Bull*. 85 pp., paperbound. Dayton, Ohio, 1891. 1st ed. $150-$200. Another, rebound, front cover preserved, $120 (1966 auction).

ALMANACK and Register for the Island of Jamaica (An). Montego Bay, no date (1792). $45.

ALNWICK Castle, with Other Poems. Paperbound or unprinted boards. New York, 1827. (By Fitz-Greene Halleck.) 1st ed. $50-$75. Another copy, calf, paper covers bound in, $28.50. New York, 1836. $32.50.

ALTER, J. Cecil. *James Bridger, Trapper, Frontiersman, Scout, and Guide.* 18 plates. Clothbound. Salt Lake City, no date (1925). 1st ed. Limited and signed. $75 and $50. Columbus, 1951. $25.

ALTOWAN; or Incidents of Life and Adventure in the Rocky Mountains. 2 vols. New York, 1846. (By Sir William Drummond Stewart.) 1st ed. $100-$185.

ALVAREZ, Jose and Rafael Duran. *Itinerarios y Derroteros de la Republica Mexicana.* Mexico, 1856. $25-$100.

ALVORD, Clarence Walworth and Lee Bidgood. *The First Explorations of the Trans-Allegheny Region by the Virginians, 1650-1674.* Map, 4 facsimiles. Clothbound. Cleveland, 1912. 1st ed. One of 1,000. $35.

ALVORD, Clarence W. *The Mississippi Valley in British Politics.* 4 maps. 2 vols. Clothbound. Cleveland, 1917. 1st ed. $50.

AMERICAN Poems, Selected and Original. Vol. I (all published). Litchfield, Conn., no date (1793). 1st ed. $50. Repaired, $27.50.

AMERICAN Primer, Containing Short and Easy Lessons for Little Children (The). 19 pp., paperbound. Cincinnati, 1829. $30.

AMERICAN Repository of Useful Information (The). Paperbound. Philadelphia, 1795. $50. Philadelphia, 1797. $40.

AMERICAN Spectator, or Matrimonial Preceptor (The). Boston, 1797. (By Susanna Haswell Rowson). 1st ed. $25-$35.

AMERICAN Spy (The). 62 pp., paperbound. Albany, 1846. (By Jeptha R. Simms). 1st ed. $28.50.

AMES, Nathaniel, Jr. *An Astronomical Diary, or, an Almanack for the Year . . . 1729.* Boston, 1729. $35. For 1730, 1735, 1736 and 1760, each $25. For 1762, $15. For 1772, $50.

ANALYSE d 'un Entretien sur la Conservation des Establissemens du Bas-Canada, des Loix, des Usages, etc., de ses Habitans. Pamphlet. Montreal, 1926. (By Dennis Benjamin Viger.) $50.00.

ANDERSON, Alexander C. *Hand-book and Map to the Gold Region of Frazer's and Thompson's Rivers, etc.* Large folding map. 31 pp., boards. San Francisco, 1858. 1st ed. In morocco case, $900.

ANDERSON, Peter. *An Inaugural Dissertation on the Diarrhoea Infantum, etc.* 29 pp. New York, 1795. Errata slip pasted to back of title page, $25.

ANDERSON, Sherwood. *Windy McPherson's Son.* Clothbound. New York, 1916. 1st ed. $60-$80. Spine faded, $25.

ANDERSON, W. F. *Map of Southern Idaho and the Adjacent Regions, etc.* San Francisco, no date (1880). 1st ed. $75.

ANDREWS, Prof. E. B. *Letter on the Coal and Iron Deposits of the Upper Sandy Creek and Moxahala Valleys, in Perry County.* 44 pp., paperbound. Columbus, 1873. $25.

ANNUAL Circular of Marietta College, with the Inaugural Address of the President, July 25, 1838. 14 pp., sewed. Cincinnati, 1839. $35.

ANTI-MORMON Almanac, for 1842. 24 pp., paperbound. New York, no date (1841). $50.

APPEAL to the World (An). 37 pp. Boston, 1769. (By Samuel Adams.) 1st ed. $35.

APPLEBY, Wm. P. and others. *The Pah-Ranagat Central Silver Mining District, Nye County, Nevada.* 2 woodcut maps on one large folding tissue sheet. 32 pp., paperbound. New York, 1866. $75.

APPLEGATE, Jesse. *A Day With the Cow Column.* Chicago, 1934. One of 300, Caxton Club. $40-$50.

ARCHBOLD, Ann. *A Book for the Married and Single.* 192 pp., clothbound. East Plainfield, Ohio, 1850. 1st ed. $125. Another, $120 (1966 auction).

ARITHMETICK Vulgar and Decimal. Leatherbound. Boston, 1729. (By Isaac Greenwood.) $225.

ARMSTRONG, A. N. *Oregon: A Brief History and Description of Oregon and Washington.* Clothbound. Chicago, 1857. 1st ed. $85 and $60. Rubbed, $40 (1966 auction). Rebound, $25.

ARNY, W. F. M. *Centennial Celebration, Santa Fe, New Mexico, July 4, 1876.* (Cover title.) 64 pp., paperbound. Santa Fe, 1876. 1st ed. $35 and $45.

ARRIAGA, Pablo Jose de. *Extirpacion de la Idolatria del Piru.* Lima, 1621. $700 to $1,200.

ARTHUR MERVYN; or Memoirs of the Year 1793. By the Author of "Wieland." Leatherbound. Philadelphia, 1799. (By Charles Brockden Brown.) 1st ed. $50-$100. Second part, 1800, leatherbound, $50. Boston, 1827, 2 vols. $25.

ARTHUR, T. S. *Ten Nights in a Bar-Room, and What I Saw There.* Clothbound. Philadelphia, 1854. 1st ed., 1st issue, with the Lippincott and Bradley imprint. $65.

ARTICLES of an Association by the Name of the Ohio Company. 12 pp., boards. Worcester, 1786. 1st ed. $750 and up. A copy sold at auction for $1,700 on Dec. 3, 1958.

ASHLEY, Capt. C. B. *Gilbert the Trapper.* Paperbound. New York, 1889. (By Harry Castlemon?) 1st ed. $32.50.

ASHLEY, Clifford W. *The Yankee Whaler.* Boards. Boston, 1926. 1st ed. One of 156, boxed, signed, with original drawing. $125 and $85. Regular trade ed., $25-$50.

ASHMEAD, Henry Graham. *History of Delaware County, Pennsylvania.* Philadelphia, 1884. $30 and $45.

ASPLUND, John. *The Annual Register of the Baptist Denomination in North America.* 72 pp., unbound. Preface dated Southampton County, Va., July 14, 1791. No place, no date (Philadelphia, 1791?). 1st ed. $50-$75.

ASSASSINATION and History of the Conspiracy (The). 163 pp., yellow paperbound. Cincinnati, no date (1865). 1st ed. $50-$75. Rebound, $35-$50.

ASTRONOMICAL Diary (An), or An Almanac, 1757. Portsmouth, N. H., no date (1756). $125. Portsmouth, 1757, 2d issue (for 1758), $30.

ATLAS of Athens County, Ohio. 88 pp., clothbound. Philadelphia, 1875. $25-$50.

ATLAS of Cuyahoga County (Ohio). 119 lithographic views. Philadelphia, 1874. $25-$50.

ATLAS of Illinois. Chicago, 1876. $50-$100. Rebound, $35-$75.

ATLAS of Jackson County (Ohio). Philadelphia, 1875. $40.

ATLAS of LaSalle County and the State of Illinois. Chicago,

1876. $35-$60.

ATLAS of Macon County and the State of Illinois. Chicago, 1874. $35-$60.

ATLAS of Mahoning County (Ohio). Philadelphia, 1874. $50.

ATLAS of Wyane County (Ohio) and the City of Wooster.

ATLAS of Wayne County (Ohio) and the City of Wooster. Sunbury, 1873. $35-$50.

ATTERLEY, Joseph. *A Voyage to the Moon.* New York, 1827. (By George Tucker.) 1st ed. $175.

AUCTION Catalog of the Famous Sale and Dispersion of the Nursery Stud (stock and buildings) Held in New York, 1891. Leatherbound. No place, no date (about 1892). $50-$75.

AUDSLEY, George Ashdown. *The Art of Organ-Building.* 2 vols. Clothbound. New York, 1905. $150-$200.

AUDUBON, John James. *The Birds of America.* New York, 1840-44. 7 vols., octavo, full or half morocco; also, half calf. 1st ed. $1,000 and up ($750 and $850 at auction, 1963). New York, no date (1870), George R. Lockwood, publisher, 8 vols., fine sets, $600 and up ($588 at auction, 1963).

AUDUBON, John James and John Bachman. *The Quadrupeds of North America.* 155 colored plates. 3 vols. New York, 1849-51-54. 1st ed. $300-$400. New York, 1854. 3 vols., published by Lockwood, $75-$150.

AUSTIN, Jane G. *Standish of Standish.* Tan cloth. Boston, 1889. 1st ed. $35. Later issue, same date, gray-green cloth, $25.

AUSTIN, Mary. *Land of Little Rain.* Clothbound. Boston, 1903. 1st ed. $25. Worn, $17.50.

AUTHENTIC Account of the Barbarity of the Russians, etc. (An). 16 pp., sewed. Boston, 1769. $27.50.

AUTHENTIC and Thrilling Narrative of the Captivity of Mrs. Horn, and Her Two Children, with Mrs. Harris, by the Camanche Indians, etc. (An). Paperbound. Cincinnati, 1851. (By Mrs. Sarah Ann Horn.) 2d ed. Half leather, paper covers bound in, $210 (1966 auction). Cincinnati, no date (1853), 3d ed., paperbound, $50.

AUTHENTIC Historical Memoir of the Schuylkill Fishing Com-

pany of the State of Schuylkill. 5 plates. Clothbound. (Bound with—under separate title page—*Memoirs of the Gloucester Hunting Club.)* Philadelphia, 1830. 1st ed. (By William Milnor.) $100-$200.

AUTOCRAT of the Breakfast Table (The). Clothbound (tan and brick red). Boston, 1858. (By Oliver Wendell Holmes.) 1st ed., 1st issue, with engraved half title, and left end paper at back headed "Poetry and the Drama" and right "School Books." In preferred and presumably first binding with five rings on spine, $270 (1962 auction).

rings on spine, $270 (1962 auction). Four-ring binding, $100. Others, worn, $45 and $25.

AVERY, S. P. *Mrs. Partington's Carpet-Bag of Fun.* Clothbound. New York, 1854. 1st ed. $27.50.

BACHELLER, Irving. *Eben Holden: A Tale of the North Country.* Clothbound. Boston, no date (1900). 1st ed., 1st issue, with reading "go to fur" in line 13, page 400. $35-$50.

BADGER, Joseph. *A Memoir of.* Hudson, Ohio, 1851. 1st ed. $35-$50.

BAIRD, Spencer F., T. M. Brewer and R. Ridgway. *The Water Birds of North America.* Hand-colored illustrations. 2 vols. Clothbound. Boston, 1884. 1st ed. $250.

BAKER, Rev. Alfred. *An Address in Commemoration of George F. Emmons, etc.* 20 pp., paperbound. New York, 1884. $25.

BALDWIN, Mrs. Alice Blackwood. *Memoirs of the Late Frank D. Baldwin.* 12 plates. Los Angeles, 1929. 1st ed. $35.

BALDWIN, Joseph G. *The Flush Times of Alabama and Mississippi.* Clothbound. New York, 1853. 1st ed. $40-$100.

BALDWIN, Thomas. *Narrative of the Massacre, by the Savages, of the Wife and Children of, etc.* Folding colored frontispiece. 24 pp., paperbound. New York, 1835. 1st ed. $75 and $100. New York, 1836. 2d ed. $45 and $75. Clothbound, $35. Paperbound, $25.

BANCROFT, George and Joseph G. Cogswell. *Prospectus of a School to be Established at Round Hill, Northampton, Mass.* 20 pp., stitched. Cambridge, 1823. $27.50.

BANCROFT, H. H. *History of Alaska: 1730-1885.* San Francisco, 1886. 1st ed. $35 and $50. Worn, $25.

BANKS, Henry. *The Vindication of John Banks, of Virginia, etc.* 88 pp., sewed. Frankfort, 1826. 1st ed. $100-$300.

BARBE-MARBOIS, Francois. *The History of Louisiana, Particularly the Cession of that Colony to the U.S.A.* Clothbound. Philadelphia, 1830. 1st Am. ed. $75.

BARBER, Miss [Mary]. *The True Narrative of the Five Years' Suffering and Perilous Adventures of.* 108 pp., paperbound. Philadelphia, no date (1873). $25-$35.

BARKER, Benjamin. *Francisco, or The Pirate of the Pacific.* Paperbound. Boston, 1845. 1st ed. $35.

BARLOW, Joel. *An Oration, Delivered at the North Church.* 20 pp., blue-gray paperbound. Hartford, no date (1787). 1st ed. $27.50.

BARNES, Charles Merritt. *Combats and Conquests of Immortal Heroes.* Clothbound. San Antonio, 1910. 1st ed. $30-$50. Leatherbound, $40.

BARNES, L. D. *References to Prove the Gospel, in Its Fulness, etc.* 12 pp., sewed. No place, no date (Nauvoo, 1841). In morocco case, $250.

BARNES, Will C. *Western Grazing Grounds and Forest Ranges.* Plates. Clothbound. Chicago, 1913. 1st ed. $35-$50.

BARREIRO, Antonio. *Ojeada Sobre Nuevo-Mexico.* 3 tables. Paperbound. Puebla, 1832. 1st ed. $350-$450-$500. Rebound in half leather, $300 (1966 auction).

BARRY, Thomas. *The Singular Adventures and Captivity of.* Manchester, no date (1801?). 2d ed. $100.

BARTLETT, Joseph. *Aphorisms on Men, Manners, Principles and Things.* Boston, 1823. 1st ed. $28.

BARTON, Benjamin Smith. *New Views of the Origin of the Tribes and Nations of America.* Philadelphia, 1797. 1st ed. $50. Philadelphia, 1798. 2d ed. $35.

BASCOM, Flavel and Frederick Perkins. *A Historical Discourse: Commemorative of the Settlement at Galesburg. And a Statistical Paper.* 39 pp., sewed. Galesburg, 1866. $45.

BAUM, L. Frank. *Dorothy and the Wizard of Oz.* Clothbound. Chicago, no date (1908). 1st ed., 1st issue, with "Reilly & Britton Co." at bottom of spine. $35-$50.

BAUM, L. Frank. *The Marvelous Land of Oz.* Green cloth. Chicago, 1904. 1st ed., 1st issue, without "Published July, 1904" in copyright line. In dust jacket, $150. Another copy, lacking dust jacket, $100.

BAUM, L. Frank. *Mother Goose in Prose.* Illustrated by Maxfield Parrish. Pictorial cloth cover. Chicago, no date (1897). 1st ed. $75-$100.

BAUM, L. Frank. *A New Wonderland.* Green cloth. New York, 1900. 1st ed. $50-$75.

BAUM, L. Frank. *The Wonderful Wizard of Oz.* With Pictures by W. W. Denslow. Green cloth. Chicago and New York, 1900. 1st ed., 1st issue, with 11-line colophon (not 13) on back end paper. $875 (1960 auction), $600, $550 (1962 auction), and $625, covers faded (1965 auction). (A complex book to identify in various 1st ed. states. Ask a rare book specialist for help if you find a copy with 1900 date on title page.) Other prices: Front and back hinges broken, $550. Hinges weak, two plates loose, $117.50. Presentation copy signed by author, $600. Another copy, leaf missing, binding shabby, $25.

BAYARD, Coll. Nicholas. *An Account of the Commitment, Arraignment, Tryal, etc., of Nicholas Bayard, Esq., for High Treason.* 44 pp. New York, 1702. 1st ed. $450.

BAYLIES, Francis. *Northwest Coast of America.* 22 pp. Washington, 1826. Half morocco, $75.

BAZ, Gustavo and E. L. Gallo. *History of the Mexican Railway.* Color plates. Mexico City, 1876. $75-$150. Waterstained, $50.

BEASTALL, William. *A Useful Guide, for Grocers, Distillers, Hotel & Tavern-Keepers and Wine and Spirit Dealers.* New York, 1829. $30.

BEAUMONT, William. *Experiments and Observations on the Gastric Juice, and the Physiology of Digestion.* Boards. Plattsburgh, N.Y., 1833. 1st ed. $475 (1966 auction). $450, $400, and $200. Rebound, $175. Boston, 1834. Rebacked, rubbed. $100.

BEAUTIES of Divine Poetry, or Appropriate Hymns and Spiritual Songs. Lexington, Ky., 1817. $25.

BECK, Lewis C. *A Gazetteer of the States of Illinois and Missouri.* Folding map, 5 plates. Boards, paper label. Albany, 1823. 1st ed. In rarest state, with wide, rough edges on all sides, $500. Other copies, $425 and $300.

BEEBE, Henry S. *The History of Peru.* Errata leaf. Peru, Ill., 1858. 1st ed. $35.

BEER'S Almanac and Ephemeris . . . for the year of our Lord, 1795. 36 pp. Hartford, no date (1794). Clothbound copies, $65 and $87.50. Another, stitched, $35.

BEESON, John. *A Plea for the Indians; with Facts and Features of the Late War in Oregon.* 144 pp., paperbound. Also in boards. New York, 1857. 1st ed. $100. Another, boards, rubbed, $45 (1966 auction).

BELKNAP, Jeremy. *American Biography; or, an Historical Account of Those Persons Who Have Been Distinguished in America.* 2 vols. Boards. Boston, 1794-98. 1st ed. $75. Rebound in calf, $45.

BELL, Horace. *Reminiscences of a Ranger.* Clothbound. Los Angeles, 1881. 1st ed. $35 and $60.

BELLAMY, Edward. *Looking Backward, 2000-1887.* Clothbound. Boston, 1888. 1st ed., 1st issue, with printer's imprint of "J. J. Arakelyan" on copyright page. $85. (1966 auction). Another copy, rubbed, $60. Later issue, 1888, paperbound, $20-$25.

BELTRAMI, J. C. *La Decouverte des Sources du Mississippi et de la Riviere Sanglante, etc.* Nouvelle-Orleans, 1824. 1st ed., with errata slip. $100-$150. Also, $90 (1958 auction). Another, worn, $35.

BELTRAN De. Sta. Rosa, Fr. Pedro. *Arte Del Idioma Maya Reducido, etc.* Merida (de Yucatan), 1859. 2d ed., $25.

BENET, Stephen Vincent. *John Brown's Body.* Garden City, 1928. 1st ed. One of 201 signed large paper copies, bound in vellum and boxed. $250-$350. In defective binding, $120 (1961 auction). Another, covers spotted, box repaired, $70 at retail. 1st trade ed. Clothbound, $10-$30. Inscribed copies, in dust jacket, $25 and $35. New York, 1948. With Curry illustrations. One of 1,500, boxed. $35-$50.

BENJAMIN, Asher and Daniel Reynard. *The American Builder's Companion.* Leatherbound. Boston, 1806. 1st ed. $200-$250. $130 (1960 auction). Boston, 1826. 5th ed. Worn, $35 (at auction).

BENJAMIN, Asher. *The Country Builder's Assistant.* 37 plates. Leatherbound. Greenfield, Mass., 1805. $250-$300.

BENNETT, Emerson. *The League of the Miami.* 116 pp., paperbound. Cincinnati, 1851. 1st ed. Back missing, $65. (Catalogued in 1956 as "the only known copy.")

BENNETT, John C. *The History of the Saints.* 5 plates. Boston, 1842. 1st ed., $60. Worn, stained, $40 and $35. 2d and 3d eds., same date, $25 each.

BENSCHOTER, Geo. E. *Book of Facts Concerning the Early Settlement of Sherman County (Nebraska).* 76 pp., paperbound. Loup City, no date (about 1897). 1st ed. $30 and $35.

BENSON, Frank W. *Etchings and Drypoints.* 4 vols. Paper boards, linen backs. Boston, 1917. One of 275 sets, with frontispiece signed by Benson. Lacking dust wrapper for Vol. 1, $225. Other copies noted ranging from $150 to $200.

BENTON, Ariel. *Life and Times of.* 51 pp., boards. Peoria, 1882. 1st ed. $100.

BERLANDIER, Luis and R. Chovel. *Diario de Viage de la Comision de Limites que . . . baja la Direccion del General Manuel de Mier y Teran.* Portrait, 2 maps. Calfbound. Mexico, 1850. 1st ed. $125-$150. Another, lacking portrait, $35.

BERNARD, Auguste. *Geofroy Tory, Printer and Engraver.* Translated by George B. Ives. No place, no date (Boston, 1909). One of 370 printed by Bruce Rogers. $50-$80.

BERQUIN, Arnaud. *Le Livre de Famille, ou Journal des Enfans: The Family Book; or, Children's Journal.* 2 vols. Detroit, 1812. $150-$250. Worn, $100.

BERRY, Thomas F. *Four Years with Morgan and Forrest.* 13 plates. Oklahoma City, 1914. 1st ed. $32.50.

BESCHKE, Prof. Wm. *The Dreadful Sufferings and Thrilling*

Adventures of an Overland Party of Emigrants to California.
4 plates. 71 pp., paperbound. St. Louis, 1850. 1st ed. Dampstained, covers slightly chipped, $250. Another, 60 pp., paper-
bound. covers frayed and mended, $275.

BESSON, Maurice. *The Scourge of the Indies.* Clothbound. New
York, 1929. 1st ed. Limited. $25-$30.

BEY, Ali. *Extracts from a Journal of Travels in North America,
etc.* Boston, 1818. (By Samuel L. Knapp.) 1st ed. $27.50.

BEYER, Ed. *Album of Virginia.* 40 plates and text (oblong vol.
of plates and octavo vol. of text). Richmond, 1856. 1st ed.
$600-$1,000. Richmond, 1857. Oblong folio. $600 and up.
Richmond, 1858. Oblong folio. Up to $500. (All issues scarce
and valuable and may bring higher prices than indicated.)

BICKERSTAFF'S Boston Almanack, for . . . 1778. 24 pp., sewed.
Danvers, no date (1777). (By Benj. West.) $25.

BIDWELL, John. *A Journey to California with Observations
About the Country, Climate, and the Route to this Country.*
48 pp., boards. San Francisco, 1937. $45 and $75.

BIERCE, Ambrose. *Tales of Soldiers and Civilians.* Clothbound.
San Francisco, 1891. 1st ed. $75-$100. Some copies imprinted
"Compliments of" on preliminary leaf and signed by Bierce—
the so-called "limited" edition. $125-$150.

BIERCE, Gen. L. V. *Historical Reminiscences of Summit County.*
Akron, 1854. 1st ed. $37.50 and $50.

BIGELOW, Jacob. *American Medical Botany.* 60 color plates.
3 vols. Boston, 1817-1818-1820. 1st ed. $150-$200. Lacking
half-title to second section of Vol. 2, $95. Another set, covers
loose, spines worn off, $75.

BIGLER, John. *Annual Message of the Governor of California
with the Accompanying Documents; Delivered at the Commencement of the Seventh Session of the Legislature, January,
1856.* 35 pp., paperbound. No place (Sacramento), December,
1855. Uncut, unopened, $250.

BIGLER, John. *Governor's Annual Message to the Legislature of
the State of California, Assembled at Sacramento, January 1,
1855.* 40 pp., paperbound. Sacramento, no date (1855). Uncut,
$250.

BILL Jones of Paradise Valley, Okla., etc. Kingfisher, Okla., 1914. $30.

BIOGRAPHICAL Sketch of the Life of Capt. Michael Cresap (A). 124 pp. Cumberland, Md., 1826. (By John J. Jacob.) 1st ed. Leatherbound, $475 (1966 auction).

BIOGRAPHICAL Sketch of the Life of William B. Ide (A). No place, no date (Claremont, N.H., 1880). (By Simeon Ide.) 1st ed. $137.50 and $250. Autographed, $295.

BIRCH, W. *The Country Seats of the United States.* Part I (all published). 20 color plates. Springland, Pa., 1808. 1st ed. $300 and up.

BIRKBECK, Morris. *Notes on a Journey in America from the Coast of Virginia to the Territory of Illinois.* Boards. Philadelphia, 1817. 1st ed. $55 and $45.

BISHOP, Richard E. *Bishop's Birds.* Clothbound. Philadelphia, 1936. Limited ed., 135 signed, with signed Bishop etching tipped in, boxed. $75-$100.

BLACK, Nellie P. *Richard Peters, His Ancestors and Descendants.* Leatherbound. Atlanta, 1904. Rubbed, $27.50.

BLACKWATER Chronicle (The). Clothbound. New York, 1853. (By John Pendleton Kennedy?) 1st ed. $35-$50.

BLAIR, J. and J. Maginn. *Communications in Relation to the Entrance of the Columbia River.* 8 pp., clothbound. Washington, 1846. $25.

BLAKE, William. *America, a Prophecy.* Paperbound. Edmonton, Alberta, Canada, 1887. One of a few hand-colored copies of an edition of 50, signed by William Muir. $75-$100.

BLAKE, William. *Genesis.* Cummington, Mass., 1952. One of 170. $35-$50.

BLAND, Richard. *An Inquiry into the Rights of the British Colonies, etc.* 31 pp. Williamsburg, no date (1766). 1st ed. $250.

BLASDEL, H. G. *Inaugural Address of the Governor of Nevada, Delivered at Carson City, Dec. 5, 1864, etc.* 26 pp., calfbound. Carson City, 1865. 1st ed, $125. Second inaugural address, Carson City, 1867, $25 at auction in 1966.

BLEEKER, Leonard. *The Order Book of Capt. Leonard Bleeker.*

New York, 1865. 1st ed. $25.

BLEDSOE, A. J. *Indian Wars of the Northwest.* San Francisco, 1885. 1st ed. $125-$150.

BLUNT, Edmund M. *The American Coast Pilot.* New York, 1842. 14th ed. Internal water stains, joints cracking, $27.50.

BLUNT, Edmund M. *Traveller's Guide to and Through the State of Ohio, with Sailing Directions for Lake Erie.* 16 pp., leatherbound. New York, 1832. 1st ed. $300-$400. New York, 1833. 28 pp., leatherbound, with folding colored map, $300.

BOALES, Daniel M. *Scott's Exercises and Manoeuvres of Infantry. etc.* Cincinnati, 1825. $25.

BOARDING School (The). Boston, 1798. (By Hannah Webster Foster.) 1st ed. $25.

BOGAERTS, Felix. *The Butchers of Ghent.* Paperbound. No place, no date (New York, 1842). 1st ed. $45.

BOGGS, Mrs. Mae (editor). *My Playhouse Was a Concord Coach.* No place, no date (Oakland, Calif., 1942). 1st ed. $125.

BOLLER, Henry A. *Among the Indians.* Folding map, clothbound. Philadelphia, 1868. 1st ed. $200. Another copy, lacking map, $130 (auction).

BOLTON, Herbert Eugene. *Athanase de Mezieres and the Louisiana-Texas Frontier.* Map, 2 facsimiles. 2 vols. Clothbound. Cleveland, 1914. 1st ed. $50.

BONNELL, George W. *Topographical Description of Texas.* 150 pp., boards. Austin, 1840. 1st ed. $675 (1966 auction). Other copies catalogued in $350-$450 range.

BONNER, T. D. (editor). *The Life and Adventures of James P. Beckwourth, Mountaineer, Scout and Pioneer, etc.* Clothbound. New York, 1856. 1st ed. $150-$175. Soiled copy, $35 (at auction).

BOLTON, Herbert Eugene. *The Rim of Christendom.* 12 plates, 3 facsimiles. Clothbound. New York, 1936. 1st ed. $35-$50.

BONNEY, Edward. *The Banditti of the Prairies.* Plates. 195 pp., paperbound. Chicago, 1850. 1st ed. $600-$900. Philadelphia, no date (1855). $75. Philadelphia, 1856. 3d ed. $150. Chicago, 1856, $200. Chicago, 1858. 13 plates, paperbound. $120 (1966 auction). Also, $225 at retail in catalogue.

BOOK of Commandments, for the Government of the Church of Christ, etc. (A). 160 pp. With or without ornamental border on title page. Zion (Independence, Mo.), 1833. (By Joseph Smith.) 1st ed. $3,000 and up. (A bookseller paid $2,600 for an imperfect copy of this, with title page in ornamental border, at a New York auction in 1963.)

BOOK of Common Prayer, etc. (The). Boston, 1930. One of 520 printed by D. B. Updike. $75-$100.

BOOK of the Law of the Lord (The). Saint James, A. R. I. (Beaver Island, Lake Michigan), no date (1851). (By James Jesse Strang.) 1st ed. $1,000 and up (only three copies known). 2d ed., lacking title page (some supplied in modern type), $250-$450.

BOOK of Ruth (The). King James Version. Introduction by Mary Ellen Chase. New York, 1948. $35-$50.

BORGIA, Experience (pseudonym). *The Confessions of a Magdalen.* 31 pp., sewed, or paperbound. New York, 1831. 1st ed. Front cover missing, $55. Another copy, $13 (at auction).

BORZOI 1920 (The). New York, 1920. 1st ed. One of 100 on San Marco paper, uncut. $35-$50.

BOSTON Prize Poems, and Other Specimens of Dramatic Poetry. Printed boards, uncut. Boston, 1824. 1st ed. $100. Another copy, covers loose, spine chipped, $37.50. Another copy, $32.50.

BOURKE, John G. *An Apache Campaign in the Sierra Madre.* 11 plates. 112 pp., paperbound. New York, 1886. 1st ed. $125 (1966 auction). Another, clothbound, $60 at retail.

BOURKE, John G. *The Snake-Dance of the Moquis of Arizona.* 31 plates, many colored. Clothbound. New York, 1884. 1st ed. $60-$80. New York, 1891. $50-$60.

BOWDITCH, Nathaniel. *Mathematical Papers, etc.* 18 pp., paperbound. Cambridge, 1820. 1st ed. $45.

BOWDITCH, Nathaniel. *The New American Practical Navigator.* 7 plates and maps, one folding. Boards or leatherbound. Newburyport, 1802. 1st ed. Rebacked calfbound copy, $850 (1963 auction). Other copies have been catalogued in recent years in the $250-$500 range. Copies with defects have been noted at $100 (half of map missing) and $225 (rebacked and with stamp on title page). New York, 1817. 4th ed. (described as 1st stereotype ed.). Rebacked, $40 (1957 auction). New York, 1821. Calfbound, worn, $25.

BOWEN, Clarence Winthrop. *The History of the Centennial Celebration of the Inauguration of George Washington.* Clothbound. New York, 1892. $25-$50.

BOWEN, J. B. (compiler). *The Wheeling Directory and Advertiser.* Wheeling, 1839. 1st ed. $75. Rebacked, $35.

BOWNAS, Samuel. *An Account of the Life, Travels, and Christian Experiences of Samuel Bownas.* Stamford, 1805. $25 and $27.50.

BOWNAS, Samuel. *Journals of the Lives and Travels of Samuel Bownas and John Richardson.* Calfbound. Philadelphia, 1759. 1st Am. ed. $75-$100.

BOYD, Lucinda. *The Sorrows of Nancy.* Richmond, 1899. 1st ed. Flyleaf loose, hinges cracked, $25.

BOYNTON, Charles B. and T. B. Mason. *A Journey Through Kansas.* Map. 216 pp., paperbound. Cincinnati, 1855. 1st ed. $50. Also, clothbound, $25-$50.

BRACKENRIDGE, Henry M. *Views of Louisiana.* Calfbound. Pittsburgh, 1814. 1st ed. $150. Other copies at $115 and $100. Rebound copies, $50 and $100. Baltimore, 1817. $50.

BRADFORD, John. *The General Instructor; or the Office, Duty, and Authority of Justices of the Peace, etc.* Lexington, 1820. With both the indexes (sometimes lacking), $45.

BRADFORD, Maj. Ward. *Biographical Sketches of.* Portrait. Paperbound. No place (Fresno, Calif.?), no date (1893). 1st ed. In morocco case, $125.

BRADLEY, William Aspenwall. *The Etching of Figures.* Marlborough-on-Hudson, 1915. One of 250. $50-$75.

BRAINARD, Maj. J. *The Death-Face; or, the Enchantress of the Wilderness; an Episode of the Recent Indian Troubles in the West.* 92 pp., sewed. New York, 1864. $25.

BRAND *Book of the Montana Stock Growers' Association.* 152 pp., paperbound. No place (Miles City, Mont.), 1908. $25.

BRAYTON, Matthew. *The Indian Captive, etc.* 68 pp., paperbound. Cleveland, 1860. 1st ed. $450-$650. Also, boards,

$200-$400. Fostoria, Ohio, 1896. 2d ed. Boards. $75.

BRETON, Nicholas. *The Twelve Months and Christmas Day.* New York, 1951. One of 100, signed by Bruce Rogers. $35.

BRETT, Capt. Wilford. *Hints on Bivouac and Camp Life.* Halifax, no date (1855). $75.

BREVE Noticia del Actual Estado del Territorio de la Alta California. Folding table. 8 pp., paperbound. Mexico, 1833. (By Jose Maria Guzman.) $400-$550.

BREWER, William H. *Up and Down California in 1860-64.* Map, 32 plates. Clothbound. New Haven, 1930. 1st ed. $35-$50.

BRIDAL Eve (The): A Tale. By a Youth. Mobile, 1833. (By William Russell Smith.) $75.

BRIGGS, Richard. *The New Art of Cookery.* Philadelphia, 1792. 1st Am. ed. $60. Philadelphia, 1798. 2d Am. ed. $45.

BRIGHAM, Clarence S. *Paul Revere's Engravings.* Clothbound. Worcester, 1954. 1st ed. $40-$60.

BRINTON Family (The). 60 pp., clothbound. No place, no date (Media, 1878). (By D. G. Brinton.) $37.50.

BRITTON, Rollin J. *Early Days on Grand River and the Mormon War.* Columbia, Mo., 1920. 1st ed. $40.

BROOKE, Rupert. *1914 and Other Poems.* New York, 1915. 1st Am. ed. One of a few copies (out of an issue of 87) bound in morocco (others being paperbound). $75-$100. Paperbound, $35-$50.

BROUILLET, J. B. A. *Authentic Account of the Murder of Dr. Whitman and Other Missionaries.* 108 pp., paperbound. Portland, 1869. 2d ed. (1st ed. with this title). $450. Also, $350 (1966 auction).

BROWN, C. Exera. *Brown's Gazetteer of the Chicago and Northwestern Ry., etc.* Map. Chicago, 1869. 1st ed. $150. Spine missing, $125. Another copy, ex-library, $50.

BROWN, J. Henry. *Brown's Political History of Oregon: Vol. 1, Provisional Government* (all published). Map, 2 portraits, 2 facsimiles. Portland, 1892. 1st ed. $175-$200. Another, autographed, $150.

BROWN, John Henry and W. S. Speer. *The Encyclopedia of*

the New West. Leatherbound. Marshall, Tex., 1881. 1st ed. $75-$125.

BROWN, John H. *Reminiscences and Incidents of the "Early Days" of San Francisco.* Map. Clothbound. San Francisco, no date (1886). 1st ed. $325. Also, $250 (1963 auction). Another, rebound, $175 at retail. San Francisco, no date (1933). Grabhorn Press ed. One of 500. $35.

BROWN, William R. *The Horse of the Desert.* New York, 1929. One of 750. Derrydale Press ed. $50-$60.

BROWNE, J. Ross. *Adventures in the Apache Country.* Clothbound. New York, 1869. 1st ed. $75-$100. New York, 1874. $30.

BRYANT, Edwin. *What I Saw in California.* Clothbound. New York, 1848. 1st ed. $60-$125. Santa Ana, 1936. Half morocco, $25.

BRYANT, William Cullen. *Poems.* Brown printed boards. Also in printed brown paper covers. Cambridge, 1821. 1st ed. Fine copies, up to $1,000. Chipped and defective, $600. Another copy, $575. Another, lacking ad leaf following title page, $225. Another, rebacked, $85. Another, spine chipped and name cut from title page, $97.50. New York, 1832. 2d ed. Boards. Worn, $50. New York, 1836. 3d ed. $35-$50.

BUCHANAN, Rev. Claudius. *Christian Researches in Asia, etc.* Warren, 1816. $27.50.

BUCK, William J. *History of the Indian Walk, etc.* Philadelphia, 1886. 1st ed. $50.

BUCKINGHAM, Nash. *De Shootinest Gent'man and Other Tales.* New York, no date (1934). 1st ed. One of 950. $100-$150.

BUCKSKIN Mose: or, Life from the Lakes to the Pacific. 12 plates. New York, 1873. (By George W. Perrie.) 1st ed. $30-$40.

BUEL, J. W. *Heroes of the Plains.* Clothbound. St. Louis, 1881. 1st ed. $25-$35.

BULLEN, Henry Lewis. *The Nuremberg Chronicle, etc.* San Francisco, 1930. One of 300 copies with leaf from 1493 ed. laid in. $80, $60, and $47.50.

BUNN, Matthew. *Narrative of the Life and Adventures of, etc.* 71 pp., paperbound. Batavia, 1827. Reprint ed. $100-$300.

Note: The 1st ed. of this book, Providence, no date (1796), is a rarity worth $5,000 or more. Any ed. before 1830 is rare and worth in the hundreds of dollars, depending, of course, on condition.

BUNN, William. *Biennial Message of the Governor of Idaho to the 13th Session of the Legislative Assembly.* 32 pp., paperbound. Boise City, 1884. $35.

BUNTLINE, Ned. *Magdalena, The Beautiful Mexican Maid.* New York, 1846 (really 1847). (By Edward L. C. Judson.) 1st ed. $50.

BUNYAN, John. *The Doctrine of the Law and Grace Unfolded.* Boston, 1742. 1st Am. ed. $75-$100.

BURDELL, Harvey and John Burdell. *Observations on the Structure, etc., of the Teeth.* New York, 1838. 1st ed. Badly stained binding, waterstained throughout, $32.

BURGESS, Gelett. *The Purple Cow!* Paperbound. No place, no date (San Francisco, 1895). 1st ed., 2d state, printed on one side of leaf only. $50. Another copy, $35. (Only one known copy of 1st state printing on both sides of leaf.)

BURK, John. *The History of Virginia.* 4 vols. Petersburg, 1804-16. 1st ed. $200-$400. Modern half morocco, $210 (1963 auction).

BURKE, John. *Dreams and Derisions.* Illustrated by Rockwell Kent. Half morocco. No place (New York), 1927. (By Ralph Pulitzer.) 1st ed. One of 100 (of an edition of 300) signed by Kent, boxed. $35.

BURKE, William S. (compiler). *Military History of Kansas Regiments.* Leavenworth, 1870. 1st ed. $100.

BURNETT, Frances Hodgson. *The Drury Lane Boys' Club.* 78 pp., blue paperbound. Washington, 1892. 1st ed. One of 800. $60-$100.

BURNETT, Frances Hodgson. *Little Lord Fauntleroy.* Gray-blue or brown cloth. New York, 1886. 1st ed., 1st issue, with the DeVinne imprint on back of last page of text. $100-$200. Worn copies much less.

BURNETT, Peter H. *Recollections and Opinions of an Old Pioneer.* Clothbound. New York, 1880. 1st ed. $75-$100.

BURNHAM, George P. *The Game Fowl, etc.* Melrose, Mass.,

1877. 1st ed. $35.

BURNS, John H. *Memoirs of a Cow Pony, as Told by Himself.* Plates. Boston, no date (1906). 1st ed. $35.

BURROUGHS, John. *Notes on Walt Whitman as Poet and Person.* New York, 1867. 1st ed., 1st issue, with leaves trimmed to 6-9/16 inches tall. Clothbound, $100-$150. Blue paperbound. $75-$100-$150. Later, 1867, clothbound, leaves 7¼ inches. $35.

BURROWS, J. M. D. *Fifty Years in Iowa.* 2 portraits. Clothbound. No place (Davenport), 1888. 1st ed. $75. Another, $55.

BURROUGHS, John. *Wake-Robin.* Green or terra cotta clothbound. New York, 1871. 1st ed. $25-$50.

BUTLER, Gen. B. F. *General Orders from Headquarters, Department of the Gulf, Issued by Gen. Butler from May 1, 1862, to the Present Time (Nov. 9, 1862).* 35 pp., sewed. New Orleans, 1862. $45.

BUTLER, Mann. *A History of the Commonwealth of Kentucky.* Portrait. Calfbound. Louisville, 1834. 1st ed. $45-$75. Ex-library copy, repaired, $37.50.

BUTTERFIELD, C. W. *History of the Girtys.* Clothbound. Cincinnati, 1890. 1st ed. $60-$125. Worn, $25 and $35.

BUTTERFIELD, C. W. *History of the Discovery of the Northwest, etc.* Cincinnati, 1881. 1st ed. $40-$50.

BUTTERFIELD, C. W. *History of Seneca County.* Clothbound. Sandusky, 1848. 1st ed. $50. Another, $37.50.

BYRD, William. *The Writings of "Colonel William Byrd of Westover in Virginia, Esqr."* Edited by John Spencer Bassett. New York, 1901. One of 500. $65-$85. Worn, $35-$50.

BYRNE, Donn. *Stories Without Women.* Red ribbed cloth. New York, 1915. 1st ed. $50-$100. Worn, $25.

CABALLERIA y Collell, Juan. *History of the City of Santa Barbara from Its Discovery to Our Own Days.* Translated by Edmund Burke. 111 pp., paperbound. Santa Barbara, 1892. 1st ed. $100. Another, title page repaired, $75. Another, worn, $55.

CABELL, James Branch. *Gallantry.* Gray clothbound. New York,

1907. 1st ed. Fine, in original box, $25.

CABEL, James Branch. *Jurgen.* Brown clothbound. New York, 1919. 1st ed., 1st issue, measuring 3/4 inches across top. In dust jacket, $60. In dust jacket and autographed, $70. Other copies, lacking dust jacket, $25 and (signed) $50.

CABINET of Natural History and American Rural Sports (The). 3 vols. Philadelphia, 1830-32-33. 1st book ed. Published by J. and T. Doughty. Includes 29 monthly parts (dated 1830 to 1834); 57 plates, 54 colored. $1,000-$1,500. Another set, 3 vols. in 2, $450 (at auction). Incomplete set, Vols. 1 and 2 only, $130 (1960 auction). Philadelphia, 1832. Vol. 1 only. 24 colored plates. $110 (1964 auction). Sets in parts are very rare and expensive.

CABLE, George W. and George E. Waring, Jr. *Tenth Census of the United States.* 15 plates, folded chart. 99 pp., gray-green paperbound. Washington, 1881. 1st ed. $50.

CABLE, George W. *Old Creole Days.* Clothbound. New York, 1879. 1st ed., 1st issue, with no ads at end. $200. Other copies, $50-$100. Worn, stained, $35 and $50.

CAIN, Joseph and Arieh C. Brower. *The Mormon Way-Bill, to the Gold Mines, etc.* 40 pp., unbound. G.S.L. City (Great Salt Lake City), 1851. 1st ed. $3,400 (1948 auction). One of two copies known. Another copy would bring perhaps $5,000 or more in today's market.

CALDWELL, Charles. *Medical and Physical Memoirs.* Unbound. Lexington, 1826. $25.

CALDWELL, Erskine. *The Bastard.* New York, no date (1929). 1st ed. One of 200 signed (in an edition of 1,100 numbered copies). $75 (1963 auction). Unsigned copies, about $25.

CALIFORNIA Sketches, etc. 57 pp., paperbound. Albany, 1850. (By Leonard Kip.) 1st ed. $125.

CALL, Richard Ellsworth. *The Life and Writings of Rafinesque.* 2 plates, 3 facsimiles. 227 pp., paperbound. Louisville, 1895. 1st ed. $35-$50.

CAMPBELL, Albert H. *Report Upon the Pacific Wagon Roads.* House Doc. 108. 6 maps. 125 pp., sewed. No place, no date (Washington, 1859). 1st ed. $50-$75.

CAMPBELL, Alexander. *Delusions. An Analysis of the Book of Mormon.* 16 pp., sewed. Boston, 1832. 1st ed. $75-$125.

CAMPBELL, J. A. *Sunbeams: Some Poems and Essays on Various Topics.* Chehalis, 1886. $50.

CAMPBELL, John P. (editor). *The Southern Business Directory and General Commercial Advertiser.* Vol. 1 (all published). Clothbound. Charleston, 1854. 1st ed. $45-$50.

CANFIELD, Thomas Hawley. *Life of, etc.* Portrait. 48 pp., clothbound. Burlington, Vt., 1889. 1st ed. $25-$35.

CANFIELD, William H. *Guide Book to the Wild and Romantic Scenery in Sauk County.* 14 pp., sewed. Baraboo, Wis., 1873. $35-$50.

CANTONWINE, Alexander. *Star Forty-six, Oklahoma.* Frontispiece. No place (Oklahoma City), 1911. 1st ed. $50.

CAREY, Charley. *The Lady of the Green and Blue.* Boston, 1847. 1st ed. $30.

CARLIN, Thomas. *Message of the Governor, Transmitting the Report of the Board of Commissioners of the Illinois and Michigan Canal to the Legislature of Illinois.* Folding table. 93 pp., paperbound. Vandalia, 1839. $60.

CARMAN, Bliss. *Low Tide on Grand Pre.* 13 pp., paperbound. Toronto, no date (1889 or 1890?). 1st ed., 1st issue, with name misspelled "Carmen." $75. New York, 1893. 1st Am. ed. Lavender clothbound. $20-$25. Worn, $12.50.

CARO, Ramon M. *Verdadera Idea de la Primera Campana de Tejas y Sucesos Occurridos Despues de la Accion de San Jacinto.* Mexico City, 1837. 1st ed. $150.

CAROLINA Folk-Plays. Second Series. New York, 1924. 1st ed. In dust jacket, $75-$100. Others, lacking jacket, $35 and $45. (This was Thomas Wolfe's first book appearance.) New York, no date (1941). Clothbound. (1st, 2d, and 3d series.) $20 (at auction).

CARR, John. *Pioneer Days in California.* Portrait. Clothbound. Eureka, 1891. 1st ed. $75-$100.

CARR, Spencer. *A Brief Sketch of La Crosse.* 28 pp., sewed. La Crosse, Wis., 1854. 1st ed. $60.

CARRINGTON, Col. Henry B. *The Dacotah Tribes: Their Beliefs, and Our Duty to Them Outlined.* 7 pp., paperbound. Salem, 1881. Uncut, unopened, $45.

CARRINGTON, Henry B. *The Indian Question.* Map. 32 pp. Boston, 1884. 1st ed. $50.

CARROLL, Lewis. *Alice's Adventures in Wonderland.* 42 illustrations by John Tenniel. Red clothbound. New York, 1866. 1st Am. ed. $500. Other copies, less fine, $350 and $300; worn, $275 and $150; binding defective, $100. Boston, 1869. $50.

CARROLL, Lewis. *Through the Looking-Glass.* Introduction by Carl Van Doren. Blue morocco. Mt. Vernon, 1935. $25.

CARSON, J. H. *Early Recollections of the Mines.* Map. 64 pp., paperbound. Stockton, 1852. 1st ed. $250. Also, $550 (at auction). Note: This is 1st ed. despite its identification on cover as 2d ed., an earlier appearance having been as a newspaper supplement.

CARSON, Kit. *The Life and Times of Christopher Carson.* Paperbound. New York, 1861. 1st ed., dated title page. $40.

CARTER, E. S. *The Life and Adventures of.* St. Joseph, Mo., 1896. 1st ed. $175.

CARTER, Susannah. *The Frugal Housewife: or, Complete Woman Cook.* Philadelphia, 1802. Edges of two engraved plates ragged, parts of two pages missing, $37.50.

CARUS, Paul. *The History of the Devil & the Idea of Evil.* Clothbound. Chicago, 1900. 1st ed. $30-$40.

CASENDER, Don Pedro. *The Lost Virgin of the South.* Tallahassee, 1831. (By Michael Smith.) $235.

CASES *Decided in the Courts of Common Pleas in the Fifth Circuit of the State of Ohio, etc.* No place, no date (Steubenville, 1818). (Issued without a title page.) Hinges weak, $65.

CASKODEN, Edwin. *When Knighthood Was in Flower.* Clothbound. Indianapolis, 1898. (By Charles Major.) 1st ed., 1st issue, with 1897 copyright and no notice of reprints on copyright page. $75 and $60. Very good, $45.

CASLER, John O. *Four Years in the Stonewall Brigade.* Folding facsimile. Clothbound. Guthrie, 1893. 1st ed. $60-$80.

CASSIN, John. *Illustrations of the Birds of California, Texas,*

Oregon, etc. 50 colored plates. Philadelphia, 1856. 1st ed. $150-$250. Philadelphia, 1862. $90-$150.

CASTLEMON, Harry. *Frank on the Lower Mississippi.* Cincinnati, 1867. 1st ed. $42.50.

CASTRO, Lorenzo. *The Republic of Mexico in 1882.* New York, 1882. $35.

CATALOGUE of Some of the More Important Books, Manuscripts and Drawings in the Library of Harry Elkins Widener. Philadelphia, 1910. One of 102. $40-$60.

CATHER, Willa. *April Twilights.* Boards, paper label. Boston, 1903. 1st ed. $150-$200. Freak copy, sheets bound upside down, $125. Worn copy, $57.50. Other copies, in varying condition, have been catalogued in the $50-$100 range. New York, 1923. 1st revised ed., boards, one of 450 signed copies. $25.

CATHER, Willa. *My Antonia.* Brown clothbound. Boston, 1918. 1st ed., 1st issue, with illustrations on glazed paper inserted. Up to $150 at retail. Other copies, less than fine, have ranged at retail from $30 to $100.

CATHER, Willa. *Obscure Destinies.* Clothbound. New York, 1932. 1st ed. One of 260. $35-$50. 1st trade ed. $5-$10.

CATHER, Willa. *O Pioneers!* Clothbound. Boston, 1913. 1st ed., 1st issue, in tan or cream-colored ribbed cloth. Mint, in dust jacket, $100. Another, lacking jacket, $35. 2d issue copies, dark brown cloth, $10. Worn 1st issue copies, as low as $10-$15, worn 2d issue copies, as low as $2-$3.

CATHER, Willa. *Sapphira and the Slave Girl.* Boards. New York, 1940. 1st ed. One of 520 signed copies. $25-$35. 1st trade ed. Clothbound. $5-$10.

CATHER, Willa. *Shadows on the Rock.* New York, 1931. 1st ed., advance issue, mislabled "Second Edition" on copyright page. $25. One of 619 signed copies, marbled cloth, $30. Another one, bound in full orange vellum, one of 199 on vellum, signed, $65. 1st trade ed. Clothbound, $10. Autographed, $30. Worn copies, $5.

CATHER, Willa. *The Troll Garden.* Crimson clothbound. New York, 1905. 1st ed., 1st issue, with "McClure, Phillips & Co." at foot of spine. Up to $150.

CATHERWOOD, Mrs. Mary Hartwell. *Spanish Peggy.* Red clothbound. Chicago, 1899. 1st ed. $25-$35.

CATLIN, George. *Letters and Notes on the Manners, Customs, etc., of the North American Indians.* 2 vols. New York, 1841. 1st Am. ed. $75-$100. Philadelphia, 1857. $40-$60.

CATLIN, George. *O-Kee-Pa, a Religious Ceremony.* 13 colored lithographs. Clothbound. Philadelphia, 1867. 1st Am. ed. $325 (1963 auction). Worn and soiled, $57.50 at retail.

CELEBRATED Ada Elmore Gold and Silver Mine of South Boise, Idaho Territory (The). 38 pp., sewed. No place, no date (1866). (By Wilson Waddingham.) In morocco case, $150.

CENTAUR (The). Translated by George B. Ives from the French of Maurice de Guerin. No place (Montague, Mass.), 1915. One of 125. $100.

CENTENNIAL Guide to Southeastern Kansas and Southwestern Missouri, Via the Missouri River, Fort Scott & Gulf Railroad, etc. 24 pp., in 3 columns, paperbound. Kansas City, 1876. $45.

CERVANTES, Miguel de. *The History of the Valorous and Witty Knight-Errant, Don Quixote of the Mancha.* Vierge illustrations. 4 vols. New York, 1906. One of 140 on Japan paper, with duplicate plates. $100. Another issue, 845 copies, $40-$50.

CHAGALL, Marc. *Illustrations for the Bible.* New York, no date (1956). $150-$200.

CHALKLEY, Thomas. *A Journal, or, Historical Account of the Life, Travels, and Christian Experiences of.* Philadelphia, 1749. Last two leaves missing, $25.

CHAMBERLAIN, Joshua L. (editor). *Universities and Their Sons.* Boston, 1898-1900. $25.

CHAMBERS, Andrew Jackson. *Recollections by.* 40 pp., half morocco. No place, no date (1947). 1st ed. Various copies: $150, $77.50, $75, and $60. Another copy, stapled, blank paper covers, $100.

CHAMBERS, Margaret White. *Reminisences* (sic). 48 pp., half morocco. No place, no date (1903). (By Mrs. Andrew Jackson Chambers.) 1st ed. $100-$150. Another copy, stapled, $75.

CHANCELLOR, William Estabrook. *Warren Gamaliel Harding, President of the United States.* No place, no date (Wooster, Ohio, 1922.) $150.

CHANUTE, O. *Aerial Navigation.* A Lecture Delivered to the Students of Sibley College, Cornell University. Paperbound. New York, 1891. 1st ed. $35-$50.

CHAPLIN, Charles. *Charlie Chaplin's Own Story.* Indianapolis, no date (1916). 1st ed. In dust jacket, $50.

CHAPMAN, John Ratcliffe. *Instructions to Young Marksmen, etc.* 7 plates. New York, 1848. 1st ed. $25 and $35.

CHAPELLE, Howard I. *The Baltimore Clipper, etc.* 35 plates. Boards. Salem, 1930. One of 97 numbered copies. $80-$115.

CHARLESS' Magazine Almanac for 1818. No. 1. 60 pp., sewed. St. Louis, 1817. Last six leaves in photostat, $27.50.

CHARTER and By-Laws of the Chamber of Commerce of the City of Fargo, D. T. 39 pp., clothbound. Fargo, 1883. $75.

CHASE, Bishop Philander. *Address Delivered Before the Convention of the Protestant Episcopal Church, Springfield, Ill., June 16, 1845.* 27 pp., paperbound. St. Louis, 1845. Back cover missing, $125.

CHAUCER, Geoffrey. *The Canterbury Tales.* Illustrated by Arthur Szyk. Brattleboro, 1946. $35. Another: New York, 1930. 2 vols., illustrated by Rockwell Kent. One of 75, signed by Kent. $75-$100.

CHESTER, Walter T. *Chester's Complete Trotting and Pacing Record.* New York, 1884. $25.

CHICAGO Illustrated. (Cover title.) Oblong folio of 52 tinted plates. Published by Jevne & Almini. No place, no date (Chicago, 1866-67). 1st ed. $3,000 (1966 auction). New York, 1952. Portfolio of plates reprinted. $75-$100.

CHITTENDEN, L. E. *The Emma Mine.* 76 pp., sewed. New York, 1876. $45.

CHIVERS, Thomas Holley. *Eonchs of Ruby. A Gift of Love.* Printed white boards. New York, 1851. 1st ed. $125.

CHRISTIAN Almanac for Mississippi for the Year 1832 (The). 36 pp., paperbound. Natchez, no date (1831). $25.

CHRISTY, David. *Letters on Geology.* Rossville, 1848. New blank paper covers, $25.

CHURCHILL, Winston. *Broadcast Addresses to the People of Great Britain, Italy, Poland, Russia and the United States.* San Francisco, 1941. One of 250. Grabhorn Press. $100-$150.

CICERO, M. T. *Cicero's Cato Major.* Philadelphia, printed by B. Franklin, 1744. 1st ed. 1st issue, with "only" misspelled on page 27. $500 and up.

CINCINNATI Directory (The). By a Citizen. No place (Cincinnati), 1819. (By Oliver Farnsworth.) 1st ed. $200.

CLAIBORNE, J. F. H. *Mississippi as a Province.* 7 portraits. Jackson, Miss., 1880. 1st ed. $35.

CLAIBORNE, Nathaniel H. *Notes on the War in the South.* 112 pp., paperbound. Richmond, 1819. 1st ed. $75-$100. Rebound in cloth, paper covers bound in, $45.

CLARK, C. M. *A Trip to Pike's Peak and Notes by the Way.* Clothbound. Chicago, 1861. 1st ed. $300 and $325. Another, morocco, $385. Another, $210 (1966 auction).

CLARK, Daniel. *Proofs of the Corruption of Gen. James Wilkinson.* Philadelphia, 1809. 1st ed. $45 (1966 auction). Another copy, rebound in half leather, $62.50 at retail.

CLARK, Jonas. *Opening of the War of the Revolution, 19th of April, 1775.* Boston, 1875. $25.

CLARK, Joseph G. *Lights and Shadows of Sailor Life.* Clothbound. Boston, 1847. 1st ed. $35.

CLARKE, Asa B. *Travels in Mexico and California.* 138 pp., paperbound. Boston, 1852. 1st ed. $250-$400. Leather and cloth, $150-$300.

CLASS Poem. 52 pp., tan paperbound. No place (Cambridge), 1838. (By James Russell Lowell.) 1st ed. $55, $80, $100, $110. Another, in new paper covers, $25.

CLAVERS, Mrs. Mary. *A New Home—Who'll Follow?* New York, 1839. (By Caroline M. Kirkland.) 1st ed. $35-$50.

CLAY, John. *My Life on the Range.* Clothbound. Chicago, no date (1924). 1st ed. $75-$100.

CLAYTON, W. *The Latter-Day Saints' Emigrants' Guide, etc.*

24 pp., paperbound. St. Louis, 1848. 1st ed. $1,800 (1963 auction)—for a copy with only part of the front cover preserved.

CLEARWATER, Alphonso T. *History of Ulster County, New York.* Kingston, 1907. $25.

CLELAND, Robert Glass. *The Cattle on a Thousand Hills.* Map, 2 illustrations. Clothbound. San Marino, 1941. 1st ed. Mint, in dust jacket, $25-$35.

CLYMAN, James. *James Clyman, American Frontiersman.* Clothbound. San Francisco, 1928. 1st ed. $150-$250.

COBB, Joseph B. *Mississippi Scenes; or, Sketches of Southern and Western Life and Adventure, etc.* Philadelphia, 1851. 1st ed. Foxed, $35.

COBB, Sylvanus, Jr., *The Gunmaker of Moscow.* New York, 1888. 1st ed. $37.50.

COBURN, Wallace D. *Rhymes from the Round-Up Camp.* Clothbound. No place, 1899. 1st ed. $140 (auction)—for a copy with warped covers. Great Falls, 1899. 2d ed. $62.50.

CODY, William F. *The Life of Hon. William F. Cody, Known as Buffalo Bill, etc. An Autobiography.* Clothbound. Hartford, no date (1879). 1st ed. (Attributed variously to Frank E. Bliss and Ned Buntline, pseudonym of Edward L. C. Judson.) 1st ed. $75 and $37.50. Another copy, signed by Cody, $80 (auction).

COLBURN, J. G. W. (editor). *The Life of Sile Doty.* 3 plates. Toledo, 1880. 1st ed. $100-$150. Another, worn, $75.

COLE, George Watson (editor). *Catalogue of Books Relating to the Discovery and Early History of North and South America.* 5 vols. Clothbound. New York, 1907. One of 150. $350-$500. Also, $325 (1963 auction).

COLE, J. R. *History of Greenbrier County.* Clothbound. Lewisburg, W. Va., no date (1917). 1st ed. $27.50-$40.

COLECCION de Constitutiones de los Estados Unidos Mexicanos. 3 vols. Mexico, 1828. $350.

COLLECTION of Sacred Hymns, for the Church of Jesus Christ of Latter Day Saints. Selected and published by Charles A. Adams. Bellows Falls, 1845. $125.

COLLEY, James (editor). *The Thrilling Adventures of Alice Dunbar, the Celebrated Horse Thief, and Female Jack Sheppard, etc.* 62 pp., paperbound. Philadelphia, no date (1869). $25.

COLLINS, Dennis. *The Indian's Last Fight, or the Dull Knife Raid.* 8 plates. Clothbound. Girard, Kan., no date (1915). 1st ed. $85, $100, and up.

COLLINS, John S. *Across the Plains in '64.* 151 pp., clothbound. Omaha, 1904. 1st ed. $75-$125. Omaha, 1904-11. 2d ed., with Part 2. $100-$150.

COLLINS, Lewis. *Historical Sketches of Kentucky.* Map. Maysville, 1847. 1st ed. $75-$100. Cincinnati, 1847. $35-$50. Louisville, 1924. 2 vols., revised by Richard H. Collins. $75-$100.

COLLINS, Lewis. *History of Kentucky.* 2 vols. Covington, 1878-82. (Revised by Richard H. Collins.) $75-$100.

COLORADO Condensed. Industrial Information for Capitalists and Immigrants, Freshly Compiled by the Rocky Mountain News. 40 pp., paperbound. Denver, 1881. 1st ed. $200.

COLTON, Walter. *Three Years in California.* Map, 12 plates, folding facsimile. Clothbound. New York, 1850. 1st ed. $100-$125.

COMBINATION Atlas Map of Licking County (Ohio). No place (Philadelphia), 1875. $35-$50.

COMBINATION Atlas Map of Seneca County (Ohio). Philadelphia, 1874. $35-$50.

COMBINATION Atlas Map of Stark County (Ohio). History in English and German, business directory, biographies, 100 views and portraits. Philadelphia, 1875. $35-$50.

COMBINATION Atlas Map of Trumbull County (Ohio). Chicago, 1874. $35-$50.

COMMERCIAL Directory of the Western States and Rivers. St, Louis and Chicago, 1867-8. 1st ed. $50.

COMPTON, Frances Snow. *Esther: A Novel.* Green clothbound. New York, 1884. (By Henry Adams.) 1st ed., "American Novel Series—No. 3." $225.

CONARD, Howard Louis. *"Uncle Dick" Wooton.* Frontispiece, 65 plates. Clothbound. Chicago, 1890. 1st ed. $50-$100. Columbus, Ohio, 1950. One of 500. $35-$50.

CONFEDERATE Spelling Book (The). Richmond, 1865. $35-$50.

CONFESSIONS of an English Opium Eater. Philadelphia, 1823. (By Thomas De Quincey.) 1st Am. ed. Rebound, $50.

CONKLING, Edgar. *Benton's Policy of Selling and Developing the Mineral Lands, etc.* 14 pp., sewed. Cincinnati, 1864. $25.

CONNELLEY, William E. *Quantrill and the Border Wars*. Portrait, 2 maps. Clothbound. Cedar Rapids, 1910. 1st ed. In dust jacket, $50-$60.

CONRAD, Henry S. *The Waterlilies*. Washington, 1905. $40.

CONRAD, Joseph. *The Arrow of Gold*. Clothbound. New York, 1919. 1st ed., 1st issue, with uncorrected errors, line 16, page 5, and line 24, page 15. $25.

CONSIDERATIONS sur L'Artillerie, etc. Oblong. St. Christopher, 1786. $40.

CONSIDERATIONS sur les Effets qu' ont Produit en Canada, la Conservation des Etablissemens du Pays, les Moeurs, l'Education, etc. de ses Habitans; etc. Pamphlet. Montreal, 1809. (By Dennis Benjamin Viger.) Leaf torn, signature, $50.40.

CONSTITUCION Politica del Estado Libre de Coahuila y Tejas, etc. Pamphlet. Leona Vicario, no date (1829). $500.

CONSTITUTION and By-Laws of the Historical Society of the City of Chicago. 14 pp., paperbound. Chicago, 1856. $75.

CONSTITUTION of the State of California. 19 pp., sewed. San Francisco, 1849. $2,500 and $1,500. Also, $800 (1964 auction). San Jose, no date (1850). 27 pp., bound with five other rare California items, sold for $9,000 at auction in 1959.

CONSTITUTION of the State of Colorado, etc. (The). 65 pp., paperbound. Denver, 1876. $150.

CONSTITUTION of the State of Tennessee. 33 pp., paperbound. Philadelphia, 1796. $250.

CONTEMPLATION Upon the Mystery of Man's Regeneration in Allusion to the Mystery of Printing (A). Vellum. San Francisco, 1928 (1927). (By James Watson.) One of 125. Grabhorn Press. Christmas keepsake. $30-$40.

CONWAY, Miles W. *Geodoesia, or a Treatise on Practical Surveying.* Lexington, Ky., 1807. $125.

CONWAY, Thomas W. *The Freedmen of Louisiana.* 37 pp., paperbound. New Orleans, 1865. 1st ed. $75.

COOK, G. & D. *Illustrated Catalogue of Carriages, etc.* New York, 1860. $35-$50.

COOK, Capt. James and Capt. James King. *A Voyage to the Pacific Ocean, etc.* 4 vols. Leatherbound. Printed by Benjamin Gomez. New York, 1796. 1st Am. ed. Worn, spine chipped, $100.

COOK, John R. *The Border and the Buffalo.* Clothbound. Topeka, 1907. 1st ed. $25 and $35.

COOK, James H. *Fifty Years on the Old Frontier.* Clothbound. New Haven, 1923. 1st ed. $25-$35.

COOKE, Philip St. George. *Scenes and Adventures in the Army.* Clothbound. Philadelphia, 1857. 1st ed. $100. Worn, end paper lacking, $75. Philadelphia, 1859. 2d ed. $25.

COOKE, R. L. *A Description of Weyer's Cave.* 36 pp., sewed. Staunton, 1836. 2d ed., $35.

COOPER, I. N. *The Gathering: or, the Plans and Principles That Should Govern Latter Day Saints, etc.* 20 pp., calfbound. Plano, Ill., 1877. 1st ed. $125.

COOPER, J. Fenimore. *The Battle of Lake Erie.* 118 pp., paperbound. Cooperstown, 1843. 1st ed. $50-$75. In modern leather, $25.

COPE, E. D. *The Batrachia of North America.* Washington, 1889. $25-$35.

CORBETT, William. *Proposals for Publishing by Subscription, a New, Entire, and Neat Edition of Porcupine's Works.* 8 pp., paperbound. No place, no date (Philadelphia, 1799). $37.50.

CORNELIUS, Elias. *The Little Osage Captive.* 2 plates. Boards. Boston, 1822. 1st ed. $25-$35. Boston, 1832. Paperbound. $12.50.

CORRESPONDENCIA que ha Mediado entre La Legacion Extraordinaria de Mexico y el Departamento de Estado De Los Estados-Unidos, etc. Mexico, 1837. $82.50.

COUTANT, C. G. *History of Wyoming.* Map, 76 plates. Leather-bound. Vol. 1 (all published). Laramie, 1899. 1st ed. $80-$100. Another, binding defective, $65 (1966 auction). Another copy, spine nicked, $40. Another, rebacked, $60.

COWAN, Robert E. *A Bibliography of the History of California and the Pacific West.* Boards, cloth spine. San Francisco, 1914. One of 250. $150-$200. San Francisco, 1933. Three vols. in one, clothbound. One of 650. $100-$150. Columbus, Ohio, 1952. Clothbound. $40-$50.

COWAN, Robert E. (compiler). *The Library of William Andrews Clark, Jr.* San Francisco, 1921. One of 150. $37.50.

COX, James (editor). *Historical and Biographical Record of the Cattle Industry, etc.* 16 plates, colored frontispiece. St. Louis, 1895. 1st ed. $800 (1966 auction) and up. New York, 1959. Reprint ed. $100-$200.

COX, Ross. *Adventures on the Columbia River.* Clothbound or boards. New York, 1832. 1st Am. ed. $75-$100. Worn, $50-$75.

COYNER, David H. *The Lost Trappers.* Concinnati, 1847. 1st ed. $60. Worn, $35. Cincinnati, 1850. Clothbound. $22.50. Cincinnati, 1859. $25.

CRADLEBAUGH, John. *Mormonism.* 18 pp., double column, sewed. No place, 1877. $25.

CRAIG, Neville B. (editor). *Washington's First Campaign, Death of Jumonville, and the Taking of Fort Necessity.* Map. 32 pp., paperbound. Pittsburgh, 1848. 1st ed. $75. Rebound, $45.

CRAKES, Sylvester. *Five Years a Captive Among the Blackfeet Indians.* 6 plates. Columbus, 1858. 1st ed. $150-$250. Worn, $125.

CRAMER'S *Pittsburgh Almanac, for the Year of Our Lord 1815.* 72 pp., sewed. Pittsburgh, no date (1814). $27.50 and $50. For 1816, $45. For 1817, 1818, each $25.

CRANE, Stephen. *The Black Riders and Other Lines.* Boards. Boston, 1895. 1st ed. 500 copies. $60-$80. Worn, $25 and $30. One of 50 printed in green ink on Japan paper, bound in boards. Also 3 copies supposedly bound in vellum. $100-$150.

CRANE, Stephen. *The Red Badge of Courage.* Clothbound. New

York, 1895. 1st ed., 1st state, with perfect type in last line on page 225. In dust jacket, $350-$400. Another copy in dust jacket, bookplate removed, former owner's name on front leaf, $200. Another, "immaculate," $185. Five copies, lacking jacket, $100-$200, sometimes more. Worn, stained, etc., $50-$150. Another, broken type, page 225, $50. Another, with type fixed but "d" slanting, $25.

CRAWFORD, Charles H. *Scenes of Earlier Days in Crossing the Plains to Oregon.* Portrait. Petaluma, Calif., 1898. 1st ed. $45-$75.

CREIGH, Alfred. *History of Washington County (Pennsylvania).* No place, no date (Washington, Pa., 1870). 1st ed. $40.

CREMONY, John C. *Life Among the Apaches.* Clothbound. San Francisco, 1868. 1st ed. $150. Rebacked, $130 (1966 auction).

CROCKETT, David. *Col. Crockett's Exploits and Adventures in Texas, etc. Written by Himself.* Portrait. Philadelphia, 1836. 1st ed. $75. Another copy, name clipped from title page, $60. Another, spine worn, $27.50. (Probably written by Richard Penn Smith, according to Wright Howes' *U.S.-iana.*)

CROCKETT, David. *Pictorial Life and Adventures of Davy Crockett. Written by Himself.* 193 pp., double column, sewed. Philadelphia, no date (about 1865), $25. (Another of numerous probably spurious Crockett books under various titles. Author unknown.)

CROSS, Maj. Osborne. *A Journal of the March of the Regiment of Mounted Riflemen to Oregon.* (Extracted from Quartermaster General's report of 1850.) Half morocco. Washington, 1850. $40-$50.

CRUMRINE, Boyd (editor). *History of Washington County (Pennsylvania).* 8 maps, 71 plates. Morocco. Philadelphia, 1882. 1st ed. $50.

CRUSTALINA; a Fairy Tale. New York, 1816. (By John M. Harney.) One hinge broken, $27.50.

CULVER, Henry B. *Contemporary Scale Models of Vessels of the Seventeenth Century.* Boards. New York, 1926. 1st ed. One of 1,000. $40-$50. One of 100. Morocco. $60-$75.

CUMING, Fortescue. *Sketches of a Tour to the Western Country, etc.* Calfbound. Pittsburgh, 1810. 1st ed. $75, $100, $125.

Rebacked, stains on title page, $125.

CUMINGS, Samuel. *The Western Pilot.* Cincinnati, 1825. $125. Cincinnati, 1829. $75. Another copy, worn and dampstained, $37.50. Cincinnati, 1834. Back scuffed, $35. Cincinnati, 1836. $50 and $35. Cincinnati, 1848. $30.

CURRY, George L. *Governor's Message, and Accompanying Documents.* 26 pp., half calf. Salem, Ore., 1858. $50.

CURTIS, Edward S. *The North American Indian.* 40 vols. (20 vols. of text and 20 portfolios of plates.) New York, 1907-30. 500 sets printed. $2,500. Also, $1,750 (1961 auction). 20 vols. of text only, $320 (1961 auction).

CURWOOD, James Oliver. *The Great Lakes and the Vessels That Plough Them.* 72 plates. Clothbound. New York, 1901. 1st ed. $35-$50. Another, hinges repaired, $20.

CUSTER, George Armstrong. *My Life on the Plains.* 8 plates. Clothbound. New York, 1874. 1st ed. $60-$80. New York, 1876. Clothbound. $25.

CUTRIGHT, W. B. *The History of Upshur County, W. Va.* No place, no date (Buckhannon, W. Va., 1907). $50-$75. Worn, $47 (at auction).

CUTTS, James Madison. *The Conquest of California and New Mexico.* 2 portraits, map, 3 plans. 264 pp., paperbound. Philadelphia, 1847. 1st ed. $175 (1966 auction), $90 (1966 auction). Worn copies at retail, $60, $75, $100.

DALCHO, Frederick. *An Historical Account of the Protestant Episcopal Church in South Carolina.* Charleston, 1820. 1st ed. New cloth, $100.

DALE, Edward Everett. *The Range Cattle Industry.* Plates. Clothbound. Norman, Okla., 1930. 1st ed. One of 500. $40-$60.

DALE, Harrison Clifford (editor). *The Ashley-Smith Explorations.* Maps and plates. Clothbound. Cleveland, 1918. 1st ed. One of 750. $50-$80. Glendale, Calif., 1941. Revised ed., limited to 750. Clothbound. $27.50.

DALTON Brothers and Their Astounding Career of Crime (The). By an Eyewitness. Paperbound. Chicago, 1892. Tears in blank margins of a few leaves, $45.

DANA, E. *Geographical Sketches of the Western Country: Designed for Emigrants and Settlers.* 312 pp., boards. Cincinnati, 1819. 1st ed. $85. Other copies, $70, $40, and $35.

DANA, James D. *Conspectus of the Crustacea of the Exploring Expedition Under Capt. C. Wilkes.* Pp. 116-125, sewed. Philadelphia, 1852. Author's separate ed. $45.

DANA, J. G. and R. S. Thomas. *A Report of the Trial of Jereboam O. Beauchamp.* 153 pp. Frankfort, Ky., no date (1826). 1st ed. $150.

DANIEL, John W. *Character of Stonewall Jackson.* Lynchburg, 1868. 1st ed. $35-$50.

DANIELS, William M. *A Correct Account of the Murder of Generals Joseph and Hyrum Smith, at Carthage, on the 27th Day of June, 1844.* 24 pp., paperbound. Nauvoo, 1845. 1st ed., 1st issue. $1,500-$2,000. 2d issue, with two woodcut engravings added. Morocco (original paper covers bound in), $1,100 (1966 auction).

DARBY, William. *A Geographical Description of the State of Louisiana, etc.* Map. Philadelphia, 1816. 1st ed. $35 and $75. New York, 1817. 2d ed., with 2 maps and large folding map in separate folder. $50-$75.

DARLINGTON, Mary Carson (editor). *Fort Pitt and Letters from the Frontier.* 3 maps, 3 plates. Pittsburgh, 1892. One of 100 large paper copies. $50-$75. One of 200 regular copies, $35-$50.

DARLINGTON, William M. *Christopher Gist's Journals.* 7 maps. Pittsburgh, 1893. 1st ed. One of 100. $50.

DAVENPORT, Homer. *My Quest of the Arab Horse.* Clothbound. New York, 1909. 1st ed. $35-$60. Writing on flyleaf, $25.

DAVIDSON, Gordon Charles. *The North West Company.* 5 folding maps. Berkeley, 1918. 1st ed. $75-$100.

DAVIDSON, J. H. *Muh-He-Ka-Ne-Ok, a History of the Stockbridge Nation.* Milwaukee, 1893. $25.

DAVIDSON, Samuel C. *Camp Meeting Songster, or a Collection of Hymns and Spiritual Songs, etc.* Knoxville, Tenn., 1832. Four pages missing, part of three leaves missing, one page with hole, $27.50.

DA VINCI, Leonardo. *Thoughts on Art and Life*. Boston, 1906. One of 303. $25.

DAVIS, Edmund W. *Salmon-Fishing on the Grand Cascapedia*. Half vellum. No place (New York), 1904. 1st ed. One of 100 on Imperial Japan paper. $100-$150.

DAVIS, M. *Report on the Petition of T. H. Perkins and His Contract with the British Northwest Fur Company*. 15 pp., sewed. Washington, 1837. $45.

DAVIS, William Heath. *Sixty Years in California*. Clothbound. San Francisco, 1889. 1st ed. $40-$50. San Francisco, 1929. 2d ed. 44 maps and plates. Half morocco. One of 2,000 (with title changed to *Seventy-five Years in California*). $50-$75. Same place and date, Argonaut Ed., one of 100, with added plates and a page of the author's original manuscript. $75-$125.

DAVY Crockett; or, The Lion-Hearted Hunter. 96 pp., paperbound. New York, no date (about 1875). $45.

DAVY Crockett's Almanac, of Wild Sports in the West, etc. (For 1837). Nashville, no date (1835). $100 and up. For 1836, $35-$50. For 1837, $120 (1966 auction). For 1838, $30. For 1840, $60. For 1841, $30. For 1846, Boston, $110 (1966 auction). For 1854, Philadelphia, $50. Complete run, Nashville, 1835-1841. 7 vols., with Boston, 1842, ed., $2,450 (1962 auction).

DAWSON, Moses. *A Historical Narrative of the Civil and Military Services of Maj-Gen. William Henry Harrison*. Boards. Cincinnati, 1824. 1st ed., 1st issue, with 15-line errata slip. $125-$200. Another, rebacked, $150 (1963 auction). Another, lacking errata slip, $90 (1962 auction). With 24-line errata slip, $65-$90 at retail.

DAWSON, Nicholas. *Narrative of Nicholas "Cheyenne" Dawson*. Half clothbound. San Francisco, 1933. One of 500. $37.50 and $50.

DAWSON, Thomas F. and F. J. V. Skiff. *The Ute War: A History of the White River Massacre, etc.* 184 pp., paperbound. Denver, 1879. 1st ed. $350-$500. $425 (1966 auction). Rebound in half morocco, title page repaired, $130 (1964 auction). Another, lacking front paper covers, $475 (in dealer catalogue).

DEAN, Bashford. *Catalogue of European Daggers.* 85 plates. Half clothbound. New York, 1929. $50-$100.

DEATH of Gen. Montgomery, etc. (The). Norwich, 1777. (By Hugh Henry Brackenridge.) Joints weak, title page repaired, $50.

DEBAR, J. H. *The West Virginia Handbook and Immigrant's Guide.* Folding map. Parkersburg, 1870. 1st ed. $50-$100.

DE BARTHE, Joe. *The Life and Adventures of Frank Grouard, Chief of Scouts.* 67 plates. Half leatherbound. St. Joseph, Mo., no date (1894). 1st ed. $85, $100, $125 and $90 (1964 auction).

DE BENAVIDES, Alonso. *The Memorial of Fray Alonso de Benavides, 1630.* Cloth-backed boards. Chicago, 1916. One of 300. $65, $75, $100 and $70 (soiled copy, 1966 auction).

DECALVES, Don Alonso. *New Travels to the Westward.* 34 pp., sewed. No place, 1795. $125. Another, no place, 1797, 81 pp., $350. Another, Greenwich, Mass., 1805, 48 pp., sewed, $75. (Three of many reprints of a rare work published first in Boston in 1788.)

DE CORDOVA, J. *Lecture on Texas.* (Also a paper read by him before the New York Geographical Society.) 32 pp., paperbound. Philadelphia, 1858. 1st ed. $30-$50.

DECREE of the Star Chamber Concerning Printing, etc. (A). Full red levant. No place, no date (New York, 1884). One of 150. Grolier Club. $50.

DEERSLAYER (The). 2 vols. Purple clothbound, paper labels. Philadelphia, 1841. (By James Fenimore Cooper.) 1st ed. $80, $120, and $150.

DE FOREST, John W. *Miss Ravenel's Conversion from Secession to Loyalty.* Clothbound. New York, 1867. 1st ed. $35.

DE FOREST, John W. *Playing the Mischief.* 185 pp., paperbound. New York, 1875. 1st ed. $35. New York, 1876. 2d printing, bound in wrappers left over from 1st printing. $25.

DE HASS, Wills. *History of the Early Settlement and Indian Wars of Western Virginia.* 5 plates. Wheeling, 1851. 1st ed. $50-$75. Rebound, $30.

DELAFIELD, John, Jr. *An Inquiry into the Origin of the Antiq-

uities of America. 11 plates, including 18-foot long folding plate. New York, 1839. 1st ed. $50-$100. Rebound, $60-$80. Cincinnati, 1839. $25-$35.

DELANO, Alonzo. *Life on the Plains and Among the Diggings.* 4 plates. Clothbound. Auburn, 1854. 1st ed., 1st issue, with page 219 misnumbered 119. $135-$150. Another, $75. Another, marked "3d thousand," $25.

DELANO, Judah. *Washington (D.C.) Directory.* Washington, 1822. 1st ed. $75.

DELANO, Reuben. *Wanderings and Adventures of.* 3 plates. 102 pp., paperbound. Worcester, 1846. 1st ed. $50-$75.

DE LINCY, A. J. V. LeRoux. *Researches Concerning Jean Grolier, His Life and His Library.* New York, 1907. $200.

DEMOCRATIC Vistas. Paperbound. Washington, 1871. (By Walt Whitman.) 1st ed., 1st issue, with Whitman's name only in copyright notice on back of title page. $50-$75. Worn, $35-$50.

DENISON, Jesse. *First Annual Report to the Stockholders of the Providence Western Land Company.* 8 pp., paperbound. Providence, 1857. $25.

DENNY, Arthur A. *Pioneer Days on Puget Sound.* Clothbound. Seattle, 1888. 1st ed., with errata slip. $50-$75.

DE QUILLE, Dan. *History of the Big Bonanza.* Plates. Hartford, 1876. (By William Wright.) 1st ed. $27.50, $35, and $50.

DESCRIPTION of Central Iowa (A), With Especial Reference to Polk County and Des Moines, the State Capital. 32 pp., sewed. Des Moines, 1858. $75.

DESCRIPTIVE Account of the City of Peoria (A). 32 pp., paperbound. Peoria, 1859. $45.

DESCRIPTIVE, Historical, Commercial, Agricultural, and Other Important Information Relative to the City of San Diego. 51 pp., paperbound. San Diego, 1874. $150.

DESCRIPTIVE Scenes for Children. 14 pp., stitched. Boston, no date (1828). $56.

DE SHIELDS, J. T. *Border Wars of Texas.* Clothbound. Tioga, Tex., 1912. 1st ed. $50.

DE SHIELDS, J. T. *Cynthia Ann Parker*. Frontispiece, 3 portraits. Clothbound. St. Louis, 1886. 1st ed. $40 and $47.50.

DE SMET, Pierre Jean. *Letters and Sketches*. Frontispiece, 11 plates, folding allegorical leaf. Clothbound. Philadelphia, 1843. 1st ed. $60, $125, $140. Also, calfbound, signed, $80 (at auction).

DE SMET, Pierre Jean. *Oregon Missions and Travels Over the Rocky Mountains*. Folding map, 12 plates. Clothbound. New York, 1847. 1st ed. $100-$150. Worn, $45. Rebound, $30 (auction).

DE VINNE, Theodore L. *The Invention of Printing*. New York, 1876. 1st ed. $35.

DE VOTO, Bernard. *Across the Wide Missouri*. 81 plates, some in color. Boston, 1947. 1st ed. One of 265, boxed. $40-$50. 1st trade ed. Clothbound. $25.

DE VRIES, David P. *Voyages From Holland to America, 1632-1644*. New York, 1853. $35-$50.

DE ZAVALA, Lorenzo. *Ensayo Historico de las Revoluciones De Megico, etc*. 2 vols. (Vol. 1, Paris, 1831.) Vol. 2, New York, 1832. The set, 1st eds. $135-$150. Also, $115 (at auction).

"DICKENS, Charles." *Sister Rose*. Paperbound. Philadelphia, no date (1855). (By Wilkie Collins.) 1st ed. $35-$50.

DICKENSON, Luella. *Reminiscences of a Trip Across the Plains in 1846*. Clothbound. San Francisco, 1904. 1st ed. $300-$400. ($300 at auction, 1966.)

DICKERSON, Oliver M. *American Colonial Government, 1696-1765*. Cleveland, 1912. 1st ed. $25-$35.

DICKERSON, Philip J. *History of the Osage Nation*. 144 pp., paperbound. No place, no date. (Pawhuska, Okla., 1906). 1st ed. $75. $35 (1966 auction). Lacking covers, $50.

DICKINSON, Emily. *Poems*. Gray or white cloth, green spine. Boston, 1890. 1st ed. $80-$150. Worn, soiled, etc., $35, $50, and $100.

DICKINSON, Emily. *Poems: Second Series*. Boston, 1891. 1st ed. Half tan calf and boards, $64, $100, $225. Gray or green and white cloth, $100. Another copy, binding soiled, $32.50.

DICKINSON, Emily. *Poems: Third Series.* Boston, 1896. 1st ed., with spine imprinted "Roberts Bros." Gray or green spine, white sides. $75. Half calf and boards, $80. Another copy, green cloth, $25.

DICKINSON, Emily. *The Single Hound: Poems of a Lifetime.* Boards, white cloth spine. Boston, 1914. 1st ed. One of 595. $100-$150. Other copies, $60 and $75; covers soiled, $47.50 and $32.50. Boston, 1915. 2d ed. $15.

DICKINSON, Jonathan. *Narrative of a Shipwreck in the Gulf of Florida.* Stanford, N. Y., 1803. (By Jonathan Dickenson.) $60. Burlington, N. J., 1811, $30. Salem, Ohio, 1826 *(Shipwreck and Dreadful Sufferings of Robert Barrow).* $35-$50. (All these are variant titles of a rare book, *God's Protecting Providence,* first published in Philadelphia in 1699 and of which only four perfect copies are known.)

DIEHL, Edith. *Bookbinding: Its Background and Technique.* 2 vols., clothbound. New York, 1946. 1st ed. $75-$100.

DIETZ, August, Sr. *The Postal Service of the Confederate States of America.* 2 color plates. Richmond, 1929. 1st ed. $50.

DILWORTH, Thomas. *The Schoolmaster's Assistant.* Philadelphia, 1796. $35.

DIMSDALE, Thomas J. *The Vigilantes of Montana.* 228 pp., paperbound. Virginia City, 1866. 1st ed. $500 and up. Lacking back cover and spine, $475 (1963 auction). Rebound in cloth, printed label, $250 (1960 auction). Rebound in half morocco and lacking ads, $275 (1959 auction). Other rebound copies, $350 and $250. Virginia City, 1882, 2d ed. 241 pp., paperbound. $75-$125. Rebound in leather, $95. Helena, no date (1915). 3d ed. 26 plates and 4 facsimiles. $30. Helena, 1915. 4th ed. $27.50.

DIOMEDI, A. *Sketches of Modern Indian Life.* 79 pp., paperbound. No place, no date. (Woodstock, Md., 1894?). 1st ed. $75-$100.

DIRECTORY of the City of Mineral Point for the Year 1859. Map. 64 pp., sewed. Mineral Point, Wis., 1859. $30.

DISCARDS (The). By Old Wolf. 22 pp., paperbound. No place, 1920. (By Lucullus V. McWhorter.) $35-$50.

DISCOURSE, on the Aborigines of the Valley of the Ohio (A). Map. 51 pp., sewed. Cincinnati, 1838. (By William Henry Harrison.) 1st ed. $25-$35.

DOCUMENTS, 1862 and 1863. (Binder's title.) Boards (collection of pamphlets, bound). Richmond, Va., no date (1863). $50.

DODDRIDGE, Rev. Dr. Joseph. Notes, on the Settlement and Indian Wars, of the Western Parts of Virginia & Pennsylvania, etc. Calfbound. Wellsburgh, Va., 1824. 1st ed. $100-$150. Worn, $75. Presentation copy signed by author, waterstained, $55 (1964 auction). Rebound in modern calf, $50 (at auction). Other copies, worn, repaired, etc. $40, $50, $57.50.

DODGE, Maj. Gen. Grenville M. Biographical Sketch of James Bridger, Mountaineer, Trapper and Guide. 2 plates. 10 leaves, paperbound. Kansas City, Mo., no date (1905). 1st ed., without preface. $45. New York, 1905. 3 plates, one folding. 27 pp., paperbound. $35-$50.

DODGE, J. R. Red Men of the Ohio Valley. Springfield, 1859. 1st ed. $50 and $65.

DODGE, M. E. Hans Brinker; or, The Silver Skates. Green clothbound. New York, 1866. (By Mary Mapes Dodge.) 1st ed. $150. Rebacked, $50. Another, rebacked and repaired, $45.

DODGE, Mary Mapes. Donald and Dorothy. Clothbound. Boston, 1883. 1st ed. $50.

DONKIN, R. Military Collections and Remarks. Frontispiece. 264 pp., paperbound. New York, 1777. 1st ed. $150-$300.

DORMON, Caroline. Wild Flowers of Louisiana. New York, 1934. $35.

DOS PASSOS, John. The Bitter Drink. No place, no date (San Francisco, 1939). One of 35 printed at the Grabhorn Press. $25.

DOS PASSOS, John. Ford and Hearst. San Francisco, 1940. One of 35 printed at the Grabhorn Press. $25.

DOUGHTY, William. The Physical Geography of the North Pacific Ocean and Peculiarities of its Circulation, etc. 27 pp., paperbound. Augusta, Ga., 1867. Presentation copy from author, $35.

DOUGLAS, C. L. The Gentlemen in White Hats. Dallas, 1934.

1st ed. In dust jacket, $25.

DOW, Lorenzo. *The Life and Travels of.* Leatherbound. Hartford, 1804. 1st ed. $250. Worn, foxed, signature loose, $100.

DOWNEY, Fairfax. *Indian-Fighting Army.* Clothbound. New York, 1941. 1st ed. $25-$40. New York, 1944. Clothbound. $15-$30.

DOWNIE, Maj. William. *Hunting for Gold: Personal Experiences in the Early Days on the Pacific Coast.* Frontispiece. Half leatherbound. San Francisco, 1893. 1st ed. $50. Worn, $35.

DRAFT of a Constitution Published Under the Direction of a Committee of Citizens of Colorado, etc. Denver, 1875. $45.

DRAGOON Campaigns to the Rocky Mountains. New York, 1836. (By James Hildreth.) 1st ed. $100. Foxed, $57.50. Another, worn, $50.

DRAKE, Benjamin. *The Life and Adventures of Black Hawk.* Portrait and plates. Cincinnati, 1838. 1st ed. $150.

DRAKE, Benjamin. *Life of Tecumseh, and his Brother the Prophet; etc.* Cincinnati, 1841. 1st ed. $35-$50.

DRAKE, Daniel. *An Account of Epidemic Cholera, as it Appeared in Cincinnati.* 46 pp., paperbound. Cincinnati, 1832. $45.

DRAKE, Daniel. *Natural and Statistical View . . . of Cincinnati and the Miami Country.* Cincinnati, 1815. 1st ed. $100. Other copies, $45 and $60.

DRAKE, Morgan L. *Lake Superior Railroad. Letter to the Hon. Lewis Cass.* 24 pp., paperbound. Pontiac, 1853. $100.

DRAYTON, John. *Memoirs of the American Revolution.* Portrait, 2 maps. 2 vols. Charleston, 1821. 1st ed. Margins of a few leaves damaged, $55.

DREAM Drops, or Stories from Fairy Land. By a Dreamer. Paperbound or clothbound. Boston, no date (1887). (By Amy Lowell.) 1st ed. 250 copies. Paperbound, $220 (1960 auction) and $150. Clothbound, $125.

DREISER, Theodore. *Sister Carrie.* Red clothbound. New York, 1900. 1st ed., 1st issue. $250. Autographed copy, front leaves creased, $175. Fine copy but with bookplate, $225. Spine rubbed, $70 (1963 auction). Other defective copies, $50 and up. Rebound in boards, morocco corners, original covers bound in, $25.

DRURY, Rev. P. Sheldon (editor). *The Startling and Thrilling Narrative of the Dark and Terrible Deeds of Henry Madison, and His Accomplice . . ., Miss Ellen Stevens . . . Executed by the Vigilance Committee of San Francisco.* 36 pp., paperbound, including 2 plates and cover title. Philadelphia, no date (1857). $75-$100. Philadelphia, 1865. $40.

DRYSDALE, Isabel. *Scenes in Georgia.* Frontispiece. 83 pp., cloth-backed boards, paper label. Philadelphia, no date (1827). 1st ed. $50.

DU BOIS, J. and J. Heger. *Campaigns in the West, 1856-61.* The Journal and Letters of Col. John Du Bois with Pencil Sketches by Joseph Heger. 15 (16?) plates, folding map. Boards, leather spine. Tucson, 1949. Grabhorn Press. 1st ed. One of 300, signed. $100. Also, $75 (1966 auction).

DU BOIS, John Witherspoon. *Life and Times of William Lowndes Yancey.* 9 plates. Clothbound. Birmingham, 1892. 1st ed. $50-$60. Worn, $35.

DUER, John K. *The Nautilus.* 48 pp., plain paper covers. New York, 1843. 1st ed. $25.

DUFF, E. Gordon. *William Caxton.* Boards. Chicago, 1905. One of 148 with an original leaf from *Canterbury Tales.* $200. One of 107 without the leaf. $25.

DU MAURIER, George. *Trilby.* Vellum. New York, 1894. 1st Am. ed. One of 600. In dust wrapper, $35. Clothbound, $10-$15.

DUNBAR, Paul Lawrence. *Oak and Ivy.* Blue clothbound, gold stamped. Dayton, 1893. 1st ed. $35-$50.

DUNCAN, John M. *Travels Through Part of the United States and Canada in 1818 and 1819.* 2 vols. New York, 1823. 1st Am. ed. $35-$50.

DUNIWAY, Mrs. Abigail J. *Captain Gray's Company, or, Crossing the Plains and Living in Oregon.* Clothbound. Portland, 1859. 1st ed. $250-$350. Also, $225 (1959 auction) and $275 (1963 auction).

DUNLAP, William. *The Life of Charles Brockden Brown.* 2 vols., leatherbound. Philadelphia, 1815. 1st ed. $50-$100.

DUNLAP, William. *A Narrative of the Events Which Followed Bonaparte's Campaign, etc.* Frontispiece, 5 plates. Leatherbound. Hartford, 1814. 1st ed. $50-$100.

DUNN, Jacob. *Massacres of the Mountains.* Folding map. Clothbound. New York, 1886. 1st ed, $50 and $65. Other copies, worn, $25 and $40.

DUNTHORNE, Gordon. *Flower and Fruit Prints of the 18th and Early 19th Centuries.* Clothbound. Washington, 1938. One of 750, with folding plate listing subscribers. $250-$350.

DU PONCEAU, M. *Memoire au Sujet des Pretentions du Government des Etats-Unis sur L'alluvion du la Fleuve Mississippi, etc.* Nouvelle-Orleans, 1808. 1st ed. $150.

DURANT, C. F. *Algae and Corallines of the Bay and Harbor of New York.* New York, 1950. Front cover and edge of front flyleaf stained, leather binding scuffed and cracked. $50.

DUVAL, John C. *Early Times in Texas.* Clothbound. Austin, no date, (1892). 1st ed. $35.

DWINELLE, John W. *The Colonial History of the City of San Francisco.* Map. San Francisco, 1864. 1st ed. $200 and up. $180 (1959 auction). San Francisco, 1866. 3d ed. Map, 3 plates, $500-$750. Also, $500 (1966 auction).

DYER, Mrs. D. B. *"Fort Reno," or Picturesque "Cheyenne and Arrapahoe Army Life," Before the Opening of Oklahoma.* 10 plates. New York, 1896. 1st ed. $37.50 and $50.

EARLE, Swepson and Percy G. Skinner. *Maryland's Colonial Eastern Shore.* Map. Baltimore, 1916. 1st ed. $40-$50. Shaken, $27.50.

EASTBURN, Robert. *A Faithful Narrative of the Many Dangers and Sufferings of.* Boston, 1758. $250.

EASTMAN, Mary H. *The American Aboriginal Portfolio.* Philadelphia, no date (1853). 1st ed. $75-$100. Others, worn, $30-$50.

EASTON, John. *A Narrative of the Causes Which Led to Philip's Indian War.* Map. Albany, 1858. 1st ed. $75. Others, $55 and $35.

EATON, Daniel Cady. *The Ferns of North America.* 2 vols., half morocco. Salem, 1879-80. 1st ed. $60 and $40.

EATON, Rachel Caroline. *John Ross and the Cherokee Indians.* Menasha, Wis., 1914. 1st ed. $50.

ECHO, The. No place, no date (New York, 1807). (By Theodore Dwight and Richard Alsop.) $37.50.

ECKENRODE, H. J. *The Revolution in Virginia.* Clothbound. Boston, 1916. 1st ed. $27.50 and $40.

EDGAR, Patrick Nisbett. *The American Race-Turf Register, etc.* Vol. 1 (all published). New York, 1833. 1st ed. $75.

EDWARD, David B. *The History of Texas.* Folding map. Clothbound. Cincinnati, 1836. 1st ed. $125 and $75. Lacking map, $50. Rebound, ex-library copy, $65.

EDWARDS, J. C. *Speech in Relation to the Territory in Dispute Between the State of Missouri and the United States, etc.* 20 pp., sewed. Washington, 1843. $35.

EDWARDS, John N. *Noted Guerrillas.* Frontispiece, 15 plates. Clothbound. St. Louis, 1877. 1st ed. $65-$75. Rebound, $55.

EDWARDS, Jonathan. *An Account of the Life of the Late Reverend Mr. David Brainerd.* Leatherbound. Boston, 1749. 1st ed. $50 and $30.

EDWARDS, Jonathan. *A Careful and Strict Enquiry Into . . . Freedom of the Will.* Leatherbound. Boston, 1754. 1st ed. $150. Others, $35-$100.

EDWARDS, Jonathan. *A Farewel-Sermon Preached at the First Precinct in Northampton, etc.* Boston, 1751. 1st ed. $60.

EDWARDS, Jonathan. *Marcus Whitman.* Portraits. 48 pp. Spokane, 1892. 1st ed. $40-$50.

EDWARDS, Philip L. *Sketch of the Oregon Territory; or, Emigrant's Guide.* 20 pp. Liberty, Mo., 1842. 1st ed. $5,000 estimated value. (Only one copy known.)

EDWARDS, W. F. (publisher). *Tourists' Guide and Directory to the Truckee Basin.* Truckee, 1883. 1st ed. $75-$100.

EDWARDS, Weldon. *Memoir of Nathaniel Macon, of North Carolina.* 22 pp., paperbound. Raleigh, 1862. $35.

EGE, Ralph. *Pioneers of Old Hopewell.* Portrait. Hopewell, N. J., 1908. $27.50.

EGGLESTON, Edward. *The Hoosier School-Master.* Brown or terra cotta clothbound. New York, no date (1871). 1st ed., 1st issue, with line 3 of page 71 reading "was" (not "is"). $35-$50.

EGLE, William H. *History of Dauphine and Lebanon Counties (Pennsylvania).* Philadelphia, 1883. $27.50 and $40.

ELIOT, John (translator). *Mamusse Wunneetupana-tamwe Up-Biblum God.* (The Holy Bible in Natick, American Indian, translation.) 600 unnumbered leaves, 4 blank leaves. Leatherbound. Cambridge, 1663. 1st ed. $43,000, $20,160, $7,840 and $10,500 (auction prices).

ELLICOTT, Andrew. *The Journal of.* 14 maps and plates. Half calfbound. Philadelphia, 1803. 1st ed. $125-$200. Rebound, $120 (1964 auction). Another, rebound, $100. Another, hinges cracked, maps repaired, $65. Another, repaired, $80 (1966 auction). Philadelphia, 1814. 2d ed. Half morocco. $57.50.

ELLIOT, D. G. *Monograph of the Tetraoninae, or Family of the Grouse.* 27 color plates. 5 parts in 4, boards. New York, 1864-65. 1st ed. $500-$1,250. $840 (1962 auction). $278 (1961 auction). 4 vols., morocco. $1,008 (1963 auction). $1,176 (1965 auction).

ELLIOT, W. J. *The Spurs.* No place, no date. (Spur, Tex., 1939). $25.

ELLIOTT, John and Samuel Johnson, Jr. *A Selected Pronouncing and Accented Dictionary.* Oblong. Hartford, 1800. $37.50.

ELLIS, Edward S. *The Life and Adventures of Col. David Crockett.* New York, 1861. 1st ed. $30.

EL PEREGRONI Septentrional Atlante, etc. Plate. Vellum. Mexico, 1737. (By Isidro Felix de Espinosa.) 1st ed. $300-$750. Also, $160 (1961 auction).

ELMORE, James B. *Love Among the Mistletoe, etc.* Alamo, Ind., 1899. 1st ed. $25.

ELZAS, Barnett A. *The Jews of South Carolina from the Earliest Period to the Present Day.* 11 plates. Philadelphia, 1905. $35-$50.

EMBARGO (The), or Sketches of the Times; a Satire. By a Youth of Thirteen. (Cover title.) 12 pp., leaflet, stitched. Boston 1808. (By William Cullen Bryant.) 1st ed. $500 and up. Boston, 1809. 36 pp., paperbound. With Bryant's by-line. 2d ed. $230 (1960 auction). Lacking covers, $40 (1957 auction).

EMERSON, Lucy. *The New-England Cookery.* Paper boards. Montpelier, 1808. $50.

EMERSON, Ralph Waldo. *An Address Delivered Before the Senior Class in Divinity College, etc.* Blue paperbound. Boston, 1838. 1st ed. $50-$75.

EMERSON, Ralph Waldo. *Essays.* Clothbound. Boston, 1841. 1st ed., without "First Series" on spine. $225 and $250. Rebacked, $65.

EMERSON, Ralph Waldo. *Essays: Second Series.* Clothbound. Boston, 1844. 1st ed., with "2d Series" on spine. $100. Repaired, $35.

EMERSON, Ralph Waldo. *A Historical Discourse, Delivered Before the Citizens of Concord, etc.* Blue paperbound. Concord, 1835. 1st ed. $100 and up. Front cover torn, $75.

EMERSON, Ralph Waldo. *Memorial R G S.* Boards, leather spine. Cambridge, 1864. 1st ed. $125.

EMERSON, Ralph Waldo. *The Method of Nature.* Printed tan paperbound. Boston, 1841. 1st ed. $50-$80.

EMERSON, Ralph Waldo. *Poems.* Yellow boards, paper label. Boston, 1847. 1st ed. $150-$200. Another, spine missing, $25.

EMERSON, Ralph Waldo. *Representative Men.* Black or brown clothbound. Boston, 1850. 1st ed., 1st printing, with hourglass design on front and back cover, $35-$50.

EMMART, Emily Walcott (translator). *The Badianus Manuscript.* By Martinus de la Cruz. 118 colored plates. Clothbound. Baltimore, 1940. $100-$150.

EMMONS, George T. *The Emmons Journal.* 11 pp., paperbound. Eugene, no date (1925). $35.

EMMONS, Dr. (Richard). *Tecumseh: Or, The Battle of the Thames.* 36 pp., paperbound. New York, 1836. $50.

EMORY, William H. *Notes of a Military Reconnaissance.* 68

plates, 6 maps and plans. Clothbound. Washington, 1848. House version. 1st ed. $50-$100. Same place and date, Senate version. $50-$100. Worn copies of each of these editions sell for much less.

ENGLISH, William B. *Rosina Meadows, the Village Maid.* Paperbound. Boston, 1863. 1st ed. Covers torn, $32.50.

ENGLISHMAN'S Sketchbook (An). New York, 1828. (By Simeon DeWitt Bloodgood.) 1st ed. Worn, $32.50.

ENSIGN & Thayer's Traveller's Guide Through Ohio, Michigan, Indiana, Illinois, Missouri, Iowa and Wisconsin. (A series with varying titles.) New York, 1851. Folding map, leatherbound. $45. Buffalo, 1853, $25 and $50. New York, 1853, $40. New York, 1854. $45.

ESSAY on the Use and Advantages of the Fine Arts (An). 16 pp., pamphlet. New Haven, no date (1770). (By John Trumbull.) 1st ed. $50.

ESSAYS of Howard on Domestic Economy. New York, 1820. (By Mordecai Manuel Noah.) 1st ed. $37.50.

ESSAYS from Poor Robert the Scribe. Doylestown, 1815. (By Charles Miner.) $125.

ESSHOM, Frank. *Pioneers and Prominent Men of Utah.* Salt Lake City, 1913. $30.

EULOGY on the Life of Gen. George Washington (An). Paperbound. Newburyport, 1800. (By Robert Treat Paine, Jr.) 1st ed. $32.50.

EVANGELICAL Hymns. 24 pp., stitched, uncut. Greenwich, Mass., 1807. 1st ed. $25.

EVANS, Augusta Jane. *St. Elmo.* New York, 1867. 1st ed. $25.

EVANS, Elwood. *Puget Sound: Its Past, Present and Future.* 16 pp., paperbound. Olympia, 1869. $125. Half morocco, $75.

EVANS, Estwick. *A Pedestrious Tour, of 4,000 Miles, Through the Western States and Territories.* Portrait. Boards. Concord, N.H., 1819. 1st ed. $300 and up. Also, chipped, soiled, foxed, $275 (1966 auction).

EVANS, Lewis. *Geographical, Historical, Political, Philosophical and Mechanical Essays, etc.* Map. Stitched. Philadelphia,

1755. Franklin imprint. 1st ed. $300-$500. Also, $320 (1959 auction). Philadelphia, 1755. 2d ed. Map in photostat, $77.50 and $82.50.

EVENINGS in New England. By an American Lady. Brown boards. Boston, 1824. (By Lydia Maria Child.) 1st ed. $50.

EVENTS in Indian History, Beginning with an Account of the Origin of the American Indians, etc. Lancaster, 1843. (By James Wimer). $45.

EVIL of Intoxicating Liquor (The), and the Remedy. 24 pp., sewed. Park Hill, Okla., 1844. $27.50.

EVJEN, John O. *Scandinavian Immigrants in New York, 1630-1674.* Minneapolis, 1916. 1st ed. $25.

EXAMINATION and Review of a Pamphlet, etc. Pamphlet. Washington, 1837. Waterstained, $137.

FACTS Concerning the City of San Diego, the Great Southwestern Sea-port of the United States, with a Map Showing the City and Its Surroundings. 14 pp., paperbound. San Diego, no date (1888). $45.

FACTS Respecting Indian Administration in the Northwest (The). 74 pp., paperbound. No place, no date (Victoria?, 1886). $40.

FAIRBANKS, George R. *The Spaniards in Florida.* 120 pp., paperbound. Jacksonville, 1868. 1st ed. $50. Lacking back cover, $35.

FAIRCHILD, T. B. *A History of the Town of Cuyahoga Falls, Summit County.* 39 pp. Cleveland, 1876. $35.

FALL of British Tyranny (The). Philadelphia, 1776. (By John Leacock.) 1st ed. $125.

FANNY. 49 pp., gray paperbound. New York, 1819. (By Fitz-Greene Halleck.) 1st ed. $75-$100. Worn, $75 (in recent catalogue). (There also exists a pirated 1819 ed., 67 pp.).

FANSHAWE: A Tale. Brown boards, paper labels. Boston, 1828. (By Nathaniel Hawthorne.) 1st ed. $2,600 (1958 auction price). Previously: Another copy, $1,800. Another, four lines in facsimile on page 139 and four on page 140, lower part of 140 renewed, flyleaves not original, writing on covers, stains, $500.

FARNHAM, Thomas J. *Travels in the Californias.* Map and plate. 4 parts. Paperbound and boards. New York, 1844. 1st ed. $225, $150, and $72.50. Another, morocco, front cover loose, library stamp on title page, $112.50.

FARNHAM, Thomas J. *Travels in the Great Western Prairies.* 197 pp. Poughkeepsie, 1841. 1st ed. $150. Dampstained, $57.50. New York, 1843. Paperbound, $35. Boards, $85. Ploughkeepsie (sic), 1843. Half calfbound, $100. Also $35 (at auction).

FARQUHARSON, Martha. *Elsie Dinsmore.* New York, 1867. (By Martha Finley.) 1st ed., with publisher's address misprinted "605" for "506" Broadway on title page. $150.

FAULKNER, William. *Absalom, Absalom!* New York, 1936. 1st ed. Boards, cloth spine. One of 300, signed. $150-$200. 1st trade ed. Clothbound. $75-$100.

FAULKNER, William. *As I Lay Dying.* Clothbound. New York, no date (1930). 1st ed., 1st state, with dropped "I" on page 11. Mint in dust jacket, $100-$150.

FAULKNER, William. *The Marble Faun.* Boards, printed labels. Boston, no date (1924). 1st ed. One of 500. In dust jacket (torn), $1,700 (1963 auction). Another, lacking jacket, $650 (1963 auction). Defective copies, $350 and $475 (at auction).

FAULKNER, William. *Miss Zilphia Gant.* Reddish brown clothbound. No place (Dallas), 1932. 1st ed. One of 300. $400. Also, $325 (1963 auction) and, at retail, $125-$300 for copies in varying states of condition.

FAULKNER, William. *Pylon.* Blue clothbound. New York, 1935. 1st ed. $75-$100. Spine faded, $50. One of 310, signed. Boards, boxed. $200.

FAULKNER, William. *Salmagundi.* Paperbound. Milwaukee, 1932. 1st ed. One of 525 numbered copies. $150-$300. Also, $220 (1964 auction).

FAULKNER, William. *These Thirteen.* Blue and gray clothbound. New York, no date (1931). 1st ed., 1st issue, with "280" for "208" in table of contents. Clothbound. $75-$100. One of 299, signed. Clothbound. $150-$200.

FELLOWS-JOHNSTON, Annie. *The Little Colonel.* Boston, 1896. 1st ed. $45. Another copy, less fine, $25.

FERTILE and Beautiful Palouse Country in Eastern Washington and Northern Idaho (The). 32 pp., oblong paperbound. St. Paul, 1889. $45.

FIELD, Eugene. *Culture's Garland.* Clothbound or paperbound. Boston, 1887. 1st ed. Clothbound. $25. One of six (or 12?) copies with leaves untrimmed, paperbound. $50 and up. Other paperbound copies, $25-$35.

FIELD, Eugene. *A Little Book of Western Verse.* Blue-gray boards, white cloth spine. Chicago, 1889. 1st ed., limited to 250 copies on hand-made paper, with list of subscribers. $100 and $75. New York, 1890. 1st trade ed. Clothbound. $25.

FIELD, Eugene. *Love Songs of Childhood.* Blue clothbound. New York, 1894. 1st ed. $25. One of 15 on Japan paper. $75. One of 106 on Van Gelder paper. $25-$35.

FIELD, Eugene. *Tribune Primer.* Gray-blue paperbound. No place, no date (Denver, 1881). 1st ed. $125-$300. Rebound in leather, $260 (1959 auction).

FIELD, Stephen J. *Personal Reminiscences of Early Days in California.* No place, no date (San Francisco, 1880?). 1st ed. $60-$80. Another copy, spine faded and worn, $35. Another, no place (Washington), 1893. $27.50.

FILISOLA, Gen. Vicente. *Evacuation of Texas.* 68 pp. Columbia, Tex., 1837. 1st ed. in English. $1,250.

FILLEY, William. *Life and Adventures of.* 7 plates and half-page cut. 96 pp., paperbound. Chicago, 1867. Printed by Fergus. 1st ed. $750 and up. Chicago, 1867, 112 pp., paperbound, printed by Filley & Ballard. 2d ed. $50-$100.

FILSON, John. *The Discovery, Settlement and Present State of Kentucke.* 118 pp., leatherbound. Wilmington, Del., 1784. 1st ed. With separately printed map, $1,000 and up. Lacking map, $850 (1966 auction). New York, 1793. 2d ed. Morocco. $50.

FINNEY & Davis (pub.). *Biographical and Statistical History of the City of Oshkosh.* 76 pp. Oshkosh, 1867. 1st ed. $50.

FIRST Catalogues and Circulars of the Botanical Garden of Transylvania University, etc. 24 pp., sewed. Lexington, Ky., 1824. (By C. S. Rafinesque.) $75.

FIRST Settlement and Early History of Palmyra, etc. (The).

10 pp., paperbound. Palmyra, N. Y., 1858. Repaired, $45.

FIRST Settlers of Virginia (The). New York, 1806. (By John Davis.) 2d ed. $25-$50.

FISH, Daniel. *Lincoln Bibliography*. Red clothbound. New York, no date (1906). One of 75, signed. $35.

FISHER, George. *Memorials of, etc.* Houston, 1840. 1st ed. $100-$200.

FISHER, R. S. *Indiana: Its Geography, Statistics, County Topography*. New York, 1852. $40.

FISHER, Vardis. *In Tragic Life*. Morocco. Caldwell, Idaho, 1932. 1st ed. One of 25, signed. $25-$50. 1st trade ed. Clothbound. In dust jacket, $7.50-$12.50. Later Garden City ed. of minor value ($5-$10).

FISHER, William (compiler). *An Interesting Account of the Voyages and Travels of Captains Lewis and Clark*. Baltimore, 1812. 2 portraits. $35-$50. Baltimore, 1813. 2 portraits, 4 (sometimes 3) plates. $25-$35.

FISKE, Nathan. *Remarkable Providences to be Gratefully Recollected, etc.* Boston 1776. $75.

FITCH, Elijah. *The Beauties of Religion*. Providence, 1789. 1st ed. $27.50.

FITCH, Samuel Sheldon. *A System of Dental Surgery*. Philadelphia, 1835. 2d. ed. Worn. $28.

FITHIAN, Philip Vickers. *Journal and Letters, 1767-1774*. 8 plates. Princeton, 1900. 1st ed. $35.

FITZGERALD, Edward (translator). *The Rubaiyat of Omar Khayyam*. Cambridge, 1900. One of 300 printed by Bruce Rogers. $50-$75.

FITZGERALD, F. Scott. *This Side of Paradise*. Green clothbound. New York, 1920. 1st ed. $75-$150. Presentation copy, signed by the author, $150. Worn $35-$50.

FLEMING, Walter L. *Documentary History of Reconstruction*. 9 facsimiles. 2 vols. Cleveland, 1906-07. 1st ed. $50-$60.

FLEURY, Claude. *A Short Catechism, Containing a Summary of Sacred History, and Christian Doctrine*. Detroit, 1812. $725 (1958 auction).

FLINT, Timothy. *A Condensed Geography and History of the Western States, or the Mississippi Valley.* 2 vols., tan paper boards, paper labels. Cincinnati, 1828. 1st ed. $75-$100. Another, label missing from Vol. 2, $50. Another, rebound in leather, $45 (auction).

FLINT, Timothy. *Lectures Upon Natural History.* Clothbound. Boston, 1833. 1st ed. Worn, $27.50.

FLINT, Timothy. *Recollections of the Last Ten Years.* Tan paper boards, paper label. Boston, 1826. 1st ed. $75-$100. Others, worn, $30 and $40. Another copy, small piece missing from blank edge of title page, $27.50.

FLORIDA and Texas: A Series of Letters Comparing the Soil, Climate, and Productions of These States, etc. 40 pp., paperbound. Ocala, 1866. (By Dr. B. M. Byrne.) 3d ed. $150.

FOGG Art Museum. *Collection of Mediaeval & Renaissance Paintings.* Half clothbound. Cambridge, 1919. 1st ed. $25.

FOLEY, P. K. *American Authors, 1795-1895.* Clothbound. Boston, 1897. One of 500. $50-$60. One of 75. $75-$100.

FOOTE, Henry Stuart. *Texas and the Texans.* 2 vols., clothbound. Philadelphia, 1841. 1st ed. $100-$150.

FORBES, Alexander. *California.* Map, 10 plates. San Francisco, 1919. 1st Am. ed. One of 250, signed by publisher. $80-$100. San Francisco, 1937. $30. San Francisco, 1939. $25.

FORBES, James Grant. *Sketches, Historical and Topographical, of the Floridas.* Map (not in all copies). Boards, paper label. New York, 1821. 1st ed. $100-$200. Another copy, half leatherbound, $60 (auction). Another, calfbound, $85. Another, rebound in modern cloth, $120 (at auction). Hinges broken, $25.

FORBUSH, Edward Howe. *Our American Game Birds.* 18 color plates by Hunt. Wilmington, no date (1917). (Published by E. I. Du Pont de Nemours & Co.) Lacking binding, $27.50.

FORD, Paul Leicester. *The Honorable Peter Stirling, etc.* New York, 1894. 1st ed., 1st issue, with "Stirling" spelled correctly on title page but misspelled "Sterling" on front cover and spine. $50-$100. Worn, $40.

FORD, Thomas. *Message of the Governor to the General Assembly, Dec. 2, 1844.* 12 pp., sewed. Springfield, 1844. Uncut, $35.

FORE and Aft; or, Leaves from the Life of an Old Sailor. By "Webfoot." Paperbound (?) and clothbound. Boston, 1871. (By W. D. Phelps.) 1st ed. $80 (1966 auction).

FOREMAN, Grant (editor). *Indian Justice.* (By John Payne.) Harlow, Okla., 1934. 1st ed. In dust wrapper, $25.

FOREMAN, Grant. *Indians and Pioneers.* Map, 8 plates. New Haven, 1930. 1st ed. In dust jacket, $25.

FOREMAN, Grant. *Pioneer Days in the Early Southwest.* Folding map. Clothbound. Cleveland, 1926. 1st ed. $40-$60.

FORESTER, Frank. *Frank Forester's Horse and Horsemanship of the United States, etc.* 2 vols., clothbound. New York, 1857. 1st ed. $50.

FORESTER, Frank. *My Shooting Box.* Philadelphia, 1846. (By Henry William Herbert.) 1st ed., 1st issue, with "mattler" for "matter" in last line of page 35. $150-$250.

FORESTER, Harry. *Ocean Jottings from England to British Columbia.* Vancouver, 1891. $45.

FORESTERS (The); an American Tale. Boston, 1792. (By Jeremy Balknap.) 1st ed. $100-$150.

FORT Braddock Letters. Worcester, 1827. (By John Gardiner Calkins Brainard.) $25.

FORT Pitt and Letters from the Frontier. Pittsburgh, 1892. One of 100. $35.

FOSTER, George G. (editor). *The Gold Regions of California.* Map. New York, 1848. $50-$75.

FOSTER, G. G. *New-York by Gaslight.* Paperbound. New York, 1850. 1st ed. Foxed, $35.

FOURTEENTH Anniversary of the Society of California Pioneers. Paperbound. San Francisco, 1864. $75.

FOX, John, Jr. *The Little Shepherd of Kingdom Come.* Red clothbound. New York, 1903. 1st ed., 1st issue, with "laugh" for "lap" in line 14 of page 61. $10-$15. Worn, $5. One of 100. $25. New York, 1931. One of 512, signed by artist N. C.

Wyeth. $25-$35.

FRAGMENTS of the History of Bawlefredonia, etc. No place, 1819. (By Jonas Clopper.) 1st ed. $40.

FRA Luca de Pacioli of Borgo S. Seplocro. New York, 1933. One of 390. $30.

FRANCHERE, Gabriel. *Narrative of a Voyage to the Northwest Coast of America, etc.* 3 plates. Clothbound. New York, 1854. 1st ed. in English. $75-$150. Another, signed, $90.

FREE-and-Easy Songbook (The). Philadelphia, 1834. $45.

FREDERIC, Harold. *The Damnation of Theron Ware.* Green clothbound. Chicago, 1896. 1st ed. $25 and $35.

FREDERIC, Harold. *Seth's Brother's Wife.* Tan clothbound. New York, 1887. 1st ed., 1st issue, 1886 copyright and no ads. $25 and $35. (Reprints so designated on copyright page.)

FREEBETTER'S New-England Almanack, for the Year 1776. Paperbound. New London, no date (1775). $35.

FREEMAN, George. *Midnight and Noonday.* Caldwell, Idaho, 1892. $40.

FREMAUX, Leon J. *New Orleans Characters.* 17 color plates. No place (New Orleans), 1876. 1st ed. $200.

FREMONT, John Charles. *Geographical Memoir Upon Upper California.* Senate Misc. Doc. No. 148. Folding map (not in all copies). 67 pp., paperbound. Washington, 1848. 1st ed. $40-$50. Lacking map, $30.

FREMONT, Brevet Capt. J. C. *Narrative of the Exploring Expedition to the Rocky Mountains, in the Year 1842, etc.* Clothbound. Syracuse, 1847. With folding map by Rufus B. Sage. $100 and $60. Repaired and recased, $50 (1957 auction). (This is one of several reprints of FREMONT: *Report of the Exploring Expedition, etc.,* which see.)

FREMONT, John Charles. *Report on an Exploration of the Country Lying Between the Missouri and the Rocky Mountains, etc.* Senate Doc. 243. 6 plates, folding map. Paperbound. Washington, 1843. 1st ed. $120 (1964 auction). Worn, $35-$50. Repaired, $22.50.

FREMONT, John Charles. *Report of the Exploring Expedition*

to the Rocky Mountains in the Year 1842. Senate ed. 22 plates, 5 maps, one folding. Clothbound. Washington, 1845. 1st ed. $50-$100. Another copy, large folding map missing, rubbed, $25. House ed., same date. $50 and $17.50. (See FREMONT: *Narrative of the Exploring Expedition, etc.)*

FRENEAU, Philip. *The American Village, A Poem.* 27 pp., paperbound. New York, 1772. 1st ed. $1,050 (auction).

FRENEAU, Philip. *The Miscellaneous Works of Mr. Philip Freneau.* Philadelphia, 1788. 1st ed. $35-$50.

FRINK, F. W. *A Record of Rice County, Minnesota, in 1868, with an Appendix Brought Down to 1871.* 32 pp., paperbound. Faribault, 1871. 2d ed. $45.

FROM Ocean to Ocean in a Winton. Winton Motor Carriage Co. 36 pp., paperbound. Cleveland, 1903. $28.50.

FROST, John. *History of the State of California.* Auburn, 1850. 1st ed. $45.

FROST, Robert. *Mountain Interval.* Clothbound. New York, no date (1916). 1st ed., 1st issue, with line 7, page 88, repeated. $50 and $37.50.

FRY, Frederick. *Fry's Traveler's Guide, and Descriptive Journal of the Great North Western Territories.* 264 pp. and 12 pp. of ads. Clothbound. Cincinnati, 1865. 1st ed. $200-$250. Signed, $185. Rebound in half leather, $100.

FULLER, Emeline. *Left by the Indians.* (Cover title.) 41 pp., paperbound. No place, no date (Mt. Vernon, 1892). $150-200. New York, 1936. Facsimile reprint. $10-$15.

FULTON, A. R. *The Red Men of Iowa.* 26 plates. Clothbound. Des Moines, 1882. 1st ed. $50-$75. Spots on binding, recased, $37.50.

FULMORE, Z. T. *The History and Geography of Texas as Told in County Names.* No place, no date (Austin, 1915). 1st ed. $35-$50.

FUNKHOUSER, W. D. *Wild Life in Kentucky.* Frankfort, 1925. $35.

GAINE, Hugh. *The Journals of Hugh Gaine, Printer.* 2 vols. Edited by Paul Leicester Ford. New York, 1902. 1st ed. One of 350. Boards, $32.50 and $50. Also, 30 copies, clothbound, printed on Japan paper. $75.

GALE, George. *Upper Mississippi.* Portraits, 13 plates. Chicago, 1867. 1st ed. $35-$50. Another copy, some pages dampstained, $25.

GALLAHER, James. *The Western Sketch-Book.* Boston, 1850. 1st ed. $25. Rebound, $15.

GALLATIN, Albert Eugene. *Art and the Great War.* New York, 1919. One of 100. $35.

GALT, John. *Lawrie Todd; or the Settlers in the Woods.* New York, 1830. Spine scuffed, one hinge cracked, $50.

GANTT, HON. E. W. *Address of: to the People of Arkansas.* 24 pp., sewed. No place (Philadelphia), 1863. 1st ed. $65.

GARCIA y Cubas, A. *Atlas Geografico, Estadistico e Historico de la Republic Mexicana.* 33 double-page maps in color. Boards. Mexico, 1858. One of 300. $200.

GARDEN, Alexander. *Anecdotes of the Revolutionary War in America.* 1st Series. Charleston, 1822. 1st ed. $50. Charleston, 1822-28. 1st and 2d Series. 1st ed. $100.

GARDINER, G. A. *A Brief and Correct Account of an Earthquake, etc.* Poughkeepsie, 1820. $75.

GARDINER, Abigail. *History of the Spirit Lake Massacre and the Captivity of Miss Abbie Gardner.* Portrait. Clothbound. Des Moines, 1885. 1st ed. $35-$40. Covers stained, $25.

GARLAND, Hamlin. *The Book of the American Indian.* 35 Remington plates. Boards. New York, 1923. 1st ed. In dust jacket, $60-$75. Worn, $40 and $25.

GARLAND, Hamlin. *Main-Travelled Roads.* Boston, 1891. 1st ed., 1st issue, clothbound, 9/16 inches across top, excluding covers. $50-$75. Worn, $35 and $50. Also blue or gray paperbound, $75-$100.

GARRARD, Lewis H. *Wah-To-Yah, and the Taos Trail.* Clothbound. Cincinnati, 1850. 1st ed., 1st issue, with page 269 mis-numbered 26. $150-$250. $90 (1966 auction). $160 (1964 auction). Rebacked, $140 (1966 auction). San Francisco, 1936. Grabhorn Press ed. One of 550. Boards. $25-$35.

GASS, Patrick. *A Journal of the Voyages and Travels of a Corps of Discovery.* Leatherbound. Pittsburgh, 1807. 1st ed. $150-$300. $250 (1966 auction). Pittsburgh, 1807. 2d ed. $100-$200. Philadelphia, 1812. 4th ed. $130 (1966 auction).

GAY, Frederick A. *Sketches of California.* 16 pp., paperbound. No place, no date (New York, 1848). $250-$350.

GEM of the Rockies! (The). Manitou Springs. 23 pp., paperbound. Manitou Springs, no date (about 1885). $35.

GENERAL and Statistical Description of Pierce County, Wisconsin. 8 pp., sewed. No place, no date (Prescott, 1854). $45.

GENTLEMAN'S Pocket-Farrier (The). 48 pp., paperbound. Boston, 1778. (By William Burdon.) $65.

GEORGE, Alice. *The Story of My Childhood. Written for My Children.* Whittier, 1923. $75.

GEORGE, Henry. *Progress and Poverty.* Clothbound. San Francisco, 1879. 1st ed., 1st issue, with the slip asking that no reviews be printed. $250-$350. Worn, $75-$150. 2d issue, green cloth, Author's Ed., without the slip referring to reviews, $150-$200.

GEORGE Mason, The Young Backwoodsman. Tan boards, paper label. Boston, 1829. (By Timothy Flint.) 1st ed. $75-$100. Label missing, $60. Another copy, worn, front end leaf and flyleaf missing, $50.

GEORGIA Scenes, Characters, Incidents, etc., in the First Half Century of the Republic. By a Native Georgian. Brown boards, cloth back, paper labels. Augusta, 1835. (By Augustus Baldwin Longstreet.) 1st ed. $450 (at auction).

GERSHWIN, George. *Porgy and Bess.* New York, 1935. 1st ed. One of 250, signed. $50.

GIDNEY, Eleazer. *A Treatise on the Structure, etc., of the Human Teeth.* Utica, 1824. 1st ed. Slightly damaged, $87.50.

GILBERT, Benjamin. *A Narrative of the Captivity and Sufferings of Benjamin Gilbert and His Family.* 96 pp. Philadelphia, 1784. 1st ed. $250. Philadelphia, 1848. 3d ed. Sheepskin. $25.

GILLELAND, J. C. *The Ohio and Mississippi Pilot.* 16 maps. Pittsburgh, 1820. 1st ed. $150.

GILLETT, James B. *Six Years With the Texas Rangers.* 8 plates. Clothbound. Austin, no date (1921). 1st ed. $35-$50. Signed, $40 and $50. New Haven, 1925. Clothbound. $15-$20.

GIRARDEY, G. *The North American Compiler.* Rossville, Ohio, 1844. $25.

GLEANINGS, or Spirit of the Press. Cincinnati, 1841. (William Lyle Keys, editor.) 1st ed. Worn, $27.50.

GLEESON, W. *History of the Catholic Church in California.* 4 maps and plans, 9 plates. 2 vols. San Francisco, 1871-72. 1st ed. $300. San Francisco, 1872. 2d ed., 2 vols. in one. $125.

GLOVER, Mary Baker. *Science and Health, With Key to the Scriptures.* Clothbound. Boston, 1875. (By Mary Baker Eddy.) 1st ed., 1st issue, without index. Mint copy, $750. Another copy, less fine, black cloth, errata leaf tipped in at end, $237.50. Another, terra cotta cloth, $200. Another, green cloth, signature on title page and flyleaf, binding rubbed, $300. Rebound in leather, $190 (auction). Repaired copies, $210 and $250 (at auction). Lynn, Mass., 1878. 2d ed. $110 (auction). Lynn, 1881. 3d ed. 2 vols. $50 (auction). Lynn, 1882. 2 vols. $100 (auction). Boston, 1883. 2 vols. 6th ed. $20 (auction).

GOBIERNO Independiente de Mexico. Paperbound. Mexico, 1882. $400.

GODDARD, Paul B. and Joseph E. Parker. *The Anatomy, Physiology and Pathology of the Human Teeth.* Philadelphia, 1844. 1st ed. $36. New York, 1854, worn, $26.

GODEY'S Lady's Book. December, 1849. Philadelphia, 1849. Printed paper covers. $25.

GODFREY, Mary. *An Authentic Narrative of the Seminole War, etc.* New York, 1836. $150. Providence, 1836. Paperbound. Half of frontispiece missing, $100.

GOETHE, J. W. Von. *Fuast.* Translated by John Anster. Harry Clarke illustrations. Half vellum. New York, no date (about 1925). Large paper, limited ed., signed by artist. $125.

GOLDER, Frank A. *Russian Expansion on the Pacific, 1641-1850.* Maps and plates. Cleveland, 1914. 1st ed. $35-$50.

GOODWIN, Mrs. L. S. *The Gambler's Fate: A Story of California.* 50 pp., paperbound. Boston, 1864. $35.

GOOKIN, Frederick William. *Daniel Gookin.* 10 plates. Chicago, 1912. 1st ed. One of 202. $32.50.

GORIN, Franklin. *The Times of Long Ago.* Louisville, 1929. 1st ed. $25.

GOUDY Gaudeamus. In Celebration of the Dinner Given Frederic W. Goudy, etc. No place (New York), 1939. One of 195. $30.

GOULD, E. W. *Fifty Years on the Mississippi.* Frontispiece. Clothbound. St. Louis, 1889. $50-$75. Worn, $32.50. Another, with presentation inscription by the author, $57.50.

GOULDING, Francis Robert. *Marooner's Island.* Philadelphia, 1869. 1st ed. Very good, $30.

GOVE, Capt. Jesse A. *The Utah Expedition, 1857-58.* 5 plates. Half clothbound. Concord, N.H., 1928. 1st ed. One of 50 on large paper. $30-$50. Another copy, regular ed., $25.

GRABHORN, Edwin. *The Fine Art of Printing.* Paperbound. No place (San Francisco), 1933. 1st ed. One of 50. $35-$50.

GRAHAM, Tom. *Hike and the Aeroplane.* Clothbound. New York, no date (1912). (By Sinclair Lewis.) 1st ed., 1st issue, with "August, 1912" on copyright page. $250. Another, worn, $100. Another, $150. Another, cover spotted, $125.

GRAHAME, Kenneth. *The Wind in The Willows.* Introduction by A. A. Milne. Boards. New York, 1940. Arthur Rackham illustrations. One of 2,020, signed by Bruce Rogers, boxed. $100-$150.

GRAND Jury Report, and the Evidence Taken by Them in Reference to the Great Riot in New Orleans, July 30, 1866. 17 pp., sewed. New Orleans, 1866. $35.

GRANT, Arthur H. *A Genealogical History of the Descendants of Matthew Grant of Windsor, Conn., 1601-1898.* Poughkeepsie, 1898. $25.

GRAVES, H. A. *Andrew Jackson Potter, the Noted Parson of the Texan Frontier.* Clothbound. Nashville, 1883. 3d ed. $75. Nashville, 1888. $27.50.

GRAY, Alonson. *Family Record of Edward Gray and His Wife, Mary Paddock, and Their Descendants.* Rutland, 1889. $40.

GRAY, John W. *The Life of Joseph Bishop.* Nashville, 1858. 1st ed. $75. Another copy, covers soiled, front inner hinge cracked, front flyleaf lacking, last 40 pages stained, $22.50.

GREAT Steam-Duck (The) . . . *An Invention for Aerial Navigation. By a Member of the LLBB.* 32 pp. Louisville, 1841. $750.

GREAT Trans-Continental Railroad Guide. Paperbound. Chicago, 1869. 1st ed. $65.

GREAT Western Almanac for 1848. Philadelphia, no date (1848). 1st ed. $175.

GREEN, Anne Katharine. *The Leavenworth Case.* Clothbound. New York, 1878. 1st ed. $100-$150.

GREEN, Jonathan S. *Journal of a Tour on the Northwest Coast of America in the Year 1829.* New York, 1915. 1st ed. One of 150. $45. (There were 10 more printed on Japan vellum, and they are more valuable.)

GREEN Mountain Boys (The). 2 vols., boards, paper labels. Montpelier, Vt., 1839. (By Daniel Pierce Thompson.) 1st ed., 1st issue, with publisher's name misspelled "Waltton" in copyright notice of Vol. 2. $75. Another, spelling corrected, $50.

GREEN, Thomas J. *Journal of the Texian Expedition Against Mier.* 11 plates, 2 plans. Clothbound. New York, 1845. 1st ed. $60-$85. Worn, $30 and $40. Another, inscribed by author, $48.50.

GREENE, Max. *The Kanzas Region.* 2 maps. New York, 1856. 1st ed. $47.50. Rebound, modern paper covers, $30 (auction).

GREENE, Talbot. *American Nights' Entertainment.* Jonesborough, Tenn., 1860. 1st ed. $60.

GREENHOW, Robert. *The History of Oregon and California.* Map. Clothbound. Boston, 1844. $35-$50. Boston, 1845. $25. New York, 1845. Worn, $25.

GREENLEE, Ralph Stebbins and Robert Lemuel Greenlee. *Genealogy of the Greenlee Families in America, etc.* Chicago, 1908. $42.

GREENLEE, Ralph Stebbins and Robert Lemuel Greenlee. *The Stebbins Genealogy.* 2 vols. Chicago, 1904. $56.

GREER, James K. *Bois d'Arc to Barb'd Wire.* Dallas, 1936. 1st ed. $35-$50.

GREGG, Alexander. *History of the Old Cheraws.* 4 maps. New York, 1867. 1st ed. $40-$50.

GREGG, Josiah. *Commerce of the Praries.* 2 maps, one folding, 6 plates. 2 vols., brown clothbound. New York, 1844. 1st ed. $550. Other sets, $350 and $137.50. New York, 1845. 2d ed. Rebound in calf, $100.

GREGORY, John. *Industrial Resources of Wisconsin.* Clothbound. Milwaukee, 1855. 1st complete ed. (3 separate parts appeared in Chicago in 1853). $250. Another copy, $60.

GRIGGS, George B. *Norkoma.* Houston, 1906. 1st ed. $25.

GRISWOLD, N. W. *Beauties of California.* 18 color plates. Paperbound. San Francisco, 1883. 1st ed. $50. Another, covers torn, $22.50.

GROVER, LaFayette. *The Oregon Archives.* Salem, 1853. 1st ed. $250. Rebound and repaired, $130 (1966 auction).

GUIDE, Gazetteer and Directory of Nebraska Railroads, etc. Map, folding plates. Paperbound. Omaha, 1872. (By J. M. Wolfe.) 1st ed. $100.

GUIDE to Texas Emigrants. Map, plates. Boston, 1835. (By David Woodman.) 1st ed. $75-$100. Another, worn, $30.

GUILLOTINA (The), or a Democratic Dirge, A Poem. Paperbound. Philadelphia, no date (1796). (By Lemuel Hopkins.) 1st ed. $45.

GUINEY, Louise Imogen. *Songs at the Start.* Clothbound or boards. Boston, 1884. 1st ed. $35 and $25.

GUNTER, Archibald Clavering. *Mr. Barnes of New York.* Clothbound and paperbound. New York, 1887. 1st ed., 1st issue, with perfect type in copyright notice. Paperbound, $125. Clothbound, $100.

HAFEN, LeRoy and W. J. Ghent. *Broken Hand.* Map, 8 plates. Cloth-backed boards. Denver, 1931. 1st ed. Large paper issue, one of 100, signed. $150-$250. $160 (1966 auction). Another issue, one of 500. $100-$200.

HAFEN, LeRoy. *The Overland Mail, 1849-1869.* Map, 7 plates. Clothbound. Cleveland, 1926. 1st ed. Limited. $30 and $40.

HALBERT, Henry S. and Timothy H. Bell. *The Creek War of*

1813 and 1814. Portraits, folding map (not in all copies). Clothbound. Chicago, 1895. 1st ed. $35.

HALE, Lucretia P. *The Peterkin Papers*. Clothbound. Boston, 1880. 1st ed. $35 and $57.50.

HALEY, J. Evetts. *Charles Goodnight, Cowman and Plainsman*. Clothbound. Boston, 1936. 1st ed. $25 and $35.

HALEY, J. Evetts. *Fort Concho on the Texas Frontier*. Clothbound. San Angelo, 1952. 1st ed. One of 185, signed. $35-$50.

HALEY, J. Evetts. *The XIT Ranch of Texas*. 2 maps, 30 plates. Clothbound. Chicago, 1929. 1st ed. $100-$125.

HALL, Edward H. *The Great West*. Map. 89 pp., paperbound. New York, 1864. 1st ed. $150. Another, $75. New York, 1865. Clothbound. $50-$75. New York, no date (1866?). Map, 181 pp., paperbound. $25. Another copy, $35.

HALL, Frances. *Narrative of the Capture and Providential Escape of Misses Frances and Almira Hall*. No place (St. Louis), 1832. 1st ed. $60. New York, 1833. $25.

HALL, Frederick. *Letters From the East and From the West*. Washington, no date (1840). 1st ed. $50-$60. Baltimore, 1840. $50.

HALL, George Eli. *A Balloon Ascension at Midnight*. Boards. San Francisco, 1902. One of 30 on Imperial Japan vellum, signed by Hall and silhouettist Gordon Ross. $25.

HALL, J. L. (printer). *Journal of the Hartford Union Mining and Trading Company*. 88 pp. Printed aboard the Henry Lee, 1849. (By George G. Webster.) $1,000 and up. Later ed., no place, no date (Hartford? or Wethersfield, Conn.,?), 1898. 2d ed. $65 (1960 auction).

HALL, James. *Legends of the West*. Half leatherbound. Philadelphia, 1832. 1st ed. $50. Philadelphia, 1833. 2d ed. Clothbound. $25. Cincinnati, 1869. Clothbound. $25.

HALL, James. *Sketches of History, Life, and Manners in the West*. 2 vols. Philadelphia, 1835. 2d issue of Vol. 1, 1st ed. of Vol. 2. $50.

HALL, Linville J. *Around the Horn in '49*. Wethersfield, Conn., 1898. $40. San Francisco, 1932. One of 250. $27.50.

HALL, Samuel R. *Lectures on School-Keeping*. Boston, 1829.

1st ed. $35.

HALSEY, R. T. H. *Pictures of Early New York on Dark Blue Staffordshire Pottery.* Clothbound. New York, 1899. 1st ed. One of 265 on handmade paper. $67.50 and $85. One of 30 on Japan vellum, $85 and $150.

HALSTEAD, M(urat). *The Caucuses of 1860.* Columbus, 1860. 1st ed. $65. Another, chip at top of spine, $45.

HAMBLIN, Jacob. *Narrative of Personal Experiences as a Frontiersman, Missionary to the Indians, and Explorer.* Salt Lake, 1881. $25.

HAMILTON, Alexander, and others. *The Federalist: A Collection of Essays, etc.* 2 vols., boards. New York, 1788. 1st ed. In fine and uncut condition, $4,000 (1964 auction). Rebound in modern calf, $850 (1964 auction). Hallowell, Me., 1826. $45 (1962 auction). Washington, 1818. $140 (1964 auction).

HAMILTON, Alexander. *Hamilton's Itinerarium.* St. Louis, 1907. $25.

HAMILTON, Alexander. *The Speeches at Full Length of Mr. Van Ness, Mr. Caines, the Attorney-General, Mr. Harrison and General Hamilton, etc.* 78 pp., paperbound. New York, 1804. $45.

HAMILTON, W. T. *My Sixty Years on the Plains.* 8 plates (6 by Charles M. Russell). Clothbound. New York, 1905. 1st ed. $75. Other copies, $30-$50.

HAMMOND, George. *Campaigns in the West.* Tucson, 1949. 1st ed. One of 300. $60 and $75.

HAMMOND, J. H. *Two Letters on Slavery in the United States, Addressed to Thomas Clarkson.* 51 pp., sewed. Columbia, 1845. Uncut, unopened, $25.

HAMMOND, John Martin. *Colonial Mansions of Maryland and Delaware.* 65 plates. Clothbound. Philadelphia, 1914. 1st ed. Limited. $35.

HANCOCK, Jean. *President du Congress de Philadelphia, etc.* Stitched. Philadelphia, 1776. $42.50.

HAND Book of Monterey and Vicinity (The). Paperbound. Monterey, 1875. $45.

HANSON, George A. *Old Kent: The Eastern Shore of Maryland.* Baltimore, 1876. 1st ed. $40. (Some on large paper.)

HARDIN, John Wesley. *The Life of.* 144 pp., paperbound. Seguin, Tex., 1896. 1st ed., 1st issue, with portrait of Hardin's brother (mistitled "John"). $60. 2d issue, with the Hardin portrait tipped in. $35.

HARDIN, Mrs. Philomelia Ann Maria Antoinette. *Everybody's Cook and Receipt Book.* Cleveland, 1842. $40.

HARGRAVE, Catherine Perry. *A History of Playing Cards.* Clothbound. Boston, 1930. 1st ed. In dust jacket, $100-$125.

HARLAN, Jacob Wright. *California, '46 to '88.* San Francisco, 1888. 1st ed. $75. Other copies, $40 and $45.

HARMAN, S. W. *Hell on the Border.* Portrait. Paperbound. Fort Smith, Ark., no date (1898). 1st ed. $200. Other copies, $150 and $100. Another, cover torn, $100. Another, rebound, $120 (at auction).

HARMER, Brig.-Gen. Josiah. *The Proceedings of a Court of Enquiry, Held at the Special Request of Brig-Gen. Josiah Harmer to Investigate His Conduct, etc.* 31 pp., paperbound. Philadelphia, 1791. $750 and up. Also, $672 (1958 auction).

HARMON, Daniel Williams. *Journal of Voyages and Travels in the Interior of North America.* Folding map. Andover, 1820. 1st ed., 1st issue, with map placed opposite title page and with no errata slip. $150-$250. $160 (1966 auction). Another, map in photostat, $175. Later issue, same date, errata slip and portrait, map moved. $75.

HARRINGTON, Kate. *In Memoriam. Maymie.* 60 pp., clothbound. Keokuk, Iowa, 1870. 1st ed. Worn, end papers broken at folds, $50.

HARRIS, Chapin A. *The Dental Art, a Practical Treatise on Dental Surgery.* Baltimore, 1839. 1st ed. Spine gnawed away by silverfish, $50.

HARRIS, Joel Chandler. *Uncle Remus: His Songs and His Sayings.* Clothbound. New York, 1881. 1st ed., 1st issue, with "presumptive" for "presumptuous" in last line, page 9, and with no mention of this book in ads at back. $100-$125. Other copies, less than fine, $30-$75. Another, worn, $27.50. 1st ed., 2d issue. $38.50 and $20.

HARRIS, Sarah Hollister. *An Unwritten Chapter of Salt Lake, 1851-1901.* Clothbound. New York, 1901. 1st ed. $200. Also, $85 (1966 auction).

HARRIS, Thaddeus Mason. *The Journal of a Tour into the Territory Northwest of the Alleghany Mountains.* 4 maps (3 folding) and a folding plate. Marbled boards, paper spine and paper label. Boston, 1805. 1st ed. $150-$200. Also, $110 (1967 auction).

HARRIS, W. B. *Pioneer Life in California.* 98 pp., paperbound. Stockton, 1884. 1st ed. $250.

HARRIS, W. R. *The Catholic Church in Utah.* Map, 25 plates. Salt Lake City, no date (1909). 1st ed. $50. (Also issued in 2 vols.)

HARRIS, William Charles. *The Fishes of North America That Are Captured on Hook and Line.* Vol. 1 (all published). Half leatherbound. New York, 1898. Ex-library, $50.

HARRISON, E. J. *The Thrilling, Startling and Wonderful Narrative of.* 30 pp., paperbound. Cincinnati, 1848. 1st ed. $850 (at auction).

HARRISON, E. S. *Central California, Santa Clara Valley.* San Jose, no date (1887). $45.

HARRISON, Fairfax. *Virginia Land Grants.* Richmond, 1925. 1st ed. $35.

HARRISON, William W. *Harrison, Waples and Allied Families: Being the Ancestry of George Leib Harrison of Philadelphia and of His Wife Sarah Ann Waples.* Full morocco. Philadelphia, 1910. One of 100. $35-$50.

HART, John A. *History of Pioneer Days in Texas and Oklahoma.* 12 plates. No place, no date (Guthrie, 1906). 1st ed. $50-$75.

HART, Joseph C. *The Romance of Yatching.* Clothbound. New York, 1848. 1st ed. $50. Ex-library, $25.

HARTE, Bret. *The Lost Galleon and Other Tales.* Clothbound. San Francisco, 1867. 1st ed. $90-$125. Also, $60 (1962 auction). Another, autographed, worn and faded, $250.

HARTE, Bret. *The Luck of Roaring Camp and Other Sketches.* Clothbound. Boston, 1870. 1st ed., 1st issue, without the story, "Brown of Calaveras." $100-$200. Also, $120 (1962 auction). Another, worn and faded, $72.50.

HARTE Bret. *The Story of Enriquez.* Boards. San Francisco, 1924. One of 100. $40.

HARVEY BELDEN: or a True Narrative of Strange Adventures. Cincinnati, 1848. (By Nathaniel A. Ware.) $50.

HASKELL, Burnette G. *Kaweah, a Co-operative Commonwealth.* 16 pp., paperbound. San Francisco, 1887. $75.

HASKINS, C. W. *The Argonauts of California.* Clothbound. New York, 1890. 1st ed. $70 and $40.

HASTINGS, Lansford W. *The Emigrants' Guide to Oregon and California.* 152 pp., paperbound. Cincinnati, 1845. 1st ed. Rebound in full leather, $4,700 (1959 auction). Another, rebound in facsimile paper covers, $4,000 (1963 auction). Rebound in calf, rebacked, washed, title page scuffed, 33 pp. supplied from a 2d ed. copy, $3,000.

HASTING, Sally. *Poems, on Different Subjects. To Which is Added a Descriptive Account of a Family Tour to the West; in the Year 1800.* Leatherbound. Lancaster, Pa., 1808. 1st ed. $175-$200. Also, $120 (1967 auction).

HASTINGS, Mrs. Susannah Willard Johnson. *A Narrative of the Captivity of Mrs. Johnson.* Windsor, Vt., 1807. $50.

HASWELL, Anthony (editor). *Memoirs and Adventures of Capt. Matthew Phelps.* Leatherbound. Bennington, Vt., 1802. 1st ed. $200-$300. Also, $200 (1966 auction).

HAVEN, Charles T. and Frank A. Belden. *History of the Colt Revolver.* Clothbound. New York, 1940. 1st ed. $75-$100.

HAWKESWORTH, John. *A New Voyage, Round the World in the Years 1768, 1769, 1770, 1771, etc.* Folding map, 2 folding plates by Paul Revere. 2 vols., calfbound. New York, 1774. 1st Am. ed. of Capt. Cook's first voyage. $900.

HAWKINS, A. *Picture of Quebec; with Historical Recollections.* Quebec, 1834. Foxed, worn, $56.

HAWLEY, Zerah. *A Journal of a Tour Through Connecticut, Massachusetts, New York, etc.* Leatherbound. New Haven, 1882. 1st ed. $200-$300. Also, $180 (1966 auction).

HAWTHORNE, Nathaniel. *Grandfather's Chair.* Clothbound. Boston, 1841. 1st ed. $75-$150. Another, $35. Another, ex-library, $25. Another, binding faded, $30.

HAWTHORNE, Nathaniel. *The House of the Seven Gables.* Brown clothbound. Boston, 1851. 1st ed., 1st issue, with ads dated March. $140 (1962 auction). Other copies, $100 and $75 at retail. Worn, $25 and $35.

HAWTHORNE, Nathaniel. *The Scarlet Letter.* Brown cloth. Boston, 1850. 1st ed., 1st issue, with readings of "reduplicate" in line 20, page 21; "characterss" in line 5, page 41, and "catechism" in line 29, page 132. $600 (1960 auction) "in very fine condition." Others at retail, $200-$400. Also, $300 (1962 auction). Another, in morocco slipcase, $165. Another copy, bookplate, $150. Another, rebound, $50. New York, 1928. Angelo woodblocks. One of 980. $25.

HAWTHORNE, Nathaniel. *Tanglewood Tales, for Girls and Boys.* Clothbound. Boston, 1853. 1st Am. ed., 1st issue, with ads at page 2 reading "In press." $100-$150. Worn copies, $50-$100. Average copy, $67.50 (in recent catalogue).

HAWTHORNE, Nathaniel. *Twice-Told Tales.* Purple clothbound. Boston, 1837. 1st ed., 1st issue, with 2 leaves of ads at front, 8 at back. $1,250 (1960 auction) "in unusually fine condition . . . lettering on backstrip in brilliant gilt." Another, $550 (1958 auction). Another, $275 (1963 auction). No recent catalogue prices seen, but previously, $90-$200; rebound in full leather, $59.50.

HAWTHORNE, Nathaniel. *A Wonder-Book for Girls and Boys.* 6 plates. Clothbound. Boston, 1852. 1st ed., 1st issue, with gilt decorations at top of spine only and with no ads. $200-$250. Worn, $120. Cambridge, 1893. Illustrated by Crane. Boards. One of 250. $35-$50.

HAYDEN, F. V. *Geological and Geographical Atlas of Colorado, etc.* Leatherbound. Washington, 1877. $35-$50.

HAYMOND, Henry. *History of Harrison County, W. Va.* Morgantown, W. Va., no date (1910). $35-$50.

HAYWOOD, John. *The Civil and Political History of the State of Tennessee.* Knoxville, 1823. 1st ed., with tipped-in copyright slip and inserted printed slip. $200-$250. Signed copy,

$200. Rebound in leather, $200 and $150.

HAZEL, Harry. *The West Point Cadet.* Paperbound. Boston, 1845. 1st ed. $50.

HAZEN, Gen. W. B. *Our Barren Lands.* 53 pp., paperbound. Cincinnati, 1875. 1st ed. $75-$150. $85 (1966 auction).

HEALY, Francis. *The American Calculator, or Countinghouse Companion.* 29 pp., paperbound. New York, 1787. $125.

HEAP, Gwinn Harris. *Central Route to the Pacific.* Folding map (not in all copies), 13 tinted plates. Clothbound. Philadelphia, 1854. 1st ed. $100-$200. $130 (1965 auction). Others, in catalogues, $150 and $125. Lacking map, $50.

HEARN, Lafcadio. *Chita: A Memory of Last Island.* Clothbound. New York, 1889. 1st ed. $35 and $25.

HEARN, Lafcadio. *Some Chinese Ghosts.* Clothbound. Boston, 1887. 1st ed. $100-$125. Other copies, $75 and $45 (worn).

HEARN, Lafcadio. *Stray Leaves from Strange Literature.* Clothbound. Boston, 1884. 1st ed., 1st issue, with Osgood imprint on spine. $50, $75, $80, and $100. Worn, hinges cracking, bookplate, $35.

HEART, Capt. Jonathan. *Journal of, etc.* 94 pp., paperbound. Albany, 1885. 1st ed. One of 150. $50.

HEART of the West (The). Chicago, 1871. $25.

HEATH, Maj.-Gen. (William). *Memoirs of.* Leatherbound. Boston, 1798. 1st ed. $35-$50.

HEBARD, Grace R. and E. A. Brininstool. *The Bozeman Trail.* Maps, including 2 folding maps, illustrations. 2 vols., clothbound. Cleveland, 1922. 1st ed. $75-$100. Glendale, Calif., 1960. Clothbound. $17.50.

HEBARD, Grace R. *Sacajawea.* Plates and maps. Clothbound. Glendale, Calif., 1933. 1st ed. One of 750, inscribed. $75-$100.

HEBARD, Grace R. *Washakie.* 7 maps, 16 plates. Clothbound. Cleveland, 1930. 1st ed. $40-$50.

HEBISON, W. C. *Early Days in Texas and Rains County.* 50 pp., paperbound. Emory, Tex., 1917. 1st ed. $45.

HECKEWELDER, John. *An Account of the History, Manners,*

and Customs of the Indian Nations, etc. Philadelphia, 1818. 1st ed. $75-$100. Philadelphia, 1819. 2d ed. $50. Philadelphia, 1881. $12.50.

HECKEWELDER, John. *A Narrative of the Mission of the United Brethren Among the Delaware and Mohegan Indians.* Portrait and errata slip. Philadelphia, 1820. 1st ed. $50. Cleveland, 1907. 3 maps, 15 plates. Three-quarters leather. Large paper ed. of 160. $125.

HELLER, Elinor Raas and David Magee. *Bibliography of the Grabhorn Press, 1915-1940.* San Francisco, 1940. One of 210. Half leatherbound. $300. $140 and $170 (at auction). *Bibliography . . . from 1940 to 1956.* San Francisco, 1957. Boards. $100-$200. $110 (at auction).

HELLMAN, Lillian. *Watch on the Rhine.* Leatherbound. New York, 1942. One of 50, boxed. $50.

HEMANS, Felicia. *The League of the Alps, The Siege of Valencia, The Vespers of Palermo, and Other Poems.* Boston, 1826. 1st ed. $50. Another, spine chipped at top and bottom, $25.

HEMINGWAY, Ernest. *A Farewell to Arms.* Blue-green boards, vellum spine, black label. New York, 1929. 1st ed., 1st state, without notice that "none of the characters in this book is a living person." One of 510 large paper copies, signed. $150-$250. $130 and $140 (at auction). 1st ed., 1st state, trade edition. Clothbound. In dust jacket, $50-$75. Lacking jacket, $35-$50. Same, 2d printing, in dust jacket, $35-$50. Lacking jacket, $15-$20.

HENKLE, Moses. *Gospel of Nicodemus, the Believing Jew.* 40 pp., sewed. Columbus, 1826. $35.

HENKLE, Moses. *Last Wills and Testaments of Thirteen Patriarchs, and Gospel of Nicodemus, the Believing Jew.* 67 pp., sewed. Urbana, Ohio, 1827. $35.

HENNEPIN, Father Louis. *A Description of Louisiana.* Translated by John G. Shea. New York, 1880. One of 250. $50-$100.

HENRY, Alexander. *Travels and Adventures in Canada and the Indian Territories, etc.* New York, 1809. 1st ed., with the portrait by Maverick, as preferred by collectors. Errata leaf at end. $325. Another, $250. Another, lacking the portrait, $110 (1966 auction). Boston, 1901. One of 700. $25.

HENRY, John Joseph. *An Accurate and Interesting Account of the Hardships and Sufferings of that Band of Heroes, Who Traversed the Wilderness in the Campaign Against Quebec in 1775.* Leatherbound. Lancaster, 1812. 1st ed. $150-$200. Foxed, rubbed, hinges cracked, $140. Another copy, foxed, loose in covers, $150. (Most copies of this book are badly foxed, or browned.)

HENRY, O. *Cabbages and Kings.* Clothbound. New York, 1904. (By William Sidney Porter.) 1st ed., 1st issue, with "McClure, Phillips & Co." on spine. $300. Also, $180 (1963 auction). Worn, $75.

HENRY, O. *Heart of the West.* Pictorial clothbound. New York, 1907. (By William Sidney Porter.) 1st ed. Fine copy, in dust jacket, $200 (1963 auction). Worn, $50.

HERBERT, W. H. (sic). *Ringwood the Rover, a Tale of Florida.* Printed brown paperbound. Philadelphia, 1843. (By Henry William Herbert.) 1st ed. Rebound in cloth, frayed paper covers preserved. $160 (1967 auction).

HERGESHEIMER, Joseph. *The Three Black Pennys.* Illustrations by D. Hendrickson. Vellum and clothbound. New York, 1930. One of 170, signed by author and artist. $25. (New York, 1917. 1st ed. Clothbound. $10-$15.)

HERGESHEIMER, Joseph. *Wild Oranges.* New York, 1918. One of 85 on Perusia paper, orange boards. $25.

HERNDON, William H. and Jesse W. Weik. *Herndon's Lincoln.* 63 plates. 3 vols., blue clothbound. Chicago, no date (1889). 1st ed. $200. Other copies, worn, $75-$150. Chicago, 1890. 3 vols. 2d ed. $50.

HERNE, Peregrine (pseudonym). *Perils and Pleasures of a Hunter's Life; or the Romance of Hunting.* Clothbound. Philadelphia, 1854. 1st ed. $50. Ends of spine worn, $35. New York, 1857. 11 hand-colored plates. Clothbound. $20.

HERRINGTON, W. D. *The Deserter's Daughter.* 27 pp., paperbound. Raleigh, 1865. 1st ed. $37.50.

HEWITT, Randall H. *Across the Plains and Over the Divide.* Map, portrait, 58 plates. Clothbound. New York, no date (1906). 1st ed. $85-$125. Inscribed copy, $85.

HICHBORN, Benjamin. *An Oration, Delivered March 5, 1777, etc.* 18 pp., full morocco. Boston, 1777. 1st ed. $65.

HILDEBRAND, Samuel S. *Autobiography.* 8 plates. Clothbound. Jefferson City, Mo., 1870. 1st ed. $75. Worn, $50.

HILTON, A. *Oklahoma and Indian Territory Along the Frisco.* 91 pp., paperbound. St. Louis, 1905. $25.

HIND, Henry Y. *North-West Territory.* 8 folding maps and plans. Clothbound. Toronto, 1859. 1st ed. $50-$60. Another, worn, $35. Another, $25. Another, cover loose, spine gone, $20.

HINTON, R. J. *The Hand-Book to Arizona.* 4 maps, 16 plates. Paperbound. San Francisco, 1878. 1st ed. $60. Another, clothbound, $50.

HISTORICAL Account of the Expedition Against the Ohio Indians, in the Year 1764 (An). Folding map, 2 folding plates. 71 pp. Philadelphia, 1765. (By Provost William Smith.) 1st ed. Half morocco, $3,750 (1967 auction). Earlier: Another copy, most of map missing, photostat inserted, name clipped from title page, $200. Another, map and plate in facsimile, $97.50.

HISTORICAL and Descriptive Review of the Industries of Walla Walla. 112 pp., paperbound. No place, 1891. $60.

HISTORICAL and Scientific Sketches of Michigan. Clothbound. Detroit, 1834. 1st ed. $32.50.

HISTORICAL War Map (The). 56 pp. Indianapolis, 1862. Asher & Co. $25.

HISTORY of the Brooklyn and Long Island Fair, Feb. 22, 1864. Leatherbound. Brooklyn, 1864. Brilliant copy, but one hinge of the heavily embossed roan cover weak, $25.

HISTORY of Crawford and Richland Counties, Wisconsin. Clothbound. Springfield, Ill., 1884. (By C. W. Butterfield and George A. Ogle.) 1st ed. $35-$50.

HISTORY of Dearborn and Ohio Counties, Indiana, from Their Earliest Settlement, etc. Clothbound. Chicago, 1885. 1st ed. $35-$50.

HISTORY of the Great Lakes. Plates, 5 double-page maps. 2 vols. Chicago, 1899. (Edited by John B. Mansfield.) 1st ed. $75-$100.

HISTORY of Idaho Territory. 2 maps, 69 plates, 2 facsimiles. San Francisco, 1884. 1st ed. $75-$100.

HISTORY of the Indian Wars With the First White Settlers of the United States (A). Leatherbound. Montpelier, 1812. (By Daniel C. Sanders.) 1st ed. $150-$200. Also, $100 (1967 auction). Rochester, 1828. 2d ed. (Chapter 27 omitted.) $75.

HISTORY of the Late War in the Western Country. Leatherbound. Lexington, 1816. (By Robert B. McAfee.) 1st ed., with the "extra" printed leaf (of Gen. Winchester's criticism) at end. $175-$200. Also, $120 (1967 auction). Bowling Green, Ohio, no date (1919). One of 300. Clothbound. $17.50 and $25.

HISTORY of Lawrence County (Pennsylvania). Half morocco. Philadelphia, 1877. 1st ed. $35-$50. Recased, edges rubbed, $27.50.

HISTORY of Mercer County (Pennsylvania). Half morocco. Philadelphia, 1877. 1st ed. $40-$60.

HISTORY of Montana. Map, plates. Half leatherbound. Chicago, 1885. (Edited by Michael A. Leeson). 1st ed. $80-$150. Worn, $75.

HISTORY of Nevada. 116 plates. Half leatherbound. Oakland, 1881. (Edited by Myron Angel.) 1st ed. $250. Also, $170 (1960 auction).

HISTORY of Oregon Territory. (Cover title.) 88 pp., paperbound. Cleveland, 1846. (By H. L. W. Leonard.) 1st ed. $1,000 and up. (Only three copies known.)

HISTORY of the Origin, Rise and Progress of the War in America (The). 3 vols. in one or 3 vols. in 2, leatherbound. Boston, 1780. 1st ed. $150-$300. Worn, $85.

HISTORY of Pamela (The), or, Virtue Rewarded. Norristown, 1799. (Abridged from Samuel Richardson.) $25.

HISTORY of San Luis Obispo County (California). Half leather and clothbound. Oakland, 1883. (By Myron Angel.) 1st ed. $200-$250. Also, $170 (1960 auction).

HISTORY of Santa Barbara and Ventura Counties, California. Oakland, 1883. (By Jesse D. Mason.) $65.

HISTORY of Texas: History of Milam, Williamson, Bastrop, Travis, Lee and Burleson Counties. Chicago, 1893. $65.

HISTORY of Tioga County (Pennsylvania). No place, 1897. $40-$50.

HITCHCOCK, Enos. *The Farmer's Friend.* Boston, 1793. 1st ed. $40-$60.

HOAR, A. W. *Lineage and Family Records of Alfred Wyman Hoar and His Wife Josephine Jackson.* Delano, Minn., 1898. $45.

HOBBS, G. A. *Bilbo, Brewer, and Bribery in Mississippi Politics.* No place (Memphis), 1917. 1st ed. $40.

HOBBS, Capt. James. *Wild Life in the Far West.* 20 plates, colored frontispiece. Clothbound. Hartford, 1872. 1st ed. $100-$150. Hartford, 1873. 2d ed. $80. Hartford, 1874. $35.

HODGE, Frederick W. *Handbook of American Indians North of Mexico.* Map. 2 vols., clothbound. Washington, 1907-10. 1st ed. $50-$100. Washington, 1912. $50 and $65. New York, 1959. $35-$50.

HODGES, M. C. *The Mestico.* Paperbound. New York, 1850. 1st ed. $150.

HODGSON, Adam. *Remarks During a Journey Through North America in the Years 1819-21.* Leatherbound. New York, 1823. 1st ed. $35-$50. Worn, $25.

HODGSON, Joseph. *The Alabama Manual and Statistical Register.* Montgomery, 1869. $35.

HOFER, A. F. *Grape Growing.* 32 pp., paperbound. McGregor, Iowa, 1878. $25.

HOLDEN, William C. *Alkali Trails.* Dallas, no date (1930). 1st ed. $35.

HOLDEN, William C. *Rollie Burns, etc.* Clothbound. Dallas, 1932. 1st ed., 1st issue, tan cloth. $35. 2d issue, green cloth. $12.50.

HOLDEN, William C. *The Spur Ranch.* Boston, no date (1934). 1st ed. $42.50.

HOLDER, C. F. *The Channel Islands of California.* Clothbound. Chicago, 1910. 1st ed. $25. Another copy, worn, $12.50.

HOLLEY, Mary Austin. *Texas: Observations, Historical, Geographical and Descriptive.* Folding map, 167 pp., clothbound.

Baltimore, 1833. 1st ed. $200-$300. Also, $160 (1964 auction). Lexington, Ky., 1836. 2d ed., enlarged, 410 pp. $250. Also, worn copy, $85 (1966 auction). Another, $100 (in dealer catalogue).

HOLMES, Mary J. *Tempest and Sunshine.* Gray cloth. New York, 1854. 1st ed. $40. Another copy, lacking blank front leaves, inner hinge broken, $25.

HOLMES, Oliver Wendell. *Astraea: The Balance of Illusions. A Poem.* Rough reddish brown cloth or yellow boards. Boston, 1850. 1st ed., 1st issue, with ampersand in printer's imprint on copyright page set above the line. $45. Others, $25-$35. Worn, $15-$25.

HOLMES, Oliver Wendell. *The Contagiousness of Puerperal Fever.* Paperbound. No place, no date (Boston, 1843). 1st ed. $500.

HOLMES, Oliver Wendell. *Currents and Counter-Currents in Medical Science.* Paperbound. Boston, 1861. 1st ed., 1st state, with no ads. $40.

HOLMES, Oliver Wendell and others. *The Harbinger: A May-Gift.* Clothbound. Boston, 1833. 1st ed. $25.

HOLMES, Oliver Wendell. *Over the Teacups.* Green clothbound. Boston, 1891. 1st ed., 1st state, with no price for this book on ad leaf facing title page. $57.50. Others, $25-$50.

HOLMES, Justice Oliver Wendell. *The Common Law.* Clothbound. Boston, 1881. 1st ed. $75-$125. Another copy, $35. Another, worn, $5.

HOLY BIBLE. Cleveland and New York, 1949. One of 975 printed by A. Colish, designed by Bruce Rogers. $50 to $150. One of 20 with a decorative head piece for each book. $250.

HOME of the Badgers (The) . . . *By Oculus.* 36 pp., paperbound. Milwaukie (sic), 1845. (By Josiah Bushnell Grinnell.) 1st ed. $375 (1958 auction).

HOOPER, Johnson J. *Dog and Gun.* Paperbound. New York, 1856. 1st ed., with dated title page. $25.

HOPKINS, Rev. T. M. *Reminiscences of Col. John Ketcham, of Monroe County, Indiana, by His Pastor, etc.* 22 pp., paperbound. Bloomington, 1866. Inner margins foxed, $200.

HORN, Hosea B. *Horn's Overland Guide.* Folding map. Cloth-bound. New York, 1852. 1st ed., 1st issue, 78 pp. $250 and $300. Also, $170 and $180 (both at auction). Another copy, 2d issue, 83 pp., $200. Same, lacking map, $32 (at auction). New York, no date (1853). Map (different from that in original ed). Clothbound. $185. Another, spine chipped, $125.

HOSACK, David. *Essays on Various Subjects of Medical Science.* 3 vols., half leatherbound. New York, 1824-1830. 1st eds. $125. Another set, $60.

HOSHOUR, S. K. *Letters to Squire Pedant by Lorenzo Alti-sonant, an Emigrant to the West.* Indianapolis, 1870. $30.

HOSMER, Hez. L. *Report of the Committee on Foreign Cor-respondence of the Grand Lodge of Montana, at Its Seventh Annual Communication.* 55 pp., paperbound. Helena, 1872. $75.

HOUGH, Franklin B. *Washingtonia.* 2 vols. Roxbury, 1865. $100.

HOUGHTON, Jacob. *The Mineral Region of Lake Superior.* 2 maps on one folding sheet. Buffalo, 1846. 1st ed. $75.

HOUSMAN, A. E. *A Shropshire Lad.* Philadelphia, no date (1902). (Henry Altemus, publisher.) $37.50.

HOWBERT, Irving. *The Indians of the Pike's Peak Region.* 4 plates. New York, 1914. 1st ed. $25.

HOWE, E. D. *History of Mormonism.* Painesville, Ohio, 1840. (2d ed. of HOWE: *Mormonism Unvailed,* which see.) $100-$150.

HOWE, E. D. *Mormonism Unvailed* (sic), etc. Painesville, Ohio, 1834. 1st ed. $150-$200. (For 2d ed., see HOWE: *History of Mormonism.*)

HOWE, E. W. *The Story of a Country Town.* Atchison, 1883. 1st ed., 1st issue, with "D. Caldwell, Manufacturer. Atchi-son, Kan." rubber-stamped inside front cover and no lettering at foot of spine. $75 and $45. Another, signed, $30. Another copy, lacking stamp but with name on spine, $30. Another, soiled, $25.

HRDLICKA, Ales. *The Anthropology of Florida.* Clothbound. DeLand, 1922. 1st ed. $50. Another, spine spotted, $35.

HUBBARD, Jeremiah. *40 Years Among the Indians*. Miami, Okla., 1913. 1st ed. $50. Another, slightly worn, $35.

HUBBARD, John Niles. *Sketches of Border Adventures, in the Life and Times of Maj. Moses Van Campen*. Leatherbound. Bath, N. Y., 1841. $150-$250. Bath, N. Y., 1842. Half leatherbound, $25 and $50. Another, loose in covers, $15.

HUBBARD, William. *A Narrative of the Troubles With the Indians in New-England*. Leatherbound. Boston, 1677. 1st ed., with map reading "White Hills," not "Wine Hills." An extremely rare book. A copy bound with Hubbard's sermon, *The Happiness of a People*, Boston, 1676, brought $14,000 in 1967 at the auction of Thomas W. Streeter's Americana library. The book was bound by John Ratcliff, a much esteemed early binder, and had an otherwise distinguished history. The White Hills map is the first map engraved and printed in America. Previously we had noted another copy of this book for sale at $250. Another, with title, map, and dedication in photostat, was noted at $100.

HUGHES, John T. *Doniphan's Expedition, Containing An Account of the Conquest of New Mexico*. 144 pp., paperbound (covers undated). Cincinnati, 1847. 1st ed., 1st issue, lacking words "cheap edition" on the covers. $1,300 (1966 auction). Previously this was a book that brought $200 to $500 at retail. Other auction records: $72.80 (1958) and $450, for a copy with title leaf repairs (1963). Cincinnati, 1848. 2d ed. $100. Cincinnati, 1848. 3d ed. With map. Clothbound. $70. Worn, $32.50. Cincinnati, no date, 4th ed. $40. Cincinnati, no date (about 1851). Paperbound. Rebound in calf, $60 (at auction). Topeka, 1907. $25.

HUMPHREYS, Frederick and others. *Humphreys Family in America*. Bound with Gilbert Nash: *Dorchester and Weymouth Families*. 1,115 pp., three quarters leatherbound. New York, 1883. Rubbed, $40.

HUNT, J. *An Adventure on a Frozen Lake: A Tale of the Canadian Rebellion of 1837-8*. 46 pp., paperbound. Cincinnati, 1853. $45.

HUNT, James H. *Mormonism: Embracing the Origin, Rise and Progress of the Sect*. Clothbound. St. Louis, 1844. (2d ed. of Hunt's *A History of the Mormon War*.) With errata leaf.

$125-$150. Lacking the errata leaf, $75.

HUNT, John. *Gazetteer of the Border and Southern States*. Pittsburgh, 1863. $45.

HUNT, Rev. T. Dwight. *Address Delivered Before the New England Society of San Francisco, at the American Theatre*. 20 pp., sewed. San Francisco, 1853. $45.

HUNTER, Dard. *The Literature of Papermaking, 1390-1800*. Folio in half cloth folder. No place, no date (Chillicothe, Ohio, 1925). One of 190, signed. $200-$300.

HUNTER, Dard. *Papermaking in Indo-China*. No place (Chillicothe), 1947. One of 182. $50-$75.

HUNTER, George. *Reminiscences of an Old Timer*. Half leather and clothbound. San Francisco, 1887. 1st ed. $80 and $40. Worn, $25. Battle Creek, 1888. 3d ed. Clothbound. $20.

HUNTER, George Leland. *Decorative Textiles*. 580 illustrations, 27 plates in color. Clothbound. Philadelphia, 1918. 1st ed. $50-$75. Another, $42.50.

HUNTER, John D. *Manners and Customs of Several Indian Tribes Located West of the Mississippi*. Philadelphia, 1823. 1st ed. Three quarters calfbound, $75. Another, calfbound, foxed, $37.50. Others, $35-$50.

HUNTERS of Kentucky (The). 100 pp., paperbound. New York, 1847. (By Benjamin Bilson.) 1st ed. $150-$200. Covers missing, $25.

HUNTINGTON, D. B. *Vocabulary of the Utah and Sho-shonee, or Snake Dialects, with Indian Legends and Traditions*. 32 pp., calfbound. Salt Lake, 1872. $125.

HUTCHINS, Thomas. *A Topographical Description of Virginia, Pennsylvania, Maryland and North Carolina*. Folding map, 2 plans, 2 facsimiles. Clothbound. Cleveland, 1904. One of 20 on hand-made paper. $37.50. One of 240 others. $25.

HYDE, George. *Red Cloud's Folk*. Clothbound. Norman, Okla., 1937. 1st ed. $35-$50. Worn, $25.

HYMNS for Infant Minds. Paperbound. Boston, 1814. (By Ann and Jane Taylor.) $35.

IDLENESS and Industry Exemplified, in the History of James

Preston and Ivy Lawrence. Philadelphia, 1803. (By Maria Edgeworth.) Worn, $75.

ILIAD (The). Translated from the Greek of Homer by Alexander Pope, Esq. Philadelphia, 1795. 1st Am. ed. Free halves of end papers missing, $75.

ILLINOIS Central Railroad Company (The), Offers Over 2,000,000 Acres, etc. 64 pp., sewed. New York, 1856. (By John Wilson.) $25.

IMPARTIAL Inquirer (The). 96 pp. Boston, 1811. (By John Lowell.) 1st ed. Half morocco, $45.

INCHIQUIN, The Jesuit's Letters, During a Late Residence in the U.S.A. Leatherbound. New York, 1810. (By Charles J. Ingersoll.) $32.50.

INDIANS (The): Or Narratives of Massacres and Depredations, etc. By a Descendant of the Huguenots. 79 pp. Rondout, N. Y., 1846. (By Johannes H. Bevier.) 1st ed. $100.

INCIDENTS of Border Life. 5 plates. Chambersburg, Pa., 1839. (By Joseph Pritts.) 1st ed., 1st issue, 491 pp. $35-$50.

INGLIS, Charles. *An Essay on Infant Baptism.* New York, 1768. 1st ed. $25.

INMAN, Col. Henry. *Stories of the Old Santa Fe Trail.* Pictorial clothbound. Kansas City, Mo., 1881. 1st ed. $50. Worn, $25.

INQUIRY into the Nature and Uses of Money, etc. (An). Boston, 1740. Title page repaired, last leaf of text written by hand, bound in three quarters morocco, $37.50.

INTERSTING Appendix to Sir William Blackstone's Commentaries on the Laws of England (An). Philadelphia, 1773. $25.

IRENE the Missionary. Green or brown clothbound. Boston, 1879. (By John W. DeForest.) 1st ed. $50.

IRVING, Washington. *Voyages and Discoveries of the Companions of Columbus.* Boards, paper label. Philadelphia, 1831. 1st ed. $50. Worn, $25.

ISELIN, Isaac. *Journal of a Trading Voyage Around the World, 1805-1808.* No place, no date (New York, about 1897). 1st ed. $80 and $125.

IVINS, Virginia W. *Pen Pictures of Early Western Days.* Clothbound. No place (Keokuk, Iowa), 1905. 1st ed. $30. Same place, 1908. 2d ed. $25. Worn, $15.

JACKSON, A. P. and E. C. Cole. *Oklahoma! Politically and Topographically Described.* Map (not in all copies). Kansas City, no date (1885). 1st ed. Map reinforced, $60.

JACKSON, Helen Hunt. *Ramona.* Green clothbound. Boston, 1884. 1st ed. $65. Another, $50. Worn, $25.

JACOB, J. G. *The Life and Times of Patrick Gass.* 4 plates. Clothbound. Wellsburg, Va., 1859. 1st ed. $75. Another, spine mended, $60.

JAEGER, Benedict. *Life of North American Insects.* Providence, 1854. $30.

JAMAICA Almanack and Register (The). 14 pp., calfbound. Kingston, no date (1787). $35.

JAMES, Edwin. *Account of an Expedition from Pittsburgh to the Rocky Mountains.* 2 maps, chart, 8 plates (one in color). 3 vols., including atlas, boards and leather. Philadelphia, 1823-22. 1st ed. $275 (1966 auction). Other sets, in catalogues, $250 and $200; less than fine, $75-$150.

JAMES, Edwin (editor). *A Narrative of the Captivity and Adventures of John Tanner, etc.* Portrait. Boards, cloth spine. New York, 1830. 1st ed. $150-$200. $120 (1966 auction). Recent catalogue prices: Rebound, $125; another copy, $100; another, $135; badly worn, $82.50.

JAMES, Henry, Jr. *Daisy Miller.* Gray paperbound or brown clothbound. New York, 1879. 1st ed., 1st issue, with last number in list of works on page 4 being 79. Paperbound, $135. Clothbound, $100.

JAMES, Henry, Jr. *An International Episode.* Paperbound or clothbound. New York, 1879. 1st ed. Paperbound, $50. Clothbound, $40.

JAMES, Thomas. *Three Years Among the Indians and Mexicans.* 12 plates. Clothbound. St. Louis, 1916. 2d ed. $85-$100. Shaken, $65.

JAMES, W. S. *Cowboy Life in Texas.* Paperbound. Chicago, no date (1893). 1st ed. $50-$75. Chicago, no date (1898). Clothbound, $25.

JEFFERS, Robinson. *Californians.* Clothbound. New York, 1916. 1st ed. $50. Another, review copy with perforated advance copy notice on title page, $75.

JEFFERS, Robinson. *Flagons and Apples.* Boards, paper labels. Los Angeles, 1912. 1st ed. $250. Worn copies, $50 and $27.50.

JEFFERS, Robinson. *Tamar and Other Poems.* Clothbound. New York, no date (1924). 1st ed. One of 500. $75-$100. Worn, $40.

JEROME, Chauncey. *History of the American Clock Business for the Past 60 Years.* Paperbound. New Haven, 1860. $50. Worn but sound, $35. Another, $22.50.

JEWETT, Sarah Orne. *The Country of the Pointed Firs.* Clothbound. Boston, 1896. 1st ed., 1st issue, with silken cloth binding instead of linen texture. $60. Another copy, 2d issue. $25.

JOCKNICK, Sidney. *Early Days on the Western Slope of Colorado.* 25 plates. Clothbound. Denver, 1913. 1st ed. $150-$200. Also, $135 (1966 auction).

JOHNSON, Benj. F. (of Boone). *"The Old Swimmin'-Hole" and 'Leven More Poems.* Paperbound. Indianapolis, 1883. (By James Whitcomb Riley.) 1st ed. $200-$350. $210 (1960 auction). $140 (1961 auction). Other copies offered by dealers at $150 and $175. (There is a 1909 facsimile, which lacks the "W" in "William" on page 41.)

JOHNSON, F. M. *Forest, Lake and River.* 2 vols., bound in suede. Boston, 1902. One of 350. Without separate atlas and without ties of strings, leads, and hooks. $50, $60, and $80.

JOHNSON, Overton and William H. Winter. *Route Across the Rocky Mountains, etc.* Cloth-backed boards. Lafayette, Ind., 1846. 1st ed. $850. Another copy, rebacked and repaired, $825. Another, $650 (1963 auction).

JOHNSTON, Charles. *A Narrative of the Incidents Attending the Capture, Detention, and Ransom of, etc.* Half clothbound. New York, 1827. 1st ed. $50-$100.

JOHNSTON, George. *The History of Cecil County, Maryland.* Folding map. Elkton, 1881. $40.

JONES, Charles Colcock, Jr. *The Siege of Savannah in December, 1864.* 184 pp., paperbound. Albany, 1874. 1st ed., with errata slip. One of 10 on large paper, with autograph letter inserted. $50. Regular issue, $25.

JOHNSTON, William G. *Experiences of a Forty-niner.* Portrait, 13 plates. Clothbound. Pittsburgh, 1892. 1st ed. (With later, separately issued, folding map and an extra portrait.) $250-$300. Another copy, worn, $150. Another, $160 (1960 auction).

JOHONNOT, Jackson. *The Remarkable Adventures of.* Greenfield, 1816. $75.

JONES, Charles H. *Genealogy of the Rodman Family, 1620 to 1886.* Philadelphia, 1886. $27.50.

JONES, Charles Jesse. *Buffalo Jones' 40 Years of Adventure.* Clothbound. Topeka, 1899. 1st ed. $35-$50.

JONES, Adj. Gen. R. *General Orders, No. 16, Reporting General Court Martial Convened at Fort Kearney, Oregon Route, for Offense Committed There.* 11 pp., sewed. Washington, 1851. $25.

JONES, Samuel. *Pittsburgh in the Year Eighteen-Hundred and Twenty-six.* Plate. Boards. Pittsburgh, 1826. 1st ed. $850 (1967 auction). This copy had the frontispiece and front cover detached.

JONES, Thomas A. *J. Wilkes Booth.* Clothbound. Chicago, 1893. 1st ed. $30 and $25.

JONES, William Carey. *Letters of, in Review of Attorney General Black's Report to the President of the U. S., on the Land Titles of California.* 31 pp., paperbound. San Francisco, 1860. $100. (There was a reported sale at $325 in 1925.)

JONES, William Carey. *Report on the Subject of Land Titles in California.* 60 pp., paperbound. Washington, 1850. 1st ed. $150-$200.

JOURNAL Historique de l'Establissement des Francais a la Louisiane. Nouvelle-Orleans, 1831. $30.

JOURNAL of an Excursion Made by the Corps of Cadets, etc., Under Capt. Partridge. Marbled paper covers. Concord, 1822. $27.50.

JOURNAL of the Missouri State Convention, Held at Jefferson

City, July 1861. Bound with: *Proceedings, etc.* St. Louis, 1861. Rebacked, $25.

JOURNAL of the Proceedings in the Detention of the Conspiracy . . . for Burning the City of New York (A). By the Recorder of the City of New York. New York, 1744. (By Daniel Horsmanden.) 1st ed. $200-$300. Washed copy in new leather binding, $170 (1962 auction).

JOURNAL of the Proceedings of a Convention of Physicians, of Ohio, Held in Columbus, Jan. 5, 1835. Daniel Drake, Chairman. 30 pp., paperbound. Cincinnati, 1835. (Main report by Drake.) $75.

JOURNAL of the Senate of South Carolina Being the Session of 1863. 190 pp., unbound. Columbia, 1863. $25.

JOURNAL of a Tour From Boston to Savannah, etc. (A). Cambridge, 1849. (By Daniel Nason.) 1st ed. $35.

JOYCE, James. *Ulysses.* Colored reproductions of drawings by Matisse. Buckram. Limited Editions Club. New York, 1935. One of 250 signed by Joyce as well as by Matisse. $1,000-$1,250. $700 (1963 auction). One of 1,250 signed only by Matisse. $400 (at auction).

JUDD, A. N. *Campaigning Against the Sioux.* 45 pp., double-column, paperbound. No place, no date (Watsonville, Calif., 1906). 1st ed. $300.

JUDD, Silas. *A Sketch of the Life and Voyages of Capt. Alvah Judd Dewey.* Boards. Chittenango, N. Y., 1838. 1st ed. $250.

JUDGES and Criminals. San Francisco, 1858. (By H. M. Gray.) 1st ed. $300-$500 (or more). (Only 2 copies known.)

JUDSON, Pheobe Goodell. *A Pioneer's Search for an Ideal Home.* Frontispiece. Bellingham, Wash., 1925. 1st ed. $100. $80 (1966 auction).

KEATING, William H. (compiler). *Narrative of an Expedition to the Source of St. Peter's River, Lake Winnepeek, etc.* Map, 2 plates. 2 vols., boards. Philadelphia, 1824. 1st ed. $150. Another, rebacked, $100.

KELEHER, W. A. *The Fabulous Frontier.* 11 plates. Clothbound. Santa Fe, no date (1945). 1st ed. $35-$50.

KELLER, George. *A Trip Across the Plains.* 58 pp., paperbound. No place, no date (Masillon, Ohio, 1851). 1st ed. $1,000 and up. (5 copies known.)

KELLEY, Hall J. *A Geographical Sketch of That Part of North America Called Oregon.* Folding map. 80 pp., paperbound. Boston, 1830. 1st ed. $600. Also, $450 and $420. Rebound in half calf, $375 (auction).

KELLY, Ebenezer B. *Autobiography.* Norwich, 1856. 1st ed. $35.

KENDALL, George Wilkins. *The War Between the United States and Mexico.* Map. 52 pp., clothbound, and 12 full-page color plates in half leather folder. New York, 1851. 1st ed. $500. Also $290 and $260 (auction prices). Another, $275. Another, rubbed and rebacked, $200.

KENDERDINE, T. S. *A California Tramp and Later Footprints.* Clothbound. Newtown, Pa., 1888. 1st ed. $60 and $45.

KENNEDY, E. G. *The Etched Work of Whistler.* 4 vols. (text vol. and 3 half cloth plate folders). New York, 1910. 1st ed. One of 400. $250 and up.

KENNEDY, W. S. *The Plan of Union: or a History of the Churches of the Western Reserve.* Hudson, Ohio, 1856. $35.

KENNEDY, William. *Texas: Its Geography, Natural History, and Topography.* 118 pp., paperbound. New York, 1844. 1st Am. ed. $75. Rebound, $25.

KENT, Henry W. (compiler). *Bibliographical Notes on One Hundred Books Famous in English Literature.* New York, 1903. One of 300. $50. (Second volume of a set under this title. See: *ONE Hundred Books, etc.)*

KENT, Rockwell. *Voyaging Southward from the Straight of Magellan.* Tan buckram. New York, 1924. 1st ed. $25. Also, Author's Autograph ed. of 110, blue boards, signed, containing extra signed woodcut by Kent and end paper maps. $50-$60.

KENTUCKIAN in New-York (The). By a Virginian. 2 vols., clothbound. New York, 1834. (By W. A. Caruthers.) 1st ed. $55.

KENYON, Frederic G. *Ancient Books and Modern Discoveries.*

Half vellum. Caxton Club. Chicago, 1927. 1st ed. One of 350. $80-$100.

KER, Henry. *Travels Through the Western Interior of the United States.* Half leatherbound. Elizabethtown, N.J., 1816. 1st ed. $40 and $30.

KERCHEVAL, Samuel. *A History of the Valley of Virginia.* Winchester, Va., 1833. 1st ed. $50-$75. Winchester, 1839. 2d ed. $45. Woodstock, Va., 1902. 3d ed. $40. Strasburg, Va., 1925. $7.50.

KERR, Hugh. *A Poetical Description of Texas, etc.* Clothbound. New York, 1838. 1st ed. $250. Another copy, soiled and worn, $180 (1966 auction).

KEWEN, Edward John Cage. *Idealina.* San Francisco, 1853. 1st ed. Spine chipped and rubbed, $25.

KEYNES, Geoffrey. *A Bibliography of William Blake.* Half leatherbound. New York, 1921. One of 250. $150-$200.

KIDDER, A. V. *An Introduction to the Study of Southwestern Archaeology.* 50 plates. Clothbound. New Haven, 1924. 1st ed. $27.50.

KILBOURN, John. *Columbian Geography.* Chillicothe, 1815. 1st ed. $200-$300.

KILBOURN, John. *The Ohio Gazetteer, or Topographical Dictionary.* 3 folding maps. Columbus, 1819. 6th ed. $27.50. Columbus, 1831. Calfbound. $20.

KILBOURNE, David W. *Strictures on Dr. I. Galland's Pamphlet Entitled "Villainy Exposed," with Some Account of His Transactions in Lands of the Sac and Fox Reservation, etc., in Lee County, Iowa.* 24 pp., sewed. Fort Madison, Iowa. 1st ed. $100-$150. Also, $55 (1964 auction). Another, bound in boards, $70 (1964 auction).

KILMER, Joyce. *Trees and Other Poems.* Gray boards, paper labels. New York, no date (1914). 1st ed., 1st state, without "Printed in U.S.A." on copyright page. Fine, in dust jacket, $75. Another copy, inscribed by author, $110.

KIMBALL, Fiske. *Domestic Architecture of the American Colonies and of the Early Republic.* Clothbound. New York, 1922. $65.

KIMBALL, Heber C. *Journal of.* Edited by R. B. Thompson. Nauvoo, Ill., 1840. 1st ed. $300-$400. $238 (1958 auction).

KING, Capt. Charles. *The Fifth Cavalry in the Sioux War of 1876. Campaigning with Crook.* 134 pp., paperbound. Milwaukee, 1880. 1st ed. $200-$300. Also, $140 (1960 auction). Also: *Campaigning with Crook.* 9 plates. Clothbound. New York, 1890. $35. Others, worn, $10 and $15.

KING, Frank M. *Wranglin' the Past.* Portrait. Leatherette. No place, no date (Los Angeles, 1935). One of 300, signed. $40.

KINO, E. F. *Historical Memoir of Primeria Alta.* 7 maps, plates. 2 vols., clothbound. Cleveland, 1919. (Translated by Herbert Eugene Bolton.) One of 750. $100. Berkeley, 1948. 2 vols. in one. Clothbound. $60.

KINZIE, Mrs. Juliette A. *Wau-Bun, the "Early Day" in the North-West.* 6 plates. Clothbound. New York, 1856. 1st ed. $35. Another copy, worn, $25.

KIPLING, Rudyard. *On Dry-Cow Fishing as a Fine Art.* Vignette. Boards. Cleveland, 1926. 1st ed. One of 176. $100-$125.

KNEEDLER, H. S. *The Coast Country of Texas.* 76 pp., paperbound. Cincinnati, 1896. $35.

KNICKERBOCKER, Diedrich. *A History of New York.* 2 vols., calfbound. New York, 1809. (By Washington Irving.) 1st ed., 1st issue, with the engraved folding plate of New Amsterdam in Vol. 1. $500. Others, $200 and $150. Rebound, $200. Washed, repaired, rebound, $100.

KNIGHT, Dr. John and John Slover. *Indian Atrocities.* (Edited by H. H. Brackenridge.) 96 pp., paperbound. Nashville, 1843. $150. Cincinnati, 1867. Paperbound. $25.

KNIGHT, Sarah K. and The Rev. Mr. Buckingham. *The Journals of Madam Knight and Rev. Mr. Buckingham.* Boards. New York, 1819. 1st ed. $40.

KNOEPFEL'S Schoharie Cave. 2 folding woodcuts. 16 pp., paperbound. New York, 1853. 1st ed. $70.

KOOP, Albert J. *Early Chinese Bronzes.* Clothbound. New York, 1924. 1st Am. ed. In dust jacket, $37.50-$50.

KROEBER, Alfred L. *Handbook of the Indians of California.* Folding map, 10 other maps, 73 plates on 38 sheets. Clothbound. Washington, 1925. 1st ed. $40, $30, and $27.50.

KUNZ, George Frederick. *Gems and Precious Stones of North America.* 8 colored plates, other illustrations. Clothbound. New York, 1890. 1st ed., with errata slip. $35. Another, $22.50.

LA CUISINE Creole. Clothbound. New York, no date (1885). (Compiled by Lafcadio Hearn.) 1st ed., 1st issue, brown cloth, with "Brûlot" (in the 9th line of introduction) instead of "Brûlot." $150-$200. Another copy, worn, front hinge cracked, one leaf defective, $95. New Orleans, 1922. 2d ed. Clothbound. $25 and $20.

LAMBOURNE, Alfred. *An Old Sketch-book. Dedicated to the Memory of My Father.* 18 plates. 17 pp. Boston, no date (1892). 1st ed. $250. Jubilee ed., retitled *The Old Journey: Reminiscences of Pioneer Days.* No place (Salt Lake City?), 1897. 18 plates, 53 pp. $25.

L'AME PENITENTE, ou Le Nouveau Pensez-y-Bien; Consideration sur les Verités Eternelles, etc. Au Detroit, 1809. (Barthelemi Baudrand, editor.) Uncut, $750. $575 (1964 auction). Another, $450.

LAMON, Ward H. *Life of Abraham Lincoln.* 15 plates, 3 facsimiles. Green or rust cloth. Boston, 1872. 1st ed. $25. Others, worn, $15.

LANCASTER, Robert A., Jr. *Historic Virginia Homes and Churches.* Clothbound. Philadelphia, 1915. 1st ed., $65. Another copy, joints cracked, $50. Another, worn, $47.50. Philadelphia, 1917. $45.

LAND Laws. Columbus, 1825. $35.

LANE, Walter P. *Adventures and Recollections of Gen. Walter P. Lane.* Portrait. 114 pp., paperbound. Marshall, Tex., 1887. 1st ed. $200.

LANG, Herbert O. (editor). *History of the Willamette Valley.* 6 plates, facsimile, errata leaf. Clothbound. Portland, 1885. 1st ed. $30.

LANGSDORFF, George H. von. *Narrative of the Rezanov Voyage to Neuva California, 1806.* Map, plates. Half clothbound. San Francisco. 1927. 1st ed. One of 260, signed. $37.50-$60.

LANGLEY, Batty and Thomas Langley. *The Builder's Jewel.* 100 engravings. Leatherbound. Charlestown, no date (1799-1800). 1st Am. ed. Rebound, $85. Another, hinges cracked, $95. Another, one plate lacking, $77.50.

LANGWORTHY, Franklin. *Scenery of the Plains, Mountains and Mines, etc.* Clothbound. Ogdensburgh, N.Y., 1855. 1st ed. $60-$100.

LANGWORTHY, Lucius Hart. *Dubuque: Its History, Mines, and Indian Legends, etc.* Clothbound. Dubuque, no date (1855). 1st ed. $150 (1966 auction). Other copies in recent catalogues, $55 to $80.

LANIER, Sidney. *Tiger-Lilies.* Green clothbound. New York, 1867. 1st ed., with lilies spelled "Lillies" on the spine and "Lilies" on the title page. $75-$100. Another, minor defects, $65. Others, $45, $40, and $22.50.

LARAMIE, Hahn's Peak and Pacific Railway System, the Direct Gateway to Southern Wyoming, Northern Colorado, and Eastern Utah. Oblong. No place, no date (1910?). $32.50.

LARIMER, Mrs. Sarah L. *The Capture and Escape; or, Life Among the Sioux.* 5 plates. Clothbound. Philadelphia, 1870. 1st ed. $35-$50.

LA SALLE, Charles E. *Colonel Crockett, the Texas Trailer.* 84 pp., paperbound. New York, 1871. $45.

LA SHELLE, Kirke. *Poker Rubaiyat.* Paperbound. No place, no date (Phoenix, 1903). 1st ed. One of 274. $75.

LAST of the Mohicans (The). 2 vols., tan boards, paper labels. Philadelphia, 1826. (By James Fenimore Cooper.) 1st ed., 1st issue, with page 89 misnumbered as page 93. Fine sets at auction: $850-$2,550. Others: worn, $400; rebacked, $80; chipped, $375 (at auction).

LASSEPAS, Ulises. *De la Colonizacion de la Baja California.* Mexico, 1859. $35.

LAW, Judge John. *Address Delivered before the Vincennes Historical and Antiquarian Society.* Folding map. 48 pp., paperbound. Louisville, 1839. 1st ed. $100-$150. $80 (1966 auction). Another, covers chipped, $45.

LAWRENCE, Richard Hoe (compiler). *History of the Society of*

Iconophiles of the City of New York. Reproductions of 119 plates. Boards. New York, 1930. 1st ed. One of 186. $50.

LAWS for the Better Government of California. 68 pp. San Francisco, 1848. $2,500.

LAWS of the Territory of Michigan, etc. Detroit, 1833. Hinges started, small piece torn from title page, not affecting text, $35.

LAY, William and Cyrus M. Hussey. *A Narrative of the Mutiny on Board the Ship Globe of Nantucket.* Calfbound. New-London, 1828. 1st Am. ed. $175. Rebacked, foxed, $50.

LAYNE, J. Gregg. *Annals of Los Angeles.* San Francisco, 1935. $30.

LEA, Pryor. *An Outline of the Central Transit, in a Series of Six Letters to Hon. John Hemphill.* 32 pp., paperbound. Galveston, 1859. $75.

LEADVILLE Chronicle Annual. 40 pp., paperbound. Leadville, 1881. Backstrip torn, $32.50.

LEACH, A. J. *Early Day Stories; the Overland Trail.* 7 plates. Clothbound. Norfolk, Neb., no date (1916). 1st ed. $40-$50.

LEATHER Stocking and Silk. Clothbound. New York, 1854. (By John Esten Cooke.) 1st ed. $25.

LEAVES of Grass. Green clothbound. Brooklyn, 1855. (By Walt Whitman.) 1st ed., 1st issue, with marbled end papers, gold stamped covers, all edges gilt, no ads or reviews, portrait on plain paper, gilt bands on covers, Whitman's name on copyright page, line 20, page 23, reading "abode" for "adobe." $3,700 (1960 auction). Others at auction have brought $1,000 to $1,600. Worn copies have sold at retail from $500 to $1,000. 2d issue, plain end papers, no gold on cover. $500. Another, $250. 3d issue, ads at front, $150. (See also: WHITMAN, Walt.)

LEAVITT, Emily W. *The Blair Family of New England.* Boston, 1900. $25.

LEBRIJA, Joaquin and Ignacio Berrera. *Analisis e Impugnacion del Proyecto de le Sobre Arbitrios para la Guerra de Tejas.* 31 pp., sewed. Mexico, 1841. $45.

LEDYARD, John. *A Journal of Capt. Cook's Last Voyage to*

the Pacific Ocean, etc. Folding map (frequently missing). Leatherbound. Hartford, 1783. 1st ed., with folding map intact. $1,200. Lacking map, $200.

LEE, Chauncey. *The American Accomptant.* Lansingburgh, 1797. 1st ed. $40-$50. Another, free end paper missing, $27.50.

LEE, Maj. Henry, Jr. *The Campaign of 1781 in the Carolinas.* Calfbound. Philadelphia, 1824. 1st ed. $75.

LEE, John D. *Journals of.* Map, 13 plates. Clothbound. Salt Lake City, 1938. 1st ed. $75.

LEE, John D. *The Life and Confessions of John D. Lee.* Paperbound. Philadelphia, no date (1888). $50.

LEE, Samuel. *The Joy of Faith.* Boston, 1687. 1st Am. ed. $75-$100.

LEEPER, David Rohrer. *The Argonauts of Forty-nine.* Clothbound. South Bend, 1894. 1st ed. $50-$60. Worn, $37.50. Columbus, 1950. $10 and $7.50.

LEIGH, William R. *The Western Pony.* 6 color plates. Clothbound. New York, no date (1933). 1st ed. One of 100. $75-$100.

LELAND, Charles G. *The Union Pacific Railway, etc.* 95 pp., paperbound. Philadelphia, 1867. 1st ed. $50-$75. Rebound, $35 (at auction). Spine and corners chipped, $47.50.

LEONARD, Zenas. *Narrative of the Adventures of.* 87 pp., paperbound. Clearfield, Pa., 1839. 1st ed. Rebound in morocco, tears in 5 leaves repaired, $5,500 (1966 auction). Rebound in half morocco, title page repaired, $5,000 (1964 auction). Other auction prices: $3,500 and $2,900. Cleveland, 1904. $60 and $40.

LES ORNEMENS de la Memoire, ou les Traits Brillans des Poetes Francois les Plus Celebres, etc. Boards. Au Detroit, 1811. (By Pons Augustin Alletz.) 1st ed., 1st issue, with "k" instead of "x" in name of printer, A. Coxshaw, $350 (1961 auction). Another, $200. Another copy, bound in half leather with: *Fables Choises, de la Fontaine,* 132 pp., plus 48 pp., $650.

LESTER, John C. and D. L. Wilson. *Ku Klux Klan. Its Origin, Growth and Disbandment.* 117 pp., paperbound. Nashville,

1884. 1st ed. $150. Another, $80. Also, $125 (1967 auction).

LETTER from the Secretary of State, Accompanying Certain Laws of the North-western and Indian Territories of the United States, etc. 53 pp., sewed. No place (Washington), 1802. $30. Another, tall copy, uncut. $50.

LETTER of Amerigo Vespucci, etc. (The). Vellum. San Francisco, 1926. One of 250. $80-$100.

LETTER to the Hon. Abraham Edwards, etc. (A). 16 pp., sewed. Detroit, 1827. (By William Woodbridge.) $25.

LETTERS from a Farmer in Pennsylvania, to the Inhabitants of the British Colonies. Boston, 1768. (By John Dickinson.) 1st Am. ed. $50-$75. Philadelphia, 1769. 3d ed. $30.

LEWIS, Alfred Henry. *Wolfville.* Frederic Remington illustrations. Yellow clothbound. New York, no date (1897). 1st ed. $50-$75. (Later printings so stated on title page.)

LEWIS, Mrs. Hannah. *Narrative of the Captivity and Sufferings of.* 24 pp., including folding plate. Boston, 1817. 1st ed. $150. Another, lacking plate, $25.

LEWIS, Meriwether and William Clark. *History of the Expedition Under the Command of Captains Lewis and Clark, etc.* Folding map and 5 charts. 2 vols., boards. Philadelphia, 1814. 1st ed. $5,200 (1963 auction). Others, less fine, have sold at auction for from $1,000 to $1,750. Rebound in leather, $500, $300 (1966 auction).

LEWIS, Sinclair. *Babbitt.* Clothbound. New York, no date (1922). 1st ed., 1st state, with "Purdy" for "Lyte" in line 4, page 49. In dust jacket, $80. Another, lacking jacket, $40. Soiled, $10. Autographed copy, $55.

LEWIS, Sinclair. *Main Street.* Clothbound. New York, 1920. 1st ed., 1st issue, with perfect folio on page 54. $25-$35. New York, 1937. Limited Editions Club. One of 1,500, boxed. $60-$75.

LIBER Scriptorum: The First Book of the Authors Club. Full morocco. New York, 1893. 1st ed. One of 251, signed by contributors. $75-$100. *Liber Scriptorum: The Second Book, etc.* New York, 1921. One of 251. $40-$50.

LIFE and Adventures of Calamity Jane. By Herself. 8 pp., paperbound. Livingston, Mont., no date (1896). $300.

LIFE Among the Indians. 80 pp., paperbound. No place, no date (New Haven, about 1870). (By Healy & Bigelow.) $25.

LIFE in California, etc. By an American. 9 plates. Clothbound. New York, 1846. (By Alfred Robinson.) 1st ed. $75-$100. San Francisco, 1897. Clothbound. $25. San Francisco, 1925. Clothbound. One of 250. $40-$50.

LIFE of MA-KA-TAI-ME-SHE-KIA-KIAK or Black Hawk. Cincinnati, 1833. (J. B. Patterson, editor.) 1st ed. $100 and $125. Another copy, muslin spine frayed, third of dedication page missing, foxed, $40. Boston, 1834. Half leatherbound. $50. Oquawka, Ill., 1882. Clothbound. $35-$50.

LIFE of Stonewall Jackson (The). By a Virginian. Paperbound. Richmond, 1863. (By John Esten Cooke.) 1st ed., with Ayres & Wade imprint, $30.

LIFE in a Man-of-War, etc. By a Fore-Top-Man. Philadelphia, 1841. (By Henry J. Mercier.) 1st ed. $50.

LIFE, and Most Surprising Adventures of Robinson Crusoe of York, Mariner, etc. (The). Philadelphia, 1803. $25.

LIFE and Scenes Among the Kickapoo Indians: Their Manners, Habits and Customs. 175 pp., paperbound. New Haven, no date (1889). $35.

LIFE, Speeches and Public Services of Abram (sic) Lincoln, Together with a Sketch of the Life of Hannibal Hamlin (The). Portrait. 117 pp., paperbound. New York, 1860. The Wigwam Edition. $200. Rebound, $30 (at auction).

LIFE and Travels of Josiah Mooso (The). Clothbound. Winfield, Kan., 1888. 1st ed. $75. Also, $45 (1966 auction).

LIN, Frank. *What Dreams May Come.* Chicago, no date (1888). (By Gertrude Atherton.) Paperbound or clothbound, $50.

LINCOLN, Abraham. *The Life and Public Service of Gen. Zachary Taylor.* Marbled boards. Boston, 1922. 1st ed. One of 435. $25.

LINCOLN, Mrs. D. A. *Frozen Dainties.* 32 pp., paperbound. Nashua, N. H., 1889. 1st ed. Lower right corner of front cover chipped off, $27.50.

LINCOLN, Joseph C. *Cap'n Eri.* Clothbound. New York, 1904. 1st ed. $65 (auction). Another copy, $45.

LINDSAY, Vachel. *The Tramp's Excuse and Other Poems*. Paperbound, tied with cord. No place, no date (Springfield, Ohio, 1909). 1st ed. $100. Another copy, inscribed for presentation, $240 (1959 auction). Another, two corners of one leaf restored, $90.

LINDSEY, Charles. *The Prairies of the Western States*. 100 pp., paperbound. Toronto, 1860. $35.

LINDSLEY, John Berrien. *The Military Annals of Tennessee*. 2 plates. Clothbound. Nashville, 1886. 1st ed. $50. Another, library marks, binding shabby, $25.

LINN, John J. *Reminiscences of Fifty Years in Texas*. Portrait, 2 plates. Clothbound. New York, 1883. 1st ed., with errata slip. $100-$150. Also, $60 (1960 auction). Worn copies, $30 and $50.

LIST *of Persons to Whom Permits to Locate Mineral Lands on the South Shore of Lake Superior Have Been Granted and Leases Issued up to June 16, 1846.* 16 pp., clothbound. No place, no date (Detroit, 1846). $65.

LITTELL, William. *Principles of Law & Equity, etc.* No place (Kentucky?), 1808. $35.

LITTLE, David. *The Wanderer and Other Poems*. 32 pp., paperbound. Los Angeles, 1880. $45.

LLOYD, James T. *Steamboat Directory, and Disasters on the Western Waters*. Cincinnati, 1856. 1st ed., 1st issue, with 326 pp. $35-$50.

LOAN *Exhibition of 18th and Early 19th Century Furniture, Glass, etc.* New York, 1929. $100.

LOCKWOOD, Luke Vincent. *The Pendleton Collection*. 102 full-page plates. Leatherbound. Providence, 1904. One of 160 on Japan vellum, signed. $225.

LOFTING, Hugh. *The Story of Doctor Dolittle*. New York, 1920. 1st Am. ed. In dust jacket, $35-$50. Lacking jacket, $25-$35. Worn, $15.

LOG *of the Cruise of Schooner Julius Webb, Which Sailed from Norwich, Ct., on July 23, 1858, etc.* 40 pp., paperbound. Worcester, 1858. (By A. B. R. Sprague.) 1st ed. $50.

LOMAS, Thomas J. *Recollections of a Busy Life*. Portraits. No place, no date (Cresco, Iowa, 1923). 1st ed. Original sheets, folded. $100. Bound in morocco, $85.

LONDON Cries For Children. Philadelphia, 1810. $27.50.

LONDON, Jack. *The Call of the Wild.* Green clothbound. New York, 1903. 1st ed., 1st issue, with vertically ribbed cloth. In dust jacket, $60-$75. Other copies, original cloth, $25, $32.50, and $35.

LONDON, Jack. *The Cruise of the Dazzler.* Clothbound. New York, 1902. 1st ed., cream-colored binding with "Published October, 1902" on copyright page. $150-$250. Other copies, $125 and $90 (worn).

LONDON, Jack. *The Son of the Wolf.* Slate-colored clothbound, silver stamping. Boston, 1900. 1st ed., $50-$75. Also, rough green cloth, silver stamping (trial binding). $25.

LONGFELLOW, Henry Wadsworth. *Christus: A Mystery.* 3 vols. in one. Boston, 1872. 1st ed., 1st issue, with reading "set sail" in line 20, page 171 of vol. 2. $50.

LONGFELLOW, Henry Wadsworth. *The Courtship of Miles Standish and Other Poems.* Brown clothbound. Boston, 1858. 1st ed., 1st state, with ads dated September and with line 3, page 124, reading "treacherous" instead of "ruddy." $75-$100. Another, in blue "gift" binding, $100.

LONGFELLOW, Henry Wadsworth. *Evangeline: A Tale of Acadie.* Gray or yellow boards, paper label. Boston, 1847. 1st ed., 1st issue, with line 1, page 61, reading "Long," not "Lo." $250 or more. "Lo" issue, up to $100 or more.

LONGFELLOW, Henry Wadsworth. *Hyperion: A Romance.* 2 vols., boards, paper labels. New York, 1839. 1st ed. $200. Another, $90. Rebound in modern cloth, $40 and $50.

LONGFELLOW, Henry Wadsworth. *The Song of Hiawatha.* Brown clothbound. Boston, 1855. 1st ed., 1st issue, with the "n" present in "one" in the fifth line from the bottom of page 279. $75-$100. Others, $50 and $80. Worn, $35-$50. In blue "gift" binding, $120-$200.

LONGFELLOW, Henry Wadsworth. *Tales of a Wayside Inn.* Clothbound. Boston, 1863. 1st ed., 1st issue, with Welch, Bigelow imprint at bottom of page 225. $50. Another, $27.50.

LORIMER, George Horace. *Letters from a Self-Made Merchant to His Son.* 36 pp., paperbound. Philadelphia, 1901. 1st ed. $25. Boston, 1902. 1st (complete) ed. Clothbound. $10 and $7.50.

LOVE, Nat. *The Life and Adventures of Nat Love.* Plates. Pictorial clothbound. Los Angeles, 1907. 1st ed. $75-$90.

LOVE, Robertus. *The Rise and Fall of Jesse James.* Frontispiece. Clothbound. New York, 1926. 1st ed. $25.

LOWELL, James Russell. *Ode Recited at the Commemoration of the Living and Dead Soldiers of Harvard University, July 21, 1865.* Gray boards with paper label. Cambridge, 1865. 1st ed. One of 50. $300 (and up). Inscribed copy, $550 (1962 auction).

LOWELL, James Russell. *The President's Policy.* Paperbound. No place, no date (Philadelphia, 1864). 1st ed., 1st state, with "crises" misspelled "crisises" in first line of text. $75.

LOWELL, James Russell. *The Vision of Sir Launfal.* Printed glazed yellow boards. Cambridge, 1848. 1st ed. $100. Another copy, cover repaired, part of spine gone, $75. Another, spine chipped, $45. Another, morocco-bound, bookplate, $57.50. Another, calfbound, $25. Another, repaired, $25.

LOWELL, James Russell. *A Year's Life.* Boards, paper label. Boston, 1841. 1st ed., without errata slip, $25; with errata slip, $35.

LUCERNE: Its Homes, Climate, Mineral Resources, etc. 37 pp., paperbound. Los Angeles, 1888. (By Theron Nichols.) $35.

LUDLOW, N. M. *Dramatic Life as I Found It.* Clothbound. St. Louis, 1880. 1st ed., $42.50. Another, $37.50.

LUMPKIN, Wilson. *Removal of the Cherokee Indians from Georgia.* 2 portraits. 2 vols. Wormsloe, Ga., 1907. One of 500. $30.

LUTTIG, John C. *Journal of a Fur-Trading Expedition on the Upper Missouri.* Map, 4 plates. Clothbound. St. Louis, 1920. 1st ed. One of 365. $50-$100.

LYMAN, Albert. *Journal of a Voyage to California.* Frontispiece. Paperbound. Hartford, 1852. 1st ed. Chipped, in folding box, $140. Another, $90.

LYON, Irving Whitall. *The Colonial Furniture of New England.* Plates. Clothbound. Boston, 1891. 1st ed. $25. Boston, 1925. 3d ed. One of 515. $25.

MacDONALD, J. *Food From the Far West.* New York, no date (1878). $25.

MacDONALD, P. and A. M'Leod. *A Surprising Account of the Captivity, etc.* 12 pp. Windsor, no date (about 1786). $250.

MacDOUGALL, William. *The Red River Rebellion.* 68 pp., paperbound. Toronto, 1876. $50.

MACGILLICUDDY, Irene. *The Tender Recollections of.* Paperbound. New York, 1878. (By Laurence Oliphant). 1st ed. $25.

MacKAY, Malcolm S. *Cow Range and Hunting Trail.* 24 plates. Clothbound. New York, 1925. 1st ed. $25-$50.

MACK, Effie. *Nevada: A History of the State.* Map, facsimiles. Glendale, Calif., 1936. 1st ed. One of 250, signed. $35 and $45.

MACK, Solomon. *A Narrative* (sic) *of the Life of.* No place, no date (Windsor, Conn, 1810 or 1811?). 1st ed. $150.

MADISON Directory and Business Advertiser. Map. Leatherbound. Madison, Wis., 1855. (By Wm. N. Seymour.) 1st ed. $45. Another, worn, $37.50.

MAGEE, Dorothy and David Magee. *Bibliography of the Grabhorn Press, 1940-1956, etc.* Boards. San Francisco, 1957. One of 225. $175. Another, $110 (at auction).

MAGNIFICENT Library of the Late Howard T. Goodwin, etc. (The). 3 vols. in one. Philadelphia, 1903. $25.

MAHAN, A. T. *The Influence of Sea Power Upon History.* Clothbound. Boston, 1890. 1st Am. ed. $75.

MAJORS, Alexander. *Seventy Years on the Frontier.* Paperbound. Chicago, 1893. 1st ed. $35-$50. Worn, $27.50. Rebacked in cloth, $35. Rebound in cloth, $30.

MAN Without a Country (The). 23 pp., paperbound. Boston, 1865. (By Edward Everett Hale.) 1st ed., 1st issue, without the publisher's printed yellow "Announcement" slip tipped in. $275. Also, $140 (1966 auction). 2d issue, with the "Announcement" slip tipped in, $200. Another, bound in cloth with paper covers bound in, $50.

MANIFIESTO al Mundo. La Justicia y la Necesidad de la Independencia de la Nueva Espana. 19 pp., sewed. Puebla, 1821. (By Manuel Barcena.) $300.

MANLY, William Lewis. *Death Valley in '49.* 4 plates. Clothbound. San Jose, 1894. 1st ed. $65. Others, $40 and $50.

MANSFIELD, H. *The Descendants of Richard and Gillian Mansfield, Who Settled in New Haven, 1639.* New Haven, 1885. $25.

MAP of Texas With Parts of the Adjoining States. 30 sections. Philadelphia, no date (1830). (Compiled by Stephen F. Austin.) 1st ed. $100.

MAPS of the District of Columbia, etc. Washington, 1852. Lacking backstrip, covers loose, rubbed, $25.

MARK Twain's Sketches. ("Number One" at top of title page.) Blue paperbound. New York, no date (1874). 1st ed., 1st issue, with blank back cover. $100-$150. *Mark Twain's Sketches, New and Old.* Blue clothbound. Hartford, 1875. 1st ed., 1st issue, with erratum slip at page 299. $75-$150.

MARKHAM, Edwin. *The Man With the Hoe.* Paperbound. San Francisco, 1899. 1st book ed. $60 and $85. (Earlier, Jan. 15, 1899: Special supplement to San Francisco Examiner, containing first printing of the poem, 4 pp., $35.) New York, 1899. Green clothbound. 2d ed., 1st issue, with "fruitless" for "milkless" in line 5, page 35. $25-$35.

MARQUIS, Thomas. *A Warrior Who Fought Custer.* Clothbound. Minneapolis, 1931. 1st ed. $25.

MARRYAT, Frank. *Mountains and Molehills.* Frontispiece. Clothbound. New York, 1855. 1st Am. ed. $50-$60.

MARSH, James B. *Four Years in the Rockies.* Portrait. Clothbound. New Castle, Pa., 1884. 1st ed. $150-$200. Worn, $45 (at auction). Lacking portrait, $40 (at auction).

MARSH, John. *Hannah Hawkins, the Reformed Drunkard's Daughter.* New York, 1844. 1st ed. $30.

MARSHALL, Humphrey. *The History of Kentucky.* Frankfort, 1812. 1st ed. $100-$150. Frankfort, 1824. 2d ed., enlarged. $75-$125.

MARSHALL, L. G. *The Arabian Art of Taming and Training Wild and Vicious Horses.* 36 pp., paperbound. No place (Circleville, Ohio), 1857. $25.

MARSHALL, Mr. Chief Justice (John). *Opinion of the Supreme Court, etc., in the Case of Samuel Worcester versus the State of Georgia.* 20 pp., sewed. Washington, 1832. 2d ed. Half calfbound, $75.

MARSHALL, O. S. *A History of the Descendants of William Marshall.* Kittanning, 1884. Worn, pages loose, $25.

MARSHALL, William I. *Acquisition of Oregon, and the Long Supressed Evidence About Marcus Whitman.* Portrait. 2 vols. Clothbound. No place (Seattle), 1905. 1st ed. $100-$150. Also, $80 (1966 auction). Portland, 1911. 2 vols. $50.

MARVEL, Ik. *Looking Back at Boyhood.* 21 pp., paperbound, reprinted from Youth's Companion. No place (Norwich, Conn.), June, 1906. (By Donald G. Mitchell.) 1st ed. $45.

MARVEL, Ik. *The Reveries of a Bachelor.* Dark blue clothbound or leatherbound. New York, 1850. (By Donald G. Mitchell.) 1st ed., with last word, "sleep," on page 29 in perfect type. $32 (at auction). Another copy, $25 at retail.

MASON, Allen C. *Tacoma.* 24 pp. No place, no date (Portland, 1888). $25.

MASON, Emily V. (editor). *The Southern Poems of the War.* Clothbound. Baltimore, 1867. 1st ed. $27.50.

MASON, Rev. George. *Ode on the Loss of the Steamship Pacific.* 4 pp., paperbound. Nanaimo, B. C., 1875. $25.

MASSIE, J. Cam. *A Treatise on the Eclectic Southern Practice of Medicine.* Philadelphia, 1854. 1st ed. $25.

MASTERS, Edgar Lee. *Spoon River Anthology.* Blue clothbound. New York, 1915. 1st ed., 1st issue, measuring exactly 7/8 inches across top. In dust jacket, $90 and $75. Others, $42.50 and $50. In dust jacket, signed, $95. Auction prices: $40, $50, $60; signed copies, $55, $80, and $100.

MATHER, Cotton and others. *A Course of Sermons on Early Piety.* Boston, 1721. 1st ed. $35. Worn copies, $8 and $10 (at auction).

MATHER, Cotton. *The Wonders of the Invisible World.* Leatherbound. Boston, 1693. 1st ed. ·$7,500 (1967 auction). Worn, $1,600 (1960 auction).

MATHER, Increase. *A Call from Heaven, etc.* Boston, 1685. Worn and stained, $125.

MATHER, Increase. *Coelestinus.* Boston, 1723. 1st ed. Rebacked, lacking last leaf of text and blank end leaves, bookplate, $32.50.

MATHER, Increase. *The Doctrine of Divine Providence, Opened and Applyed.* Boston, 1684. Margins wormed, title page pasted to front cover, $90.

MATHER, Nathanael. *A Sermon Wherein is Shewed That It is the Duty and Should Be the Care of Believers on Christ etc.* 28 pp., unbound. Boston, 1684. Tear in last leaf of text, $65.

MATHEWS, Mrs. M. M. *Ten Years in Nevada.* 2 portraits. Clothbound. Buffalo, 1880. 1st ed. $70-$100.

MAUDSLAY, A. P. (editor). *The Discovery and Conquest of Mexico, 1517-1521.* Mexico City, 1942. Limited, signed by Covarrubias and others. $47.50.

MAUGHAM, W. Somerset. *The Moon and Sixpence.* Clothbound. New York, no date (1919). 1st Am. ed., 1st state, with author's name spelled "Maughan" on front cover and spine. $25.

MAUGHAM, W. Somerset. *Of Human Bondage.* Green clothbound. New York, no date (1915). 1st Am. ed., with Doran imprint, 1st issue, with misprint in line 4, page 257. $200. Another copy, fine and in dust jacket, $140. Another copy, worn and stained and lacking jacket, $60. Later, New York, 1915, red leatherbound. $50-$75.

MAURELLE, Don Antonio. *Abstract of a Narrative of an Interesting Voyage from Manilla to San Blas, etc.* Boston, 1801. $125.

MAWE, John. *Travels in the Interior of Brazil, etc.* Philadelphia, 1816. Binding poor, frontispiece torn, foxed, $25.

MAYNARD, C. J. *The Birds of Eastern North America.* Half leatherbound. Newtonville, Mass., 1896. Revised ed. $100. Auction prices: $27.50, $40, and $45. Newtonville, 1896. Clothbound. $125. Another, $25 (at auction).

MAYO, William Starbuck. *Kaloolah, or Journeyings to the Djebel Kumri: An Autobiography of Jonathan Romer.* New York, 1849. 1st ed. Lightly foxed, $45.

McADAM, R. W. *Chickasaws and Choctaws.* Comprising the Treaties of 1855 and 1866. 67 pp., paperbound. Ardmore, 1891. 1st ed. $250.

McCAIN, Charles W. *History of the S.S. "Beaver."* No place, no date (Vancouver, 1894). 1st ed. $25.

McCALL, Hugh. *The History of Georgia.* 2 vols., boards. Savannah, 1811-16. 1st ed. $350. Another copy, rehinged, foxed, $150.

McCALLA, W. L. *Adventures in Texas.* Clothbound. Philadelphia, 1841. 1st ed. $200. Another, $110 (1966 auction).

McCLELLAN, Henry B. *The Life and Campaigns of Maj. Gen. J. E. B. Stuart.* Portrait, 7 maps. Clothbound. Boston, 1885. 1st ed. $50. Another, $40.

McCLELLAND, Nancy. *Historic Wallpapers.* Half clothbound. Philadelphia, 1924. Limited ed. $50-$80.

McCLUNG, John A. *Sketches of Western Adventure.* Boards, linen spine. Maysville, Ky., 1832. 1st ed. $150-$200. Rebacked, $150. Another, $80 (1964 auction). Philadelphia, 1832. 2d ed. (from same sheets as 1st ed.). $45.

McCLURE, S. S. *My Autobiography.* Clothbound. New York, 1914. (By Willa Cather.) 1st ed., 1st issue, with "September, 1914" on copyright page. $25-$35.

McCONNEL, Murray. *Claim to a Patent for a Tract of Land in Illinois.* 30 pp. Washington, 1857. Bound in new cloth, $45.

McCOOK, Henry C. *American Spiders and Their Spinningwork.* Portrait, 35 hand-colored plates. 3 vols., clothbound. Philadelphia, 1889-93. One of 750. $182. Another, $210.

McCORKLE, John. *Three Years With Quantrell.* 11 plates. Clothbound. Armstrong, Mo., no date (1914). 1st ed. $35-$50. Worn, $25.

McCORMICK, Richard C. *Arizona: Its Resources and Prospects.* Map. 22 pp. New York, 1865. 1st ed. $35-$50.

McCORMICK, S. J. *Almanac for the Year 1864; Containing Useful Information Relative to the Population, Progress and Resources of Oregon, Washington and Idaho.* 56 pp., paperbound. Portland, no date (1863). $75.

McCOY, Isaac. *Remarks on the Practicability of Indian Reform.*

47 pp., paperbound. Boston, 1827. 1st ed. $200 (1966 auction). New York, 1829. 2d ed. Half leatherbound. $35-$50.

McCOY, Joseph G. *Historic Sketches of the Cattle Trade of the West and Southwest.* Portraits and plates. Clothbound. Kansas City, 1874. 1st ed. $250. Auction prices: $110 and $160 (1964). Other copies at retail: Spine faded, $100; stained, repaired, new end papers, $125; rebound in leather, $72.50.

M'CREERY, John. *A Selection, from the Ancient Music of Ireland, Arranged for the Flute or Violin.* Petersburgh, Va., 1824. (John Daly Burk collaborated.) 1st ed. $75.

McCUTCHEON, George Barr. *Graustark.* Clothbound. Chicago, 1901. 1st ed., 1st issue with name "Noble" instead of "Lorry" in line 6 of page 150. $35-$50. Cover dull, $25.

McDONALD, Frank V. (editor). *Notes Preparatory to a Biography of R. H. McDonald, etc.* 32 plates. Vol. 1 (all published). Cambridge, 1881. One of 150. $200.

McDONALD, John. *Biographical Sketches of Gen. Nathaniel Massie, etc.* Cincinnati, 1838. 1st ed. $35-$50.

McGLASHAN, Charles F. *History of the Donner Party.* Clothbound. Truckee, Calif., no date (1879). 1st ed. $200-$300. Auction prices: $120, $140, and $150. San Francisco, 1880. 2d ed. Clothbound. $50. San Francisco, 1881. Clothbound. $25. Sacramento, 1907. Paperbound. $40.

McGUFFEY, W. H. *McGuffey's Rhetorical Guide; or, Fifth Reader of the Eclectic Series.* Clothbound. Cincinnati, no date (1844). Slight breaks in hinges, $25.

M'ILVAINE, William, Jr. *Sketches of Scenery and Notes of Personal Adventure, in California and Mexico.* 16 plates, engraved title page. Clothbound. Philadelphia, 1850. 1st ed. $500-$1,000. Auction prices: $400 (1963) and $675 (1966). San Francisco, 1951. One of 400. $35-$50.

McINTIRE, J. *Early Days in Texas.* 16 plates, pictorial clothbound. Kansas City, no date (1902). 1st ed. $75-$125.

McKENNEY, Thomas L. and James Hall. *History of the Indian Tribes of North America.* Map, 120 colored plates and list of subscribers. Half morocco. Philadelphia, 1836-38-44. 1st ed. $3,000 and up for fine sets. Philadelphia, 1838-42-44. 3d ed. 3 vols. Bindings broken, $1,064 (1960 auction). Other editions, each 3 vols.: Philadelphia, 1848-49-50, $195 and $220 (both at auction); Philadelphia, 1854, $110 (at auction); Philadelphia, 1855, $150 (at auction); Philadelphia, 1870, $120 (at auction).

McLEOD, Donald. *History of Wiskonsan, from Its First Discovery to the Present Period.* 4 plates, folding map. Half morocco. Buffalo, 1846. 1st ed. $150-$200. Also, $140 (1963 auction). Note: The bibliographer Wright Howes says some copies have the plates and no map and others the map and no plates.

McMASTER, S. W. *Sixty Years on the Upper Mississippi.* Paperbound. Rock Island, 1893 (printer's foreword dated Galena, 1895). 1st ed. $50-$75. Also, rebound in cloth, $60 (1966 auction).

McMURTRIE, Douglas C. and Albert H. Allen. *Early Printing in Colorado, etc.* Clothbound. Denver, 1935. 1st ed. $25.

McMURTRIE, Henry. *Sketches of Louisville and Its Environs.* Map and table. Boards. Louisville, 1819. 1st ed. Rebacked, $80 (1965 auction).

McWHORTER, Lucullus Virgil. *The Border Settlers of Northwestern Virginia from 1768 to 1795, etc.* Hamilton, Ohio, 1915. 1st ed. Title penciled on spine, $30.

MEAD, Peter B. *An Elementary Treatise on American Grape Culture and Wine Making.* Clothbound. No place (New York), 1867. 1st ed. $25.

MEAD, Spencer P. *Ye Historie of Ye Town of Greenwich.* New York, 1911. $45.

MEADE, Gen. G. G. *Report on the Ashburn Murder.* 130 pp., paperbound. No place, no date (Atlanta, 1868). With errata slip and leaf of explanation from Meade. $100.

MEANY, Edmond S. *Origin of Washington Geographic Names.* Seattle, 1923. $25.

MEEKER, Ezra. *Washington Territory West of the Cascade Mountains.* 52 pp., paperbound. Olympia, 1870. 1st ed. $150-$250. $140 (1957 auction).

MELINE, James F. *Two Thousand Miles on Horseback.* Map. Clothbound. New York, 1867. 1st ed. $75-$100. $55 (1965 auction).

MELISH, John. *A Geographical Description of the United States, etc.* 12 maps (of 14 listed). Half leatherbound. Philadelphia, 1822. 1st ed. $35-$100.

MELISH, John. *A Military and Topographical Atlas of the United States, etc.* 8 maps and plans, 5 folding. Half leatherbound. Philadelphia, 1813. 1st ed. $300-$600. Also, $450 (1966 auction) and $210 (1964 auction). Philadelphia, 1815. 12 maps and plans, 9 folding and colored in outline. $425 (1966 auction).

MELVILLE, Herman. *Battle-Pieces and Aspects of the War.* Clothbound (salmon-colored, blue, or green). New York, 1866. 1st ed., 1st issue, with "hundred" misspelled in copyright notice. $150. Also, $100 (at auction) and $65.

MELVILLE, Herman. *Moby-Dick.* Clothbound, various colors. New York, 1851. 1st Am. ed., 1st issue, red cloth binding with orange end papers. $1,050. Also, $2,500 (1967 auction). Another copy, black cloth, terra cotta end papers, worn, foxed, $675. Another, blue cloth, orange end papers, worn, faded, $750. Another, foxed, spine faded, $100. Chicago, 1930. 3 vols., limited ed. One of 1,000, Lakeside Press, in aluminum box. $150-$200. Also, $100 (1964 auction).

MELVILLE, Herman. *The Piazza Tales.* Clothbound. New York, 1856. 1st ed. $100-$150. $100 (1963 auction).

MELVILLE, Herman. *Pierre.* Clothbound or paperbound. New York, 1852. 1st ed. Clothbound, $75. Also, $32 (at auction). Paperbound, $100.

MELVILLE, Herman. *Typee.* Map frontispiece. 2 vols. in one (in cloth) or 2 vols. (paperbound). New York, 1846. 1st Am. ed., 1st issue, paperbound. $100-$200. Also, $120 (1959 auction). 2d issue, with added story, "The Story of Toby," clothbound. $100. Also, $40 and $55 (both at auction).

MELVILLE, Herman. *White-Jacket.* One vol. in cloth or 2 vols. paperbound. New York, 1850. 1st ed. Clothbound. $200-$300. Worn, $100. Also, $100, $140, $180, $185 at auction. Paperbound, 2 vols. Last price noted was $50, but the paperbound issue is scarcer and should bring very high prices in fine condition.

MEMOIRS of Lorenzo Da Ponte (The). 22 pp., stitched. New

York, 1829. 1st ed. $37.50.

MEMORIA Sobre las Proporciones Naturales de las Provincias Internas Occidentales, Causas de que Han Provenido sus Atrasos, etc. 62 pp., sewed. Mexico, 1822. Uncut in morocco case, $400.

MEMORIAL and Biographical History of McLennan, Falls, Bell and Coryell Counties, Texas. Chicago, 1893. $65.

MEMORIAL of the Illinois and Wabash Land Company, 13th January 1797. Leather-backed cloth. No place, no date (Philadelphia, 1797). (By Provost William Smith.) 1st ed. $85.

MEMORIAL to the Legislature of New York (A), Upon the Effects of the Passage of . . . Trade . . . Through the Welland and Oswego Canals, etc. 24 pp., sewed. Rochester, 1845. $25.

MENCKEN, H. L. *In Defense of Women.* Clothbound. New York, 1918. 1st ed., 1st issue, with publisher's name misspelled "Ppilip". $25.

MENCKEN, H. L. *Ventures Into Verse.* Boards or paperbound. Baltimore, 1903. 1st ed. $100.

MERCER, A. S. *The Banditti of the Plains.* Clothbound. No place, no date (Cheyenne, 1894). 1st ed. $300-$400. Another, front cover missing, marginal notes, $275. Another, sewed but unbound, $265. Another, wirestitched, blank leaves missing at each end, $200 (at auction). Another, clothbound, $170 (1964 auction). San Francisco, 1935. Grabhorn Press. $35.

MERRY-MOUNT; a Romance of the Massachusetts Colony. 2 vols., clothbound. Also, 2 vols. in one. Boston, 1849. (By John Lothrop Motley.) 1st ed. 2 vols. $50. 2 vols. in one. $25.

MERVINE, William M. *Harris, Dunlop, Valentine and Allied Families.* No place, 1920. One of 100. Slightly scuffed, loose in binding, one portrait missing, $40.

MESSAGE from the President of the U. S. 19 pp. Washington, 1813. (Covers the captivity of Mrs. Crawley among the Creek Indians.) $65.

METCALF, Samuel L. *A Collection of Some of the Most Interesting Narratives of Indian Warfare in the West.* Leatherbound. Lexington, 1821. 1st ed. $195. Another, rubbed, $150. Another, $135.

MIDGHELS, Ella Sterling. *The Story of the Files.* No place (San Francisco), 1893. 1st ed. $30. Another copy, spine chipped, $25.

MIKESELL, Thomas. (editor). *The History of Fulton County* (Ohio). Madison, Wis., 1905. $25.

MILES, Gen. Nelson A. *Personal Recollections, etc.* Plates. Clothbound or leatherbound. Chicago, 1896. 1st ed., 1st issue, with caption under frontispiece reading "General Miles." $50-$75. Worn copies, $35-$50. Rebound in cloth, $27.50. 2d issue, with rank under portrait as "Maj. Gen." $50. Chicago, 1897. 2d ed. With an added plate at end. $25.

MILLAY, Edna St. Vincent. *Conversation at Midnight.* Boards and cloth. New York, 1937. 1st ed. (so stated). One of 597 on handmade paper, signed. $10-$15. One of 36 on Japan vellum, numbered and signed. $37.50. 1st trade ed. Boards and cloth. $10.

MILLAY, Edna St. Vincent. *A Few Figs From Thistles.* Green paperbound; also other colors. New York, 1920. 1st ed. $125.

MILLAY, Edna St. Vincent. *The King's Henchman.* Half clothbound, paper label. New York, 1927. 1st ed. One of 158 on handmade paper, signed, boxed. $75-$100. One of 31 copies on vellum, signed, $100. 1st trade ed. Half clothbound. $25. Autographed, $50.

MILLAY, Edna St. Vincent. *Renascence and Other Poems.* Black clothbound. New York, 1917. 1st ed., 1st issue, with paper watermarked "Glaslan." In dust jacket, up to $200. Autographed, $250 and up. Lacking dust jacket, $75-$125. Autographed, lacking jacket, $100. Also, one of 15 (or 17?) on Japan paper, signed, bound in boards. $1,600 (1962 auction) and $950 (1960 auction).

MILLER, Andrew. *New States and Territories.* Folding map table. 32 pp., leatherbound. No place, no date (Keene, N. H., 1819). 1st ed. Map table signed by author, $1,250. Another, map table in facsimile, $87.50. Another, lacking map table, $50. 2d ed., 96 pp., folding table, marbled boards, no place, no date (Keene, 1819). $750.

MILLER, Arthur McQuiston. *The Geology of Kentucky.* Frankfort, 1919. $27.50.

MILLER, E. *The History of Page County, from the Earliest Settlement in 1843 to 1876, etc.* Folding map. Clarinda, Iowa, 1876. 1st ed. $65 (1966 auction).

MILLER, J. *Illustrated History of Montana.* Chicago, 1894. 1st ed. $35.

MILLER, J. P. and John Patterson. *Nomination of President and Vice President of the United States.* 12 pp., sewed. No place, no date (Steubenville, Ohio, 1823). Uncut, $65.

MILLER, John C. *The Great Convention.* Description of the Convention of the People of Ohio, Embracing the Speeches of the Hon. J. C. Wright, etc. 40 pp., sewed. Columbus, 1840. $25.

MILLER, John F. *A Refutation of the Slander and Falsehoods Contained in a Pamphlet Entitled SALLY MILLER, etc.* 70 pp., paperbound. New Orleans, 1845. $30.

MILLER, T. L. *History of Hereford Cattle, etc.* Chillicothe, Mo., 1902. 1st ed. $75. Another, $30.

MILLS, Robert. *Statistics of South Carolina.* Map (not in all copies). Charleston, 1826. 1st ed. $75-$100. Rebacked, $55.

MILLS, William W. *Forty Years at El Paso, 1858-1898.* Frontispiece. Clothbound. No place, no date (El Paso, 1901). 1st ed. $75. Another, $25.

MILNE, A. A. *Winnie-the-Pooh.* Decorations by E. H. Shepard. Boards, cloth spine. No place, no date (New York, 1926). One of 200, signed by author and artist, boxed. $80-$100.

MINNESOTA Guide (The). 94 pp., paperbound. St. Paul, 1869. (By J. F. Williams.) 1st ed. $50-$75. Another, $35.

MINNESOTA Year Book and Traveller's Guide for 1851. Folding map. Boards, leather spine. St. Paul, no date (1851). (By W. G. Le Duc.) $100-$200. Also, $100 (at auction). Other issues: For 1852, with plate, $50; lacking plate, $15. For 1853, folding map, $35.

MINUTES of the Proceedings of a Convention of Delegates From the Abolition Societies, etc. 30 pp., clothbound. Philadelphia, 1794. $50.

MIRROR of Olden Time Border Life. 13 plates (17 in some). Leatherbound. Abingdon, Va., 1849. (By Joseph Pritts.) $35. Another copy, foxed, two plates mended, $27.50.

MISCELLANEOUS Pieces. 24 pp., sewed. No place, no date. $25.

MISCELLANIES. By the Author of "Letters on the Eastern States." Boards. Boston, 1821. Uncut, binding defects, $30.

MITCHELL, G. R. *The Pacific Gold Company of Gilpin County, Colorado.* 19 pp., paperbound. Boston, 1866. $25.

MITCHELL, Isaac. *The Asylum; or Alonzo and Melissa.* 2 vols. Poughkeepsie, 1811. 1st ed. $250.

MITCHELL, S. Augustus. *Description of Texas, Oregon and California.* Philadelphia, 1846. $45.

MITCHELL, S. Augustus. *A New Map of Texas, Oregon and California with the Regions Adjoining.* 46 pp., text and large colored map, folding into leather covers. Philadelphia, 1846. $40-$50.

MITCHELL, S. Weir. *Mr. Kris Kringle.* Boards, cloth back. Philadelphia, 1893. 1st ed. $30.

MOKLER, A. J. *History of Natrona County, Wyoming.* Chicago, 1923. 1st ed. $37.50. Another, signed, $75.

MONKS, William. *History of Southern Missouri and Northern Arkansas.* West Plains, Mo., 1907. 1st ed. $30.

MONROE, James. *The Memoir of: Relating to His Unsettled Claims Upon the People and Government of the U. S.* 60 pp., sewed. Charlottesville, 1828. Uncut, $80.

MONT Saint Michel and Chartres. Blue clothbound. Washington, 1904. (By Henry Adams.) 1st ed. $400. Also, inscribed by the author, $750.

MONTAIGNE, Michel de. *Essays.* Translated by John Florio. 3 vols., half clothbound. Boston, 1902-04. One of 265 designed by Bruce Rogers and inscribed by him. $100-$150.

MONTANA Territory, History and Business Directory, 1879. Map. Helena, no date (1879). (By F. W. Warner.) 1st ed. $100-$200. Auction prices: $75 and $100; lacking map, $40.

MOORE, Clement C. *Poems.* New York, 1844. 1st ed. Fine, except for small portion lacking from head of spine, $200. Inscribed copies, at auction, $44 and $50.

MOORE, H. Judge. *Scott's Campaign in Mexico, etc.* Charleston, 1849. 1st ed. $57.50.

MOORE, Julia A. *The Sentimental Song Book.* 54 pp., paperbound. Grand Rapids, 1876. 1st ed. $100. Another, library stamp on front cover, $75.

MOORE, Mrs. M. B. *The Geographical Reader, for the Dixie Children.* 48 pp., boards. Raleigh, 1863. 1st ed. $45.

MOORE, S. S. and T. W. Jones. *The Traveller's Directory.* 52 pp., with 38 maps on 22 leaves. Philadelphia, 1802. 1st ed. Front hinge cracked, $37.50.

MOORE, Thomas. *Epistles, Odes and Other Poems.* Edited by Joseph Dennie. Philadelphia, 1806. 2d ed. $30.

MOREAU De Saint-Mery, Mederic Louis Elie. *Description Topographique et Politique de la Partie Espagnole de L'Isle Saint-Domingue.* 2 vols., paperbound. Philadelphia, 1796. 1st ed. $150. Also, covers defective, $70 (at auction).

MOREHEAD, James T. *Address in Commemoration of the First Settlement of Kentucky.* Frankfort, 1840. 1st ed. $50-$75.

MORGAN, John Hill and Mantle Fielding. *The Life Portraits of Washington and Their Replicas.* Clothbound. Philadelphia, no date (1931). 1st ed. One of 1,000. $45-$50. One of 100, signed, full morocco binding. $50-$75.

MORGAN, Martha M. (editor). *A Trip Across the Plains in the Year 1849.* 31 pp., paperbound. San Francisco, 1864. 1st ed. $1,500.

MORLEY, Christopher. *Parnassus on Wheels.* Gray boards, tan cloth spine. Garden City, 1917. 1st ed., 1st issue, with space between the "Y" and "e" in "Years" in line 8, page 4. In dust jacket, $100. Another, in slipcase, $35. Also, $50 and $60 (at auction).

MORPHIS, J. M. *History of Texas.* Map. New York, 1874. 1st ed. $50-$60. Worn, $35.

MORSE, Edward S. *Catalogue of the Morse Collection of Japanese Pottery.* Boards. Cambridge, 1901. 1st ed. $100-$125. Soiled copy, $62.50 (at auction).

MORSE, Jedidiah. *The American Geography.* Maps. Calfbound. Elizabethtown, 1789. 1st ed. Hinges weak, $100. Another, $50.

MORSE, Jedidiah. *Geography Made Easy.* 2 colored maps. Leatherbound. New Haven, no date (1784). 1st ed. $200-$400. Worn, $275. Another, $180. Another, map of U. S. torn in 3 parts, $310 (at auction).

MORTON, Charles. *The Spirit of Man.* Leatherbound. Boston, 1693. 1st ed. $50.

MOTLEY, John Lothrop. *Peter the Great.* Paperbound. New York, 1878. 1st ed. $30.

MOUNTAINEER (The). Harrisonburg, Va., 1812. 1st ed. (but called 2d ed., after publication in Collet's *Republican Farmer).* $75. Harrisonburg, 1818. $37.50.

MULLAN, John. *The Miners' and Travellers' Guide to Oregon, etc.* Folding colored map. Clothbound. New York, 1865. 1st ed. $75-$100. Worn, $60 (1966 auction).

MULLAN, John. *Report on the Construction of a Military Road from Fort Walla-Walla to Fort Benton.* 4 maps, 10 plates. Clothbound. Washington, 1863. $50-$60.

MULLET, J. C. *A Five Years' Whaling Voyage.* 68 pp. Cleveland, 1859. 1st ed. $100.

MUMEY, Nolie. *Calamity Jane, 1852-1903.* Plates. Denver, 1950. One of 200, signed. $50 and $60.

MUMEY, Nolie. *The Life of Jim Baker, 1818-1898.* Frontispiece and map. Half clothbound. Denver, 1931. 1st ed. One of 250, signed. $150-$200. Auction prices: $120 (1960) and $130 (1966).

MUNRO, Robert (pseudonym). *A Description of the Genesee Country, etc.* Map, 16 pp. New York, 1804. (By Charles Williamson.) 1st ed. $35.

MURDER by Deputy U. S. Marshal E. M. Thornton of E. M. Dalton Waylaid and Assassinated in Cold Blood. 16 pp., paperbound. Salt Lake, 1886. $25 and $30.

MUSICA Sacra. Leatherbound. Utica, 1815. 1st ed. $45.

MYRICK, Herbert. *Cache la Poudre.* Clothbound. New York, 1905. 1st ed. $30-$40. Also, one of 500, bound in buckskin, $50-$60.

MYSTERIES of a Convent. By a Noted Methodist Preacher. Paperbound. Philadelphia, no date (1854). $25.

MYSTERIES of Mormonism (The). A Full Exposure of its Secret Practices and Hidden Crimes. By an Apostle's Wife. Paperbound. New York, 1882. $50-$60.

MYSTERIOUS Marksman (The): or the Outlaws of New York. Paperbound. Cincinnati, no date (about 1855). (By Emerson Bennett.) $50-$60.

NARRATIVE of the Adventures and Sufferings of Capt. Daniel D. Heustis, etc. (A). 168 pp., unbound, stitched. Boston, 1847. 1st ed. Lacking frontispiece, $62.50.

NARRATIVE of Arthur Gordon Pym (The). Clothbound, paper label. New York, 1838. (By Edgar Allan Poe.) 1st ed., with May, 1838, ad in front and 14 pages of ads at end. $250. Another, stained, ex-library copy, $100.

NARRATIVE of the Captivity and Providential Escape of Mrs. Jane Lewis. (Cover title.) Woodcut plate. 24 pp., clothbound. New York, 1833. (By William P. Edwards?) 1st ed. $150. New York, 1834. Paperbound. $75.

NARRATIVE of the Captivity and Sufferings of Ebenezer Fletcher of New Ipswich (A). 26 pp. Amherst, 1798. 1st ed. $450. Windsor, Vt., 1813. 22 pp. 2d ed. $200. New-Ipswich, N. H., 1827. 3d ed (self-styled "4th" ed.) 24 pp. $135. New-Ipswich, no date (about 1828). $75.

NARRATIVE of the Captivity of Mrs. Johnson (A). 144 pp. Walpole, N. H., 1796. (By Mrs. Susannah Johnson.) 1st ed. $125. Another copy, worn, $75. Windsor, Vt., 1807. 144 pp., boards. $50 and $32.50.

NARRATIVE of the Extraordinary Life of John Conrad Shafford. Frontispiece. 24 pp., paperbound. New York, 1840. 1st ed. Foxed, $35. Another, rebound in modern cloth, $12 (at auction).

NARRATIVE of the Facts and Circumstances Relating to the Kidnapping and Presumed Murder of William Morgan (A). 36 pp. No place, no date (Batavia, N. Y., 1827). 1st ed. $25.

NARRATIVE of the Life and Adventures of Matthew Bunn, etc. 55 pp., sewed. Batavia, N.Y., 1828. 7th ed. $35.

NARRATIVE of the Massacre at Chicago. Frontispiece and map. 34 pp. Chicago, 1844. (By Mrs. Juliette A. Kinzie.) 1st ed. Full morocco, $1,400 (1966 auction). Another, in a dealer's catalogue, $600.

NARRATIVE of the Sufferings and Adventures of Capt. Charles H. Barnard, etc. Boards, cloth spine. New York, 1829. 1st ed. $100. Rebound in modern half morocco, $80 (1963 auction). Another, in original boards, $47 (1960 auction).

NARRATIVE of the Sufferings of Massy Harbison. 66 pp., leatherbound. Pittsburgh, 1825. 1st ed. $125-$300. Worn, $55. Pittsburgh, 1828. 98 pp. 2d ed. $40. Beaver, Pa., 1836. 4th ed. Half clothbound. $30 (at auction).

NASBY, Petroleum V. *The Nasby Papers.* 64 pp., paperbound. Indianapolis, 1864. (By David Ross Locke.) 1st ed. $25.

NATURE. Clothbound. Boston, 1836. (By Ralph Waldo Emerson.) 1st ed., 1st state, with page 94 misnumbered 92. In fine condition, $150-$200. Also, $150 and $140 (at auction). Worn, $75. Rebound, $35. Another copy, worn, $50. Another, spine chipped, $28.50. 2d state, error corrected. $35-$50.

NAUTICAL Reminiscences. Providence, 1832. (By Nathaniel Ames.) 1st ed. $25.

NAVIGATOR (The). Charts. Leather-backed boards. Pittsburgh, 1808. (By Zadok Cramer.) 6th ed. $325 (1967 auction). $130 (1966 auction). Pittsburgh, 1811. 7th ed. $175 (1967 auction). Pittsburgh, 1814, 8th ed., $50. Pittsburgh, 1814, 9th ed., $65. Pittsburgh, 1818, 10th ed., $40. Pittsburgh, 1821, 11th ed., $47.50. Pittsburgh, 1824, 12th ed., $35. (For earlier editions under another title see *Ohio and Mississippi Navigator.*)

NEAL, Basil Llewellin. *A Son of the American Revolution.* No place, no date (Washington, Ga., 1914). $25.

NEAL, John. *Rachel Dyer: A North American Story.* Boards, label. Portland, 1828. 1st ed. $180 (1960 auction). Another, $75. Another, dampstained, paper label chipped, $27.50. Another, $37 (at auction). Another, defective, $17 (at auction).

NEAL, Joseph Clay. *Peter Ploddy, and Other Oddities.* Philadelphia, 1844. 1st ed. $25.

NECESSITY of a Ship-Canal Between the East and West (The). 45 pp., sewed. Chicago, 1863. (By J. W. Foster.) $25.

NEESE, George M. *Three Years in the Confederate Horse Artillery.* Clothbound. New York, 1911. 1st ed. $40 and $32.50.

NEIL, John B. *Biennial Message of Governor of Idaho to the 11th Session of the Legislature of Idaho Territory.* 19 pp., paperbound. Boise City, 1880. $25.

NEIL, Julia E. *From Generation to Generation. The Genealogies of Dwight Stone and Olive Evans.* Columbus, 1907. $25.

NEW Bedford and Fairhaven Signals. New Bedford, 1834. $97.50.

NEW-England Primer Enlarged (The). Boards. Boston, 1727. Only one copy is known. The first copies of this famous old book are believed to have been printed between 1686 and 1690, but none are known to have survived.

NEW England Primer (The), or, an Easy and Pleasant Guide to the Art of Reading. Paper covered thin wooden boards. No place [New-England], no date [not after 1796]. Cover cracked and mended, $185. Philadelphia, 1797. $150. Leominster, Mass., 1804. $32.50.

NEW England Primer Improved (The). 72 pp., paperbound. New York, no date. $100. Others: Boston, 1789. $25. Boston (Loring, printer), no date (about 1815). $35. Lenox, Mass., 1829, gray paper covers, $35; Chillicothe, no date (1825-28), 36 pp., paperbound, $25. Worcester, Mass. (Allen, printer), no date (about 1835). $25.

NEW History of the Grecian States (A). Albany, 1794. $37.50.

NEW Texas Spelling Book (The). Houston, 1863. (By E. H. Cushing.) $100.

NEW Translation with Notes (A), of the Third Satire of Juvenal. New York, 1806. (By Clement Clarke Moore and John Duer.) 1st ed., with "Additional Errata" leaf. Margin of one blank page defective, $35.

NEWBERRY, J. S. *Report on the Properties of the Ramshorn Consolidated Silver Mining Company at Bay Horse, Idaho.* 16 pp., paperbound. New York, no date (1881). Lacking front cover, $45.

NEWELL, Rev. Chester. *History of the Revolution in Texas.* Folding map. Half calfbound. New York, 1838. 1st ed. $150. Other copies, $100 and $45.

NEWCOMB, Harvey. *The Wyandott Chief; or The History of Barnet, a Converted Indian, etc.* Boston, 1835. 1st ed. $25.

NEWTON, A. Edward. *The Amenities of Book-Collecting and Kindred Affections.* Half clothbound and brown boards. Boston, 1918. 1st ed., 1st issue, with reading "Piccadilly" in line 3, page 268. $50. Worn, $35 and $25.

NEWTON, J. H. (editor). *History of . . . Venango County* (Pennsylvania), *etc.* 47 plates on 33 leaves. Half morocco. Columbus, 1879. $32.50. Another copy, new backstrip, $22.50.

NIAGARA Revisited. Chicago, 1884. (By Mark Twain and others.) 1st ed. Lacking backstrip, covers and text loose, $25.

NICK of the Woods. 2 vols., purple clothbound. Philadelphia, 1837. (By Robert Montgomery Bird.) 1st ed. $375 (1962 auction). Another set, $50.

NICHOLSON, John. *The Martyrdom of Joseph Standing, etc.* Salt Lake City, 1886. $25.

NICOLLETT, Joseph Nicolas. *Report Intended to Illustrate a Map of the Hydrographical Basin of the Upper Missouri River.* Senate Doc. 237, 26th Congress, 2d session. Folding map. 170 pp., paperbound. Washington, 1843. 1st ed. $75 and $55. Washington, 1845. House Doc. 52. Smaller map. Sewed. $25-$30.

NIMMO, Joseph. *Range and Ranch Cattle Traffic.* (Caption title.) 4 folding maps, 200 pp., paperbound. Washington, 1885. 1st ed. $60. Another, lacking a map, $35. All maps lacking, $30.

NORRIS, Frank. *McTeague.* Clothbound. New York, 1899. 1st ed., 1st state, with "moment" as last word on page 106. $150-$200. Auction prices: $150, $80, $60 and $70 (for a copy with stains on spine).

NORRIS, J. Wellington. *A Business Advertiser and General Directory of the City of Chicago for the Year 1845-6.* (2d Chicago city directory.) Folding plate. 156 pp., paperbound. Chicago, 1845. 1st ed. $600 (and up). Also, $450 (1966 auction price for a copy rebound in modern boards).

NORRIS, J. W. *General Directory and Business Advertiser of the City of Chicago for the Year 1844.* (1st Chicago city directory.) 116 pp., paperbound. Chicago, 1844. 1st ed. $475 (auction price, 1959). The second issue of this book was in cloth covers.

NORTH-WEST Coast of America, Being Results of Recent Ethnological Researches from the Collections of the Royal Museum at Berlin. 15 plates, five colored. New York, no date. Half leather, $55.

NORTON, Harry J. *Wonder-Land Illustrated.* Map. 16 pp., paperbound and clothbound. Virginia City, Mont., 1873. 1st ed. Clothbound, $40. Paperbound, $65.

NOTES on California and the Placers. 2 plates (not in all copies). 128 pp., paperbound. New York, 1850. (By James Delavan.) 1st ed. $1,250.

NOTICES of Parkersburg, Virginia, As It Is in 1860. 12 pp., paperbound. Baltimore, 1860. $45.

NOTICES of Sullivan's Campaign, or the Revolutionary Warfare in Western New-York, etc. With frontispiece. Rochester, 1842. $35.

NOWLIN, William. *The Bark-Covered House, or Back in the Woods Again.* 6 plates. Clothbound. Detroit, 1876. 1st ed. $550.

NUTTALL, Thomas. *Journal of Travels Into the Arkansa Territory, etc.* Folding map, 5 plates. Three quarters leatherbound. Philadelphia, 1821. 1st ed. $200-$300. Also, $210 (1966 auction), $70 and $160 (both at auction, 1959). Other copies in catalogues at $125 (worn, signed) and $77.50 (repaired). Rebound in calf, $110 (1957 auction).

NUTTING, Wallace. *The Clock Book.* Clothbound. Framingham, Mass., 1924. 1st ed. $25-$35. Worn, $15-$20. Garden City, 1935. Clothbound. $25.

OAKES, William. *Scenery of the White Mountains.* 16 plates, sometimes colored, each with a leaf of text. Clothbound. Boston, no date (1848). 1st ed. Uncolored, $50-$75. Colored, $100-$150.

OAKLEY, Violet. *The Holy Experiment . . . Murals in the Governor's Reception Room at Harrisburg.* Elephant folio, full leather, copper clasps. No place, no date (Harrisburg, 1922). 1st ed. One of 500. $50-$75.

"OAKWOOD, Oliver." *Village Tales, or Recollections of By-*

Past Times. Trenton, N. J., 1827. (By Stacy Gardner Potts.) 1st ed. $45.

OBSERVATIONS: On the Reconciliation of Great Britain and the Colonies. 40 pp. Philadelphia, 1776. (By Jacob Green?) 1st ed. $35.

ODE on the King of Prussia (An). 15 pp., sewed. Antigua, 1760. $125.

OF the Just Shaping of Letters. From the Applied Geometry of Albrecht Durer. Decorations by Bruce Rogers. New York, 1917. One of 215. $50-$60.

OFFUTT, Denton. *The Educated Horse.* Washington, 1854. $50.

O. HENRY Calendar, 1917 (The). Paper covers, cord tie. No place, no date (New York, 1916). $35.

OHIO and Mississippi Navigator (The). 40 pp., half morocco. Pittsburgh, 1802. (By Zadok Cramer.) 3d ed. $3,500 (1967 auction). One of 4 known copies. There are no known copies of the 1st and 2d eds.

OLD Fashioned Mother Goose Melodies (The). No place (New York), 1879. (By Henry Wadsworth Longfellow.) 1st ed. $50.

OLD Soldier's History (The). Written by Himself. 20 pp., paperbound. Haverhill, 1861. (By Charles Fairbanks?) $75.

OLDER, (Mr. and Mrs.) Fremont. *Life of George Hearst.* Vellum-bound. San Francisco, 1923. 1st ed. $40.

ON the "White Pass" Pay-roll. By the President of the White Pass & Yukon Route. 15 plates. Chicago, 1908. (By S. H. Graves.) $50.

ONANIA; or, The Heinous Sin of Self-Pollution, etc. Boston 1724. 1st Am. ed. $150. Boston, 1726. 2d ed. $100.

ONE Hundred Books Famous in English Literature. 2 vols. New York, 1902-03. One of 305 sets. $50. (See: KENT, Henry W., for Vol. 2 separately.)

O'NEILL, Eugene. *Mourning Becomes Electra.* Vellum-bound. New York, no date (1931). 1st ed. Large paper ed. One of 550, signed. $50-$60. Another, worn, $35. Another, $25. 1st trade ed. Clothbound. In dust jacket, $17.50 and $12.50. Lacking jacket, $7.50-$10. Another copy, inscribed by O'Neill, $125.

O'NEILL, Eugene. *The Provincetown Plays*. Paperbound. New York, 1916. 1st ed. $37.50.

O'NEILL, Eugene. *Strange Interlude*. Vellum over boards. New York, 1928. 1st ed. Large paper ed. One of 775, signed. $50-$75. 1st trade ed. Clothbound. $10. Signed by O'Neill, $75.

O'NEILL, Eugene. *Thirst and Other One-Act Plays*. Gray boards, tan cloth spine, paper labels. Boston, no date (1914). 1st ed. In dust jacket, $150. Others, $110, $95 and $75. At auction, $90. Another, lacking jacket, $75 at retail.

ONKEN, Otto and William Wells. *Western Scenery; or, Land and River, Hill and Dale, in the Mississippi Valley*. Pictorial title page, 19 full-page lithographic views, 52 pp. of text, boards and calf. Cincinnati, 1851. 1st ed. $1,500.

OPDYKE, Charles Wilson. *The OP Duck Genealogy*. New York, 1889. $25.

OPPOSITION of the South to the Development of Oregon and Washington Territory. 8 pp., folded. No place, no date (Washington, 1859). Uncut, $45.

ORIGIN and Traditional History of the Wyandotts, etc. Toronto, 1870. (By Peter D. Clarke.) 1st ed. $25.

ORIGINAL Charades. Clothbound. Oblong. Cambridge, 1839. 1st ed. $27.50.

ORVIS, Charles F. and A. Nelson Cheney (compilers). *Fishing with the Fly*. 15 color plates. Manchester, Vt., 1883. 1st ed. Signature pulled, back faded, $25.

OSCEOLA; or, Fact and Fiction. New York, 1838. (By James Birchett Ransom). $25.

OSGOOD, Ernest Staples. *The Day of the Cattleman*. 14 plates and maps. Clothbound. Minneapolis, 1929. 1st ed. $35.

OSGOOD, Frances S. *The Poetry of Flowers and Flowers of Poetry*. New York, 1851. $50.

OTERO, M. A. *The Real Billy the Kid*. Clothbound. New York, 1936. 1st ed. $60. Another, $30.

OTIS, James. *Toby Tyler or Ten Weeks with a Circus*. Clothbound. New York, 1881. (By James Otis Kaler.) 1st ed. $100. Another, slight cover defect, $85.

PACKARD, Wellman and G. Larison. *Early Emigration to California.* 2 portraits. 23 pp., paperbound. Bloomington, Ill., 1928. One of 30. $40 (1966 auction).

PALLADINO, Lawrence B. *Indian and White in the Northwest.* 55 portraits, 90 plates, large colored map. Baltimore, 1894. 1st ed. $45. Another, $30.

PALMER, H. E. *The Powder River Indian Expedition, 1865.* 59 pp. Omaha, 1887. 1st ed. $50.

PALOU, Francisco. *Historical Memoirs of New California.* 4 vols., clothbound. Translated by Herbert Eugene Bolton. Berkeley, 1926. $100.

PALOU, Francisco. *Relacion Historica de la Vida y Apostolicas Tareas del Venerable Padre Fray Junipero Serra.* Portrait and map (folding). Limp vellum or leatherbound. Mexico, 1787. 1st ed. $850 (1962 auction—for a copy with an inserted map showing San Francisco Bay). Other copies at auction: $450 (1960) and $230 (1962). Catalogue prices noted: $450, $300, and $150 (worn).

PANTHER, Abraham. *A Surprising Narrative of a Young Woman Discovered in a Cave.* 12 pp., paperbound. Leominster, no date (about 1799). $175.

PARAPHRASE on Some Parts of the Book of Job (A). 39 pp., paperbound. Boston, 1795. (By Richard Devens.) Spine lacking, library stamps on one leaf, $40.

PARKER, A. A. *Trip to the West and Texas.* 2 plates. Clothbound. Concord, N. H., 1835. 1st ed. $75-$100. Concord, 1836. 2d ed. Colored folding map and 3 plates. $75-$125.

PARKER, Aaron. *Forgotten Tragedies of Indian Warfare in Idaho.* 10 pp., double-column, paperbound. Grangeville, Idaho, 1925. $25.

PARKER, Henry W. *How Oregon Was Saved to the U. S.* 10 pp., paperbound. New York, 1901. $25.

PARKER, John R. *The New Semaphoric Signal Book.* Boston, 1836. $42.50.

PARKER, John R. *The United States Telegraph Vocabulary.* Boston, 1832. 1st ed. Rebound, $57.50.

PARKER, Dr. M. *The Arcana of Arts and Sciences, or Farmers and Mechanics' Manual.* Washington, Pa., 1924. $25.

PARKER, W. B. *Notes Taken During the Expedition Commanded by Capt. R. B. Marcy, etc.* Clothbound. Philadelphia, 1856. 1st ed. $75-$125. Also, $55 (1966 auction).

PARKMAN, Francis. *The California and Oregon Trail.* One vol. (clothbound) or 2 vols. (paperbound). New York, 1849. 1st ed., 1st binding (brown cloth). $350-$400. $275 (1960 auction). Other auction prices: $110 and $170. 2d binding (blue cloth). $100-$200. 2d printing, blue cloth, worn type on pages 436-437. $50-$100. Paperbound copies of the 1st ed., $350-$500, possibly more.

PARKMAN, Francis. *Count Frontenac and New France Under Louis XIV.* Map. Boston, 1877. (Part 5 of *France and England in North America.*) 1st ed. One of 75 large paper copies. $25.

PARKMAN, Francis. *History of the Conspiracy of Pontiac and the War of the North American Tribes, etc.* 4 maps. Gray cloth. Boston, 1851. 1st ed. Inscribed, $30. Another copy, not inscribed, "Particularly fine," $35.

PARMLY, Levi Spear. *A Practical Guide to the Management of the Teeth.* Philadelphia, 1819. 1st ed. Repaired, $82.50.

PARTICULAR Account of the Dreadful Fire at Richmond, Dec. 26, 1811. 48 pp., sewed. Baltimore, 1812. $25.

PASADENA, Los Angeles County, Southern California, 36 pp., paperbound. Los Angeles, 1898. $25.

PATCHIN, Gen. Freegift. *The Captivity and Sufferings of.* Albany, 1833. $500.

PATHFINDER (The): or, The Inland Sea. 2 vols., green or purple muslin, or boards and cloth. Philadelphia, 1840. (By James Fenimore Cooper.) 1st ed., 1st issue, with no copyright notice in Vol. II and with the printer's imprint at the center of page 2. $150-$200. Also, $85 (at auction).

PATON, James M. (editor). *The Erechtheum. Measured, Drawn, and Restored.* By Gorham P. Stevens. Cambridge, 1927. In dust jacket, $30.

PATTIE, James Ohio. *The Personal Narrative of, etc.* 5 plates. Leatherbound. Cincinnati, 1831. 1st ed., 1st issue, published by John H. Wood. $2,300 (1963 auction). Cincinnati, 1833. 2d ed. $500-$800. Auction prices: $400, $325, $285 and $240. Worn, $170. Another copy, foxed, facsimile plates, title page stained, $175.

PATTERSON, A. W. *History of the Backwoods; or, The Region of the Ohio.* Folding map. Clothbound. Pittsburgh, 1843. 1st ed. $200. Another, spine chipped, $150. Another, at auction, $150.

PATTERSON, Lawson B. *Twelve Years in the Mines of California.* Clothbound. Cambridge, 1862. 1st ed. $65. Other copies, $40, $32.50, and $27.50.

PATTERSON, Samuel. *Narrative of the Adventures and Sufferings of, etc.* Rhode Island, 1817. 1st ed. $100. Palmer, Mass., 1817. 2d ed. $100.

PAULISON, C. M. K. *Arizona: The Wonderful Country.* 31 pp., paperbound. Tucson, 1881. 1st ed. $1,800.

PEARCE, Dutee. *Explore the Pacific Ocean.* 43 pp., sewed. Washington, 1835. $35.

PEARCE, James. *A Narrative of the Life of.* Boards. Rutland, Vt. 1825. 1st ed. $125-$150. Also, $80 (auction), $90, and $125.

PEARSON, Jonathan. *The History of the Schenectady Patent.* 28 maps and plates. Albany, 1883. 2d ed. One of 300. $32.50 and $20. There were also 50 copies on large paper, and they are worth a little more.

PECK, George Wilbur. *Peck's Bad Boy and His Pa.* Clothbound and paperbound. Chicago, 1883. 1st ed., 1st issue, with the text ending on page 196, the last word in perfect type, and with the printer's rules on the copyright page 7/8" apart. Clothbound, $50-$75. Paperbound, $75-$100.

PEET, Frederick T. *Civil War Letters and Documents of.* Newport, 1915. 50 copies. $75.

PEET, Frederick T. *Personal Experiences in the Civil War.* Half cloth and boards. New York, 1905. One of 50. $75. Another copy, signed, $35.

PENHALLOW, Samuel. *The History of the Wars of New-England.* Boston, 1726. 1st ed. $2,000 (1967 auction). Other copies, $500 and $600. Another copy, page numbers trimmed off margins, three leaves in facsimile, title page repaired, $175.

PENNELL, Joseph. *The Glory of New York.* Boards. New York, 1926. One of 350, designed by Bruce Rogers. In dust jacket, $55. Another, $45.

PENROSE, Charles W. *"Mormon" Doctrine, Plain and Simple, etc.* Salt Lake City, 1882. 1st ed. $27.50.

PERRY, John D. *Letter of John D. Perry, etc.* Paperbound. Philadelphia, 1868. $25.

PERRY, Oliver Hazard. *Hunting Expeditions of.* 3 plates. Clothbound. Cleveland, 1899. 1st ed. One of 100. $300. (1966 auction). $110 (1962 auction).

PETERS, DeWitt C. *The Life and Adventures of Kit Carson, the Nestor of the Rocky Mountains, etc.* 10 plates. Clothbound. New York, 1858. 1st ed. $75-$100. Also, $47 (at auction).

PETERS, Harry T. *California on Stone.* 112 plates. Clothbound. Garden City, 1935. $125.

PETERS, Harry T. *Currier and Ives, Printmakers to the American People.* Plates. 2 vols., clothbound. Garden City, 1929-31. 1st ed. One of 501. $200-$300. $180 (1962 auction). $120 (1960 auction). Garden City, 1942. Special ed. in one vol. $25.

PETERS, William E. *Ohio Lands and Their History.* Athens, Ohio, 1930. $25.

PETERS, William E. *Ohio Lands and Their Subdivision.* No place (Athens, Ohio), 1918. 2d ed., with folding map in pocket. $25.

PETIT, Veronique. *Plural Marriage: the Heart-History of Adele Hersch.* 99 pp., paperbound. Ithaca, 1885. $35.

PETITION of the Latter-Day Saints, Commonly Known as Mormons, etc. (The). 13 pp., sewed. Washington, 1840. $25.

PHAIR, Charles. *Atlantic Salmon Fishing.* Clothbound. New York, no date (1937). One of 950. In dust jacket, $75-$100. Also, $70 (at auction). One of 40 with examples of 200 flies. $400 (1958 auction) and $360 (1959 auction).

PHELPS and Ensign (publishers). *Traveller's Guide Through the United States, Containing Stage, Steamboat, Canal and Rail-road Routes, with the Distances from Place to Place.* 53 pp., leatherbound. Folding map. New York, 1838. 1st ed.

$35-$50. Other similar *"Traveller's Guides"*, same publishers: 1840, $40; 1850, $30; 1851, $35.

PHELPS, Noah A. *A History of the Copper Mines and New-gate Prison, at Granby, Conn.* 34 pp., paperbound. Hartford, 1845. $75.

PHILLIPS, J. V. *Report on the Geology of the Mineral Districts Contiguous to the Iron Mountain Railroad.* 14 pp., St. Louis, 1859. $25.

PICKETT, Albert James. *History of Alabama, and Incidentally of Georgia and Mississippi, etc.* Map, 3 plans, 8 plates. 2 vols., clothbound. Charleston, 1851. 1st ed. $75-$100.

PICTORIAL View of California (A). By a Returned Californian. 48 plates. Clothbound. New York, 1853. (By J. M. Letts.) Later ed of *California Illustrated.* $50-$100. Also, $95.20 (1960 auction). Other copies, worn, $30 and $45 at retail.

PICTURE Exhibition, etc. (The). Paperbound. Worcester, 1788. 1st Am. ed. $125.

PIGAFETTA, Antonio. *Magellan's Voyage Around the World.* 3 vols., clothbound. Cleveland, 1906. One of 350. $100-$125. Another set, spines faded, $40. Another, $70 (1957 auction).

PIKE, Albert. *Prose Sketches and Poems, Written in the Western Country.* Clothbound. Boston, 1834. 1st ed. Rebound in half leather, $350. Also, $250 (1963 auction). Earlier, in catalogues, $225 (for a fine copy); worn, $167.50 and $160.

PIKE, Corp. James. *The Scout and Ranger.* Portrait, 24 plates. Clothbound. Cincinnati, 1865. 1st ed., 1st issue, with errata leaf. $350. Another, $85. Another, $225 (1964 auction). Rebound in calf, $150.

PIKE, Zebulon Montgomery. *An Account of Expeditions to the Sources of the Mississippi.* Portrait, 4 maps, 2 charts, 3 tables. 2 vols., boards. Philadelphia, 1810. 1st ed. $350-$400. Rebound in calf, $250. $200 (1964 auction). Another copy, rebacked, $170 (at auction). Another, in binder's cloth, $250 (1963 auction). Another issue with maps in separate cloth atlas-folder, $120 (at auction). Another, rebound in half morocco, ex-library, $275.

PITTSBURGH Business Directory. (By Isaac Harris.) Pittsburgh, 1837. $27.50.

PILCHER, Joshua. *Report on the Fur Trade and Inland Trade to Mexico.* Washington, 1832. 1st ed. $50.

PLAIN Facts: Being an Examination into the Rights of the Indian Nations, etc. Philadelphia, 1781. (By Samuel Wharton.) $250. Another copy, $175.

PLEASANTS, J. Hall and Howard Sill. *Maryland Silversmiths, 1715-1830.* Half clothbound. Baltimore, 1930. One of 300. $100-$150. Auction prices: $84 and $45 (worn).

PLIMPTON, F. B. *The Lost Child.* (Cover title.) 79 pp., paperbound. Cleveland, 1852. 1st ed. $150.

POCAHONTAS. By a Citizen of the West. New York, 1837. (By Robert Dale Owen.) $35.

POE, Edgar Allan. *The Conchologist's First Book.* Boards. Philadelphia, 1839. 1st ed., 1st state, with colored snail plates. $50-$75. Worn, $25.

POE, Edgar Allan. *Eureka: A Prose Poem.* Black clothbound. New York, 1848. 1st ed. $75-$150. Also, $77 (1958 auction). Rebound in modern leather, $50 (1958 auction) and $35 (1959 auction).

POE, Edgar Allan. *The Prose Romances of:* . . . Uniform Serial Edition . . . No. 1. Containing The Murders in the Rue Morgue and The Man That Was Used Up. 40 pp., brown paperbound. Philadelphia, 1843. 1st ed. $25,000.

POE, Edgar Allan. *The Raven and Other Poems.* Paperbound. New York, 1845. 1st ed., 1st issue, with "T. B. Smith, Stereotyper" on copyright page. $500 and up. $500 (1961 auction— Jean Hersholt's copy). Rebound in leather, $100 and $150. Another, lacking back paper cover, most of spine gone, $425 (1963 auction).

POE, Edgar Allan. *Tales.* Buff paperbound. New York, 1845. 1st ed., 1st state, with T. B. Smith and H. Ludwig slugs on copyright page, 12 pp. of ads at back. $3,300. Rebound in leather, $120 (1961 auction). Later state, without Smith and Ludwig lines, rebound in cloth, $120 (1963 auction) and $100 (1959 auction).

POE, Edgar Allan. *Tales of the Grotesque and Arabesque.* 2 vols., purplish clothbound, paper labels. Philadelphia, 1840. 1st ed., 1st issue, with page 213 wrongly numbered. $500 and up. 2d issue, page 213 correctly numbered, $500. Another, label off Vol. I, $337.50. Another, rebound in modern leather, $110 (1958 auction).

POLLARD, Edward A. *Observations in the North.* 142 pp., paperbound. Richmond, 1865. 1st ed. $35-$50.

POLLAND, H. B. C. and Phyllis Barclay-Smith. *British and American Game-Birds.* Clothbound. New York, 1939. 1st ed. One of 125, signed by Philip Rickman, artist. $50-$100. (The auction records for this show an extraordinary range — $8.40 to $80.)

POOR Sarah. 18 pp., sewed. No place, 1843. $45.

POORE, Ben Perley. *A Descriptive Catalogue of the Government Publications of the United States.* Clothbound. Washington, 1885. $35-$50. Rubbed, hinges weakened, $32.50. Disbound, $22 (at auction). New York, 1962. 2 vols., clothbound. $75.

POPLICOLA (pseudonym—signed at end). *Monroe's Embassy, or the Conduct of the Government, in Relation to Our Claims to the Navigation of the Mississippi* (sic). 57 pp., paperbound. Philadelphia, 1803. (By Charles Brockden Brown.)

PORTALIS, Baron Roger (editor). *Researches Concerning Jean Grolier, His Life and His Library.* New York, 1907. One of 300, boxed. $25.

PORTER, Edwin H. *The Fall River Tragedy.* Plates. Clothbound. Fall River, 1893. 1st ed. $25.

PORTER, Eleanor H. *Pollyanna.* Clothbound. Boston, 1913. 1st ed. $50-$75. Also, $32 (1960 auction). Other copies, less fine, $25 and $27.50.

POSEY, Alex. *The Poems of.* Topeka, 1910. 1st ed. $35.

POSTON, C. D. *Apache Land.* Clothbound. San Francisco, 1878. 1st ed. $125 and $75. Others, at auction, $55 and $65.

POTOMAK Almanac, or, The Washington Ephemeris, for . . . 1793. George-Town (Potomak), no date (1792). $125.

POTTER, Theodore Edgar. *Autobiography.* 3 portraits. No place, no date (Concord, N. H., 1913). 1st ed.

POWELL, Willis J. *Tachyhippodamia, or, Art of Quieting Wild*

Horses in a Few Hours, etc. New Orleans, 1838. 1st ed. $40.

PRAIRIEDOM: Rambles and Scrambles in Texas. . . By A. Suthron. Map. New York, 1845. (By Frederick Benjamin Page.) 1st ed. $100-$150. $70 (1959 auction). New York, 1846. 2d ed. Leatherbound. Badly worn, $30 (1965 auction).

PRATT, Parley P. *Late Persecution of the Church of Jesus Christ, of Latter Day Saints.* Clothbound. New York, 1840. 3d ed. (of Pratt's *History of the Late Persecution*). $75. Also, $56 (1958 auction).

PRECAUTION: A Novel. 2 vols., boards or leatherbound. New York, 1820. (By James Fenimore Cooper.) 1st ed. $175 and up. Rebound in half calf, $60 (1959 auction).

PRESCOTT, George B. *The Speaking Telephone.* Clothbound. New York, 1878. 1st ed. $25.

PRESENT Political State of the Province of Massachusetts-Bay in General, and the Town of Boston, in Particular (The). By a Native of New-England. 86 pp., paperbound. New York, 1775. 2d ed. (of *Massachusettensis*). (By Daniel Leonard.) $100-$150. Soiled, $98. Another issue, same date, with added title leaf, *The Origin of the American Contest with Great Britain.* Rebound in new half calf, $45 (1959 auction). Another, disbound, $47.60 (1961 auction). Another, modern cloth, $200 (1967 auction).

PRINCE, Thomas. *A Chronological History of New-England.* Boards or leatherbound. Boston, 1736. Vol. 1 (all published as bound volume) and three 32-page pamphlets published undated (1755) as *Annals of New England*, Vol. 2 of the *Chronological History.* 1st eds. The complete set, $500. Vol. 1 alone. $50-$100. Worn copies, $25-$50. Rebound in modern leather, $35 (1959 auction). Lacking title leaf, $21 (at auction). Complete ed.: Boston, 1826. 2 vols. in one. Leatherbound or boards. $35-$50.

PRINCE, Thomas. *The Vade Mecum for America.* Boston 1732. 2d ed. $27.50.

PRINCIPLES, History, and Use of Air-Balloons, etc. (The). 48 pp., paperbound. New York, 1796. (By Jean Pierre Blanchard.) $250.

PRIVATE Journal of Aaron Burr (The). Portraits. 2 vols., half clothbound. Rochester, 1903. One of 250. $100. Another, worn, $65. Another, hinges cracked, corners rubbed, $50.

PROCEEDINGS of the Board of Mayor and Aldermen of the City of Memphis, Tenn., etc. 2 maps. 22 pp., sewed. Memphis, 1842. $25.

PROCEEDINGS of Congress, in 1796, on the Admission of Tennessee as a State, into the Union, etc. 15 pp., sewed. Detroit, 1835. $27.50.

PROCEEDINGS of the Friends of a Railroad to San Francisco, etc. 24 pp., pamphlet. Boston, 1849. $50.

PROCEEDINGS of a Meeting, and Report of a Committee of Citizens in Relation to Steamboat Disasters in the Western Lakes. 22 pp., sewed. Cleveland, 1850. $35.

PROCEEDINGS of the Republican National Convention, Held at Chicago, May 16, 17, and 18, 1860. 153 pp., paperbound. Albany, 1860. Rebound in sheepskin, $200. Another issue, Chicago, 1860. 44 pp., sewed. $37.50.

PROCEEDINGS of the St. Louis Chamber of Commerce, in Relation to the Improvement of the Navigation of the Mississippi River, etc. 40 pp., sewed. St. Louis, 1842. $40.

PROCEEDINGS of Sundry Citizens of Baltimore, Convened for the Purpose of Devising the Most Efficient Means of Improving the Intercourse Between That City and the Western States. 38 pp. Baltimore, 1827. $25 and $37.50.

PROPERT, W. A. *The Russian Ballet in Western Europe, 1909-1920.* New York and London, 1921. One of 150 for America. $45.

PROSPECTUS of Hope Gold Company. (Gold dirt lode in Gilpin County, Colorado.) 25 pp., paperbound. New York, 1864. $30.

PROSSER, R. P. (compiler). *Choice Selections of Prose and Poetry.* Cincinnati, 1857. 1st ed., with gray unprinted paper covers. $85.

PRYOR, Abraham. *Interesting Description of British America, etc.* Paperbound. Providence, 1819. $35.

PSALMS, Hymns, and Spiritual Songs, of the Old and New Testament (The). Leatherbound. Boston, 1729. 22d ed. of Bay Psalm Book. $35. Boston, 1758. (Edited by Thomas Prince.) Calfbound. $350.

PSALMS of David, etc. (The), also, The Catechism. Translated by Francis Hopkinson. New York, 1767. 1st ed., for the Reformed Protestant Dutch Church. $290 (1960 auction). Philadelphia, 1783. Printed by Aitken. Calfbound. $275. New York, 1789. $50. New York, 1937. Golden Cross Press. One of 12 illuminated by Valenti Angelo, in morocco-edged case. $75.

PUNKIN, Jonathan (pseudonym). *Downfall of Freemasonry, etc.* No place (Harrisburg), 1838. 1st ed. $100. Another, $65.

PURVIANCE, Levi. *The Biography of David Purviance.* Dayton, 1848. 1st ed. $35.

PYLE, Howard. *The Merry Adventures of Robin Hood.* Full leatherbound. New York, 1883. 1st ed. $50-$75. Worn and rubbed, $35-$50.

PYLE, Howard. *Pepper and Salt.* Clothbound. New York, 1886. 1st ed. $35.

RAFINESQUE, C. S. *Circular Address on Botany and Zoology.* 36 pp., sewed. Philadelphia, 1816. $45.

RAINES, C. W. *A Bibliography of Texas.* Clothbound. Austin, 1896. 1st ed. $35 to $50. Austin, 1934. Clothbound. $30.

RALPH, Julian. *On Canada's Frontier.* Clothbound. New York, 1892. 1st ed. $35. Another, $25.

RAMIREZ, D. Jose F. *Memorias, Negociationes y Documentos, etc.* Mexico City, 1853. $25.

RAMSAY, David. *The History of South Carolina.* 2 vols., half leatherbound. Charleston, 1809. 1st ed. $75-$100. Worn, $50. Another, $60.

RAMSDELL, Charles W. *Reconstruction in Texas.* 324 pp., paperbound. New York, 1910. 1st ed. $47.50. Another, $35.

RAMSEY, J. G. M. *The Annals of Tennessee.* Map. Charleston, 1853. 1st ed. $70. Philadelphia, 1853. 2d ed. Clothbound. Spine chipped, $45. Philadelphia, 1860. Dampstained, $35. Chattanooga, 1926. $40.

RANCK, George W. *History of Lexington, Kentucky.* Plates. Clothbound. Cincinnati, 1872. 1st ed. $35-$50.

RANDALL, Thomas E. *History of the Chippewa Valley.* Clothbound. Eau Claire, Wis., 1875. 1st ed. $35-$50.

RANDOLL, Gen. A. M. *Last Days of the Rebellion.* Sewed. San Francisco, 1883. $35.

RANKIN, M. Wilson. *Reminiscences of Frontier Days.* Denver, no date (1938). 1st ed. $35-$50.

RAREY, J. S. *The Modern Art of Taming Wild Horses.* Paperbound. Columbus, 1856. 1st ed. $250-$500. Rebound in boards, $325. Austin, 1856. 3d ed., revised and corrected. 62 pp., paperbound. Lacking front cover, $35.

READ, John K. *The New Ahiman Rezon.* Richmond, Va., 1791. 1st ed. $75.

READE, Charles. *The Cloister and the Hearth.* Clothbound. New York, 1861. 1st Am. ed. $25.

READING Made Easy, In Some Scripture Instructions For Children by Way Of Question and Answer, etc. Philadelphia, 1765. Spine chipped and last two (?) leaves missing, $25.

REDEEMED Captive (The). 40 pp. Boston, 1748. (By John Norton.) 1st ed., 1st issue, with word "taking" misspelled "taken" on title page. $800. 2d issue, "taking" correctly spelled, $500. (See WILLIAMS, John, for a similar title.)

REDMOND, Pat H. *History of Quincy [Ill.] and its Men of Mark.* Clothbound. Quincy, 1869. $25.

REDPATH, James and Richard J. Hinton. *Hand-book to Kansas Territory and the Rocky Mountains Gold Region.* 2 large folding maps in color. Clothbound. New York, 1859. 1st ed. $100-$150. Worn, mended, $75.

REED, S. G. *A History of the Texas Railroads.* Clothbound. Houston, 1941. Inscribed by author, $25.

REED, Wallace P. *History of Atlanta, Georgia.* 46 portraits. Clothbound, 2 parts in one. Syracuse, 1889. 1st ed. $40-$50.

REED, William. *Life on the Border, Sixty Years Ago.* 120 pp., paperbound. Fall River, 1882. 1st ed. $25-$50.

REES, William. *The Mississippi Bridge Cities: Davenport, Rock Island and Moline.* 32 pp., sewed. Rock Island, 1854. 1st ed. Pages trimmed close, $35.

REFLECTIONS on the Cause of the Louisianians, Respectfully Submitted to Their Agents. 77 pp., boards. No place, no date (1804). $35.

REID, J. M. *Sketches and Anecdotes of the Old Settlers and New Comers, etc.* 177 pp., paperbound. Keokuk, 1876. 1st ed. $100-$150. Also, $65 (1959 auction). Another, rebound in three-quarters leather, $100.

REIGN of Reform (The). By a Lady. Baltimore, 1830. (By Mrs. Margaret Botsford.) 1st ed. $25.

REIGN of Terror in Kanzas (The). 34 pp., paperbound. Boston, 1856. (By Charles W. Briggs.) 1st ed. $450. Another, $200. Another, worn, lacking back cover, $110 (1966 auction).

REMARKABLE History of Tom Jones, a Foundling (The). 30 pp., self wrappers. Boston, 1794. Loose, $50.

REMINGTON, Frederic. *Crooked Trails.* 49 plates. Clothbound. New York, 1898. 1st ed. $150-$200. Also, $110 (1964 auction). Worn copies, $50-$100. Also, $70 (1965 auction).

REMINGTON, Frederic. *Done in the Open.* 90 pp., cream pictorial boards. New York, 1902. 1st ed., 1st issue, with Russell imprint and with "Frederick" instead of "Frederic" on front cover. $150.Another, $50. Worn, $25. Also, 250 copies bound in leather and signed, $150-$200. Another, ex-library, $50 (at auction). Later issue, 1902, Collier imprint, clothbound. $25.

REMINGTON, Frederic. *Pony Tracks.* Clothbound or leatherbound. New York, 1895. 1st ed. Clothbound, in dust jacket, $125-$150. Also, $90 (1963 auction). Lacking dust jacket, $65 (1964 auction) and $85 (1959 auction). Leatherbound, $125-$150. Also, $60 (1960 auction).

REMINGTON, Frederic. *Drawings.* 61 plates. Oblong pictorial boards. New York, 1897. 1st ed. In original box, $100-$200. Also, $140 (1959 auction). Also, 250 copies, leatherbound. With a signed proof print. Up to $250.

REMINGTON, Frederic. *The Way of an Indian.* Clothbound. New York, 1906. 1st ed., 1st issue, February, crimson cloth, yellow lettering on spine and page 9 so numbered. $75-$100. 2d issue copies, $35-$50.

REPORT of the Board of Internal Improvements for the State of Kentucky, and Reports of the Engineers. 47 pp., sewed. No place, no date (Frankfort, 1836). $25.

REPORT of the Canal Commissioners, to the General Assembly of Ohio. 54 pp., sewed. Columbus, 1825. Uncut, $45. Another issue, 66 pp., sewed, $25.

REPORT *of the Commissioner of Public Buildings, with the Documents Accompanying the Same.* 36 pp., sewed. No place, no date (Madison, Wis., 1842). (By John Smith.) Uncut, $45.

REPORT *of the Committee to Whom Was Referred, on the 26th Ultimo, the Consideration of the Expediency of Accepting from the State of Connecticut, a Cession of Jurisdiction of the Territory West of Pennsylvania, Commonly Called the Western Reserve of Connecticut.* 31 pp., calfbound. No place (Philadelphia), 1800. $75.

REPORT *of the General Assembly Upon the Subject of the Proceedings of the Bank of the U. S., Against the Officers of State.* 37 pp., sewed. Columbus, 1820. $45.

REPORT *on the Governor's Message, Relating to the "Political Situation," "Polygamy," and "Governmental Action."* 13 pp., paperbound. Salt Lake, 1882. $35.

REPORT *Relative to the Excitements, on the Part of British Subjects, of the Indians to Commit Hostility Against the U. S., and the Late Campaign on the Wabash.* 43 pp., sewed. Washington City, 1812. Uncut, $45.

REPORT *on the Subject of a Communication between Canandaigua Lake and the Erie Canal, Made at a Meeting of the Citizens.* 23 pp., sewed. Canandaigua, 1821. Uncut, $35.

REPORT *of the Trial of Frederick P. Hill, etc.* 60 pp., paperbound. Chicago, 1864. (Allan Pinkerton, editor.) 1st ed. $75. Also, $8 (1958 auction).

REPORTS *and Resolutions of the General Assembly of the State of South Carolina.* Gathered, not sewed, but punched for stitching. Columbia, 1863. $25.

REPORTS *of Territorial Officers of the Territory of Colorado, etc.* Paperbound. Central City, 1871. $27.50.

REVERE, Joseph W. *A Tour of Duty in California.* 6 plates, folding map. Clothbound. New York, 1849. 1st ed. $90-$150. Signed, $90. Worn, $45 and $60. Another, rebound, $150.

REVIEW *of the Opinion of the Supreme Court in the Case of Cohens vs. Virginia, etc.* 78 pp., sewed. Steubenville, Ohio, 1821. (By Charles Hammond.) $35.

REYNOLDS, John. *The Pioneer History of Illinois.* Clothbound. Belleville, 1852. 1st ed. $150. Another, $100. Another, foxed and worn, $60. Rebound in calf, $50. Repaired, $50 (1964 auction).

REZANOV, Nicolai P. *The Rezanov Voyage to Nueva California in 1806.* 5 plates. Half clothbound. San Francisco, 1926. One of 200. $37.50.

RHODES, Eugene Manlove. *Say Now Shibboleth.* Clothbound. Chicago, 1921. 1st ed. One of 400. Book Fellows. $45. Another copy, $30.

RICHARDS, Laura E. *Captain January.* Clothbound. Boston, 1891. 1st ed., 1st issue. $25.

RICHARDSON, Richard. *The Genealogy of the Richardson Family of the State of Delaware.* No place, 1878. $27.50.

RICHARDSON, Rupert N. and C. C. Rister. *The Greater Southwest.* Clothbound. Glendale, 1934. 1st ed. $25.

RICHARDSON, William H. *Journal of.* 84 pp., paperbound. Baltimore, 1847. 1st ed. $3,300 (1966 auction). Also, $450 (1959 auction). New York, 1848. 3d ed. $25.

RIDINGS, Sam P. *The Chisholm Trail.* Folding map. Clothbound. Guthrie, Okla., no date (1936). 1st ed. In dust jacket, $35-$50. Another copy, $40. Another, $37, (1960 auction).

RILEY, James Whitcomb. *Poems Here at Home.* Clothbound or vellum binding. New York, 1893. 1st ed., 1st state, with "girls" spelled correctly in line 5, page 50. In dust jacket, $35. Later, $20-$25.

RILEY, James Whitcomb. *Rhymes of Childhood.* Clothbound. Indianapolis, 1891. 1st ed., 1st state, with child's head illustrated on front cover. $37.50.

RIORDAN, Joseph W. *The First Half Century of St. Ignatius Church and College.* San Francisco, 1905. $25.

ROBBINS, Aurelia. *A True and Authentic Account of the Indian War, etc.* 28 pp., paperbound. New York, 1836. $150.

ROBERTS, Oran M. *A Description of Texas.* 8 colored plates, 5 double-page maps. Clothbound. St. Louis, 1881. 1st ed. $100.

ROBERTSON, Wyndham, Jr. *Oregon, Our Right and Title.* Folding map. Paperbound. Washington, 1846. 1st ed. $350-

$500. $300 (1959 auction). Presentation copy, inscribed, $275 (1963 auction).

ROBIDOUX, Mrs. Orral M. *Memorial to the Robidoux Brothers.* Clothbound. Kansas City, Mo., 1924. 1st ed. $50-$75. Worn, $45 (1964 auction).

ROBIN, L'Abbe. *New Travels Through North America.* Translated by Philip Freneau. Philadelphia, 1783. 1st Am. ed. in English. $40. Also, in French: *Nouveau Voyage dans l'Amerique Septentrionale.* Half leatherbound. Philadelphia, 1782. 1st Am. ed. $50. Also, $25 (at auction).

ROBINSON, Edwin Arlington. *Captain Craig.* Clothbound. Boston, 1902. 1st trade ed. $75. Also issued in cloth, paper label, limited to 125 copies. $100 and up.

ROBINSON, Edwin Arlington. *The Children of the Night.* Boards. Boston, 1897. 1st ed. One of 50 on Japan vellum.$250. One of 500 on Batchworth laid paper. In dust jacket and signed, $675 (1963 auction). Another, cloth binding, $35-$50; soiled, $30. Another, $25.

ROBINSON, Edwin Arlington. *The Torrent and the Night Before.* Blue paperbound. Gardiner, Me., 1896. 1st ed. $150-$300. Rebound in leather, $125 (1959 auction). New York, 1928. One of 110. $25.

ROBINSON, Edwin Arlington. *The Town Down the River.* New York, 1910. 1st ed. In dust jacket, $35-$50. Also, $25 (1963 auction). Lacking jacket, $25.

ROBINSON, Edwin Arlington. *Tristram.* Boards and cloth. New York, 1927. 1st ed., 1st state, with "rocks" for "rooks" in line 2, page 86. One of 350 large paper copies, signed, boxed. $35-$50. Another, $30. 1st trade ed. Clothbound. $10. In dust jacket, $15-$20.

ROBINSON, Jacob S. *Sketches of the Great West.* 71 pp., paperbound. Portsmouth, N. H., 1848. 1st ed. Rebound in boards, original front cover bound in, $3,400 (1966 auction).

ROBINSON, John and George F. Dow. *The Sailing Ships of New England, 1607-1907.* 3 vols., clothbound. Series I, II, and III. Salem, 1922-1924-1928. $75, $100, and $150. Separately: Series I, 1922, and Series II, 1924, each $47.50 in 1966-67 catalogue.

ROBINSON, Rowland E. *Uncle 'Lisha's Shop.* New York, 1887. 1st ed. $30.

ROBINSON, William Davis. *Memoirs of the Mexican Revolution.* Half leatherbound. Philadelphia, 1820. $50-$60. Worn copies, $32.50 and $25.

ROCK, Marion T. *Illustrated History of Oklahoma.* 90 plates. Clothbound. Topeka, 1890. 1st ed. $60. Another, $35.

ROE, Edward Payson. *Barriers Burned Away.* Clothbound. New York, 1872. 1st ed. $40.

ROFF, Joe T. *A Brief History of Early Days in North Texas and the Indian Territory.* No place (Allen, Okla.), 1930. $35.

ROGERS, Robert. *Journals of Maj. Robert Rogers.* Map. Albany, 1883. $60.

ROOSEVELT, Franklin D. *The Happy Warrior: Alfred E. Smith.* 40 pp., black clothbound, orange label. Boston, 1928. 1st ed. In dust jacket, $35. Lacking jacket, $25.

ROOSEVELT, Franklin D. *Whither Bound?* Clothbound. Boston, 1926. 1st ed. In dust jacket, $25. Also, $9 (at auction).

ROOSEVELT, Theodore. *Hunting Trips of a Ranchman.* 20 plates. Buckram. New York, 1885. 1st ed., limited Medora ed. of 500. $35-$50. Worn, $25. New York, 1886. 1st trade ed. Clothbound. $35.

ROOSEVELT, Theodore. *Ranch Life and the Hunting Trail.* New York, no date (1888). 1st ed., 1st issue, light tan buckram, stamped green and gold. $75. Another, $50. Another, name on flyleaf, $27.50. Later binding, $25.

ROOSEVELT, Theodore. *The Value of an Athletic Training.* Paperbound. New York, 1929. 1st ed. One of 51. $25.

ROOT, Frank A. and William E. Connelley. *The Overland Stage to California.* Map. Clothbound. Topeka, 1901. 1st ed. $60-$100. $60 (1964 auction). $65 (1966 auction).

ROSE, Mrs. S. E. F. *The Ku Klux Klan.* 8 pp., paperbound. West Point, Miss., 1909. $35.

ROSEN, Peter. *Pa-Ha-Sa-Pah, or The Black Hills of South Dakota.* 27 plates. Clothbound. St. Louis, 1895. 1st ed. $50-$75. Also, $50 (1966 auction). Worn, $35 (1959 auction).

ROSENBACH, A. S. W. *Early American Children's Books.* Portland, Me., 1933. One of 88 on Zerkall Halle paper, signed, bound in morocco. $150-$200. $112 (1960 auction). Another issue, one of 585, bound in boards. $100-$150. $77 (1963 auction) and $85 (1964 auction).

ROSS, Rev. Mr. *The American Latin Grammar.* Newburyport, no date (1780). Title page stained, $25.

ROTHERT, Otto A. *A History of Muhlenburg County.* Clothbound. Louisville, 1913. 1st ed. $35-$50.

ROTHERT, Otto A. *The Outlaws of Cave-in-Rock.* 10 maps and plans. Clothbound. Cleveland, 1924. 1st ed. $40-$50. Other copies at $27.50, $30, and $35.

ROUQUETTE, Abbe Adrien. *La Nouvelle Atala ou La Fille de L'Esprit Legende Indienne Par Chahta-Ima.* Paperbound. Nouvelle-Orleans, 1879. $27.50.

RUDO Ensayo, Tentativa de Una Prevencional Descripcion Geographica de la Provincia de Sonora. Edited by Buckingham Smith. San Augustin (St. Augustine—printed in Albany), 1863. 1st ed. $150 (1966 auction). Also, one of 10 on large paper. $250.

RUGGLES, Thomas. *The Usefulness and Expedience of Souldiers As Discovered by Reason and Experience, etc.* 26 pp., sewed. New London, Conn., 1737. $75.

RULES for Regulating the Practice of the District Court of the U. S., etc. 31 pp., sewed. Pittsburgh, 1824. $32.50.

RUPP, I. Daniel. *History of the Counties of Berks and Lebanon.* 3 plates. Leatherbound. Lancaster, Pa., 1844. 1st ed. $35-$50.

RUSH, Benjamin. *Considerations Upon the Present Test-Law of Pennsylvania.* Philadelphia, 1784. $50.

RUSK, Fern H. *George Caleb Bingham.* Jefferson City, Mo., 1917. Limited ed. $35.

RUSSELL, Alex J. *The Red River Country, Hudson's Bay and North-west Territories, etc.* Paperbound. Folding map. Ottawa, 1869. 1st ed. $35. Another, covers torn, $25.

RUSSELL, Charles M. *Back-trailing on the Old Frontiers.* 56 pp., paperbound. Great Falls, 1922. 1st ed. $75-$100. Also, $60 (1960 auction).

RUSSELL, Charles M. *More Rawhides.* 60 pp., paperbound. Great Falls, 1925. 1st ed. $75-$150. Also, $80 (1960 auction) and $17 (1964 auction). Another, edges of covers frayed, $125.

RUSSELL, Osborne. *Journal of a Trapper.* 105 pp. No place, no date (Boise, 1914). 1st ed. $150. Boise, no date (1921). 2d ed. 149 pp., clothbound. $35 and $25. Portland, no date. Champoeg Press. One of 750. $25.

RUTH Whalley; or, The Fair Puritan. (Cover title.) 72 pp., pink paperbound. Boston, 1845. (By Henry William Herbert.) $50. (In some copies the author is listed as "William Henry Herbert." There is also said to be an 1844 edition.)

SACRED Writings of the Apostles and Evangelists of Jesus Christ, etc. Buffaloe, Brooke County, Va., 1826. 1st ed. $27.50.

SAGRA, Ramon de la. *Historia Economico-Politica y Estadistica de la Isla de Cuba.* Havana, 1831. 1st ed. $25.

ST. CLAIR, Maj. Gen. (Arthur). *A Narrative of the Manner in Which the Campaign Against the Indians, in the Year 1791, Was Conducted.* Half calfbound. Philadelphia, 1812. 1st ed. $50-$60.

ST. JOHN, John R. *A True Description of the Lake Superior Country.* 2 maps. Clothbound. New York 1846. 1st ed. $75-$100.

ST. LOUIS, Iron Mountain & Southern Railway Company vs. W. J. Newcom and J. F. Hudson. Brief for Plaintiff. 54 pp., paperbound. Little Rock, 1893. $25.

SAISSY, J. A. *An Essay on the Diseases of the Internal Ear.* Leatherbound. Baltimore, 1829. 1st Am. ed. $25.

SALE, Edith Tunis. *Manors of Virginia in Colonial Times.* 49 plates. Clothbound. Philadelphia, 1909. $35 and $25.

SALISBURY, Samuel. *A Descriptive, Historical, Chemical and Therapeutical Analysis of the Avon Sulphur Springs, Livingston County.* 95 pp., sewed. Rochester, 1845. $35.

SALLEY, Alexander S., Jr. *The History of Orangeburg County.* Folding map, portrait. Orangeburg, S. C., 1898. 1st ed. $35-$50.

SALT Lake City Directory and Business Guide (The). Folding map, folding view. 53-219 pp., as issued, boards. Salt Lake

City, 1869. (By Edward L. Sloan.) $75. Another copy, crudely repaired, $20 (1964 auction).

SALT Lake City: Gazetteer and Directory. (Edited by Edward L. Sloan.) Salt Lake City, 1874. $35.

SALZMANN, C. G. *Gymnastics for Youth.* Leatherbound. Philadelphia, 1802. Hinges weak, $25.

SANDBURG, Carl. *Abraham Lincoln: The War Years.* 4 vols., blue clothbound. New York, no date (1939-1941). 1st ed. One of 525 sets on all rag paper, numbered and signed. $150-$200. Auction prices: $130 (1960), $100 (1964), $110 (1961). 1st trade ed., clothbound. $25-$35. Inscribed, $50.

SANDBURG, Carl. *Steichen, the Photographer.* Clothbound. New York, no date (1929). 1st ed. One of 925, signed by author and artist. $100. Auction prices: $55 (1957) and $42 (1956).

SANDBURG, Charles A. *In Reckless Ecstasy.* Paperbound. Galesburg, 1904. (By Carl Sandburg.) 1st ed. $1,000.

SANFORD, Mrs. Nettie. *History of Marshall County, Iowa.* 5 plates. Clothbound. Clinton, 1867. $45 (1966 auction).

SARGENT, George B. *Notes on Iowa.* Map. 74 pp. New York, 1848. $150.

SAUNDERS, James E. *Early Settlers of Alabama.* Part I (all published). New Orleans, 1899. 1st ed. $35-$50. Another, $27.50.

SAUNDERS, Richard. *Poor Richard's Almanac Improved.* 36 pp. Philadelphia, no date (1757). (By Benjamin Franklin.) $1,100 (1967 auction).

SAXON, Lyle. *Lafitte the Pirate.* Clothbound. New York, no date (1930). 1st ed. Signed by author and artist, $30.

SCAMMON, Charles M. *The Marine Mammals of the North-Western Coast of North America, etc.* 27 plates. Clothbound. San Francisco, 1874. 1st ed. $500. Another, presentation copy signed by the author, $130 (1959 auction).

SCENES in the Rocky Mountains. By a New Englander. Folding map, 109 plates. Clothbound. Philadelphia, 1846. (By Rufus B. Sage.) 1st ed. $650. Another, $575. Another, $500. Also, $375 (1964 auction). Others: map repaired, $350 (1963 auction); rebound in calf and with map repaired, $350 (1964 auction);

rebound in modern calf, $250 (1959 auction).

SCHARF, John Thomas. *History of the Confederate States Navy.* 42 plates. Clothbound. New York, 1887. 1st ed. $32.50. Worn, $17.50.

SCHARF, John Thomas. *History of Western Maryland.* Map, 109 plates, table. 2 vols., clothbound. Philadelphia, 1882. 1st ed. $35-$50.

SCHATZ, A. H. *Opening a Cow Country.* Ann Arbor, 1939. $30.

SCHMIDT, G. *The Civil Law of Spain and Mexico.* New Orleans, 1851. $75.

SCHOOLCRAFT, Henry R. *An Address Delivered Before the Was-ah Ho-de-no — son-ne, or New Confederacy of the Iroquois.* 48 pp., sewed. Rochester, 1846. $45.

SCHOOLCRAFT, Henry R. *A Discourse Delivered on the Anniversary of the Historical Society of Michigan.* 44 pp., paperbound. Detroit, 1830. 1st ed. $75.

SCHOOLCRAFT, Henry R. *Historical and Statistical Information Respecting the . . . Indian Tribes, etc.* Numerous maps, plates, and tables. 6 vols., clothbound. Philadelphia, 1851-57. 1st eds. $350-$500.

SCHOOLCRAFT, Henry R. *Narrative Journal of Travels Through the Northwestern Regions of the U. S., etc.* Engraved title page, folding map, 7 plates. Half calfbound. Albany, 1821. 1st ed., with errata slip. $100 and $75. Rebound, $35.

SCHOOLCRAFT, Henry R. *A View of the Lead Mines of Missouri.* 3 plates. Half leatherbound. New York, 1819. $35-$50. Repaired, $25 and $20. Scuffed copy, $40.

SCHULTZ, Christian. *Travels on an Inland Voyage, etc.* Portrait, 2 plates, 4 (sometimes 5) maps. 2 vols., leatherbound. New York, 1810. 1st ed. $100-$150. Rebound in buckram, $37.50.

SCHWAB, John Christopher. *The Confederate States of America, 1861-1865.* New York, 1901. $30.

SCOTT, James L. *A Journal of a Missionary Tour Through Pennsylvania.* Clothbound. Providence, 1843. 1st ed. $125. Worn, $75. Rebound in modern cloth, $25 (1966 auction).

SEAVER, James E. *A Narrative of the Life of Mrs. Mary Jemi-*

son, *Who Was Taken by the Indians in the Year 1755, etc.*
Boards. Canandaigua, N. Y., 1824. 1st ed. $325 (1967 auction).
Earlier, $200-$300 at retail; worn copies at lower prices.

SELBY, Julian A. *Memorabilia and Anecdotal Reminiscences
of Columbia, S. C.* Columbia, 1905. $35.

SELECT Collection of Valuable and Curious Arts, etc. (A). Concord, 1826. (By Rufus Porter.) 1st ed. $50.

SETON, Ernest Thompson. *Boy Scouts of America: A Hand-
book of Woodcraft, Scouting, and Life-craft.* Paperbound.
New York, 1910. 1st ed., "probable earlier state," with printer's slug on copyright page. $50.

SETON, Ernest Thompson. *Wild Animals I Have Known.* Clothbound. New York, 1898. 1st ed., 1st issue, without the words
"The Angel whispered don't go" in the last paragraph on
page 265. $30 and $35.

*SEVEN Little Sisters Who Live on the Round Ball That Floats
in the Air (The).* Clothbound. Boston, 1861. (By Jane Andrews.)
1st ed. $50. Another, worn, $25.

SEWALL, Rufus King. *Sketches of St. Augustine.* 6 plates. 69
pp., clothbound. New York, 1848. 1st ed. Pages 39 and 40
removed, as with most copies. $27.50. Another, $17.50.

SEWARD, W. H. *Communication Upon the Subject of an Inter-
continental Telegraph, etc.* 52 pp., paperbound. Washington,
1864. $25.

SEXTON, Lucy Ann (Foster). *The Foster Family, California
Pioneers.* No place, no date (Santa Barbara, 1925). 1st ed. $85.

SEYMOUR, E. S. *Emigrant's Guide to the Gold Mines of Upper
California.* Folding map. 104 pp., paperbound. Chicago, 1849.
1st ed. $1,000 and, probably, much higher. There are only
two known copies.

SEYMOUR, E. S. *Sketches of Minnesota, the New England of
the West.* 281 pp., paperbound. New York, 1850. 1st ed.
$27.50. Another copy, $25.

SHAKESPEARE, William. *A Midsommer Nights Dreame.* Illustrations by Mary Grabhorn. Vellum binding. San Francisco,
1955. One of 180, boxed. $100. Also, $55 (1964 auction).

SHAKESPEARE, William. *The Poems of.* Stamford, 1939. One

of 150, with initial letters designed by Bruce Rogers, boxed. $100-$150.

SHAKESPEARE, William. *The Tempest.* Boards, cloth spine. San Francisco, 1951. One of 160. $75. Another, $50.

SHAKESPEARE, William. *The Tragedie of Macbeth.* Illustrations by Mary Grabhorn. Boards, leather spine. No place, no date (San Francisco, 1952). One of 180, boxed. $100. Also, $45 (1964 auction).

SHAKESPEARE, William. *The Tragedie of Othello.* With portraits by Mary Grabhorn. Boards, leather spine. San Francisco, 1956. One of 185. $75-$100.

SHAKESPEARE, William. *The Tragedy of Richard the Third.* Woodblocks by Mary Grabhorn. Vellum binding. No place (San Francisco), 1953. One of 180, boxed. $75-$100.

SHAKESPEARE, William. *Venus and Adonis.* Rochester, 1931. Illustrated by Rockwell Kent. One of 75 (of an edition of 1,250), signed by Kent, with 21 illustrations, mounted and boxed, issued with each of the 75 copies. $100-$125. Regular issue, without the boxed plates, $12.50 to $35.

SHALLY, Louis H. *The Book of Prices of the House Carpenters and Joiners of the City of Cincinnati.* Cincinnati, 1844. 1st ed. $35 and $25.

SHATTUCK, Lemuel. *A History of the Town of Concord.* Folding map. Boston, 1835. 1st ed. $35-$50.

SHAW, Joshua. *United States Directory for the Use of Travellers and Merchants, etc.* Leatherbound. Philadelphia, no date (1822). 1st ed. $100-$150. Also, $90 (1965 auction).

SHAW, R. C. *Across the Plains in Forty-nine.* Portrait. Clothbound. Farmland, Ind., 1896. 1st ed. $50-$75. Signed copy, $55 (1964 auction). Worn copies, $35.

SHEA, John G. *Early Voyages Up and Down the Mississippi, etc.* Albany, 1861. 1st ed., large paper. $45.

SHEPARD, A. K. *The Land of the Aztecs.* Clothbound. Albany, 1859. 1st ed. $40.

SHERWOOD, Mary Martha. *The History of Henry Milner, a Little Boy.* Leatherbound. Princeton, 1827. $30. Also, $17 (at auction).

SHINN, Charles Howard. *Mining Camps.* Clothbound. New York, 1885. 1st ed. $125. Another, $100. Another, $62.50. Also, $60 (1960 auction).

SHOBER, G. A. *A Choice Drop of Honey from the Rock Christ, or a Short Word of Advice to All Saints and Sinners.* 30 pp., paperbound. New Market, Va., 1811. $35.

SHORT History of Gen. R. E. Lee (A). 15 pp., paperbound, miniature. New York, 1888. $25.

SHORT History of T. J. Jackson (A). 15 pp., paperbound, miniature. New York, 1888. $25.

SIDNEY, Margaret. *Five Little Peppers and How They Grew.* Clothbound. Boston, no date (1880). (By Harriet M. Lothrop.) 1st ed., 1st state, with 1880 copyright and with caption on page 231 reading "said Polly." $75-$100. Also, $50 (1960 auction). Worn, $25.

SIEBERT, Wilbur Henry. *Loyalists in East Florida.* 6 maps and plates. 2 vols., clothbound. DeLand, 1929. 1st ed. $100. Worn, $45, $30, $27.50.

SIMMONS, Amelia. *American Cookery.* 47 pp., paperbound. Hartford, 1796. 1st ed. $200 (last known price, in 1948). Only two or three copies are known to exist.

SIMMS, J. R. *The American Spy, or Freedom's Early Sacrifice.* 63 pp., paperbound. Albany, 1846. 1st ed. $50. Another, worn, $28.50.

SIMON, Barbara Allan. *A Series of Allegorical Designs, Representing the Human Heart from Its Natural to Its Regenerated State.* New York, 1825. 1st ed. Rebacked, $50.

SIMPSON, George. *Journal of Occurrences in the Athabasca Department, etc.* Edited by E. E. Rich. Clothbound. Toronto, 1938. One of 550. $35-$50. Worn, $25.

SINCLAIR, Upton. *A Home Colony. A Prospectus.* 23 pp., paperbound. New York, no date (1906). 1st ed. $50.

SINCLAIR, Upton. *The Jungle.* Green clothbound. New York, 1906. 1st ed., 1st issue, Doubleday imprint and with the "1" in date on copyright page in perfect type. $85-$100. Worn, $25 and up. Later issue, 1906, Jungle Publishing Co., $25.

SINGLETON, Arthur. *Letters from the South and West.* Boards. Boston, 1824. (By Henry Cogswell Knight.) 1st ed. Spine chipped, title page repaired. $150.

SIRINGO, Charles A. *A Texas Cowboy.* Portrait. Black clothbound. Chicago, 1885. 1st ed. $100-$125. Another, $65. New York, no date (1886), paperbound, covers chipped, $35. Chicago, 1886. 2d ed., Siringo & Dobson, 8 plates, 347 pp., $35-$50. Another, $27.50. Chicago, 1886. 3d ed. Rand McNally, same collation. $50 (1960 auction). Another, $35 (in catalogue).

SIX to One; A Nantucket Idyl. Tan or gray clothbound or blue paperbound. New York, 1878. (By Edward Bellamy.) 1st ed. Clothbound, $75. Worn, stained, flyleaf gone, $50. The paperbound issue presumably is worth much more.

SKETCH of the History of South Carolina, etc (A). Clothbound. Charleston, 1856. (By William James Rivers.) 1st ed. $50-$75. Worn, $35.

SKETCH of the Seminole War, and Sketches During the Campaign. Leatherbound. Charleston, 1836. 1st ed. $100-$150. Another, $75.

SKETCHES by a Traveller. Boston, 1830. (By Silas P. Holbrook.) 1st ed. Worn, $32.50.

SKETCHES, Historical and Descriptive of Louisiana. Boards, half leather. Philadelphia, 1812. (By Amos Stoddard.) 1st ed. Worn, $100.

SKETCHES of History, Life and Manners in the United States. By a Traveller. New-Haven, 1826. (By Anne Royall.) 1st ed. $50-$100. Another, spine chipped, $27.50.

SLAUGHTER, Mrs. Linda W. *The New Northwest.* 24 pp., paperbound. Bismarck, 1874. 1st ed. $1,200 and up.

SLOAN, Robert S. *Utah Gazetteer and Directory of Logan, Ogden, Provo and Salt Lake Cities.* Clothbound. Salt Lake City, 1884. $25.

SMEDLEY, William. *Across the Plains in '62.* Map and portrait. 56 pp., boards. No place, no date (Denver, 1916). 1st ed. $75-$100. $85. Another, $40 (1959 auction).

SMITH, Alice R. H. and D. E. H. Smith. *The Dwelling Houses of Charleston.* Clothbound. Philadelphia, 1917. 1st ed. $50.

Another, hinges cracked, $42.50.

SMITH, Emma (editor). *A Collection of Sacred Hymns for the Church of the Latter Day Saints.* Kirtland, Ohio, 1835. 1st ed. $400 and up.

SMITH, F. Hopkinson. *Colonel Carter of Cartersville.* Clothbound. Boston, 1891. 1st ed., 1st issue, with no mention of this book in ads and with staircase illustration on page 1. $50. Another, spot on cover, $35. Another, worn a bit, $25. Presentation copy, signed by the author, $75.

SMITH, James. *An Account of the Remarkable Occurrences in the Life and Travels of Col. James Smith.* Folding plate, boards. Lexington, Ky., 1799. 1st ed. $10,000 (1966 auction). Philadelphia, 1831. 2d ed. Dampstained, $100. Philadelphia, 1834. $72.50. Cincinnati, 1870. Clothbound. $35. Cincinnati, 1907. Clothbound. $35.

SMITH, James F. *The Cherokee Land Lottery, etc.* New York, 1838. 1st ed. $35-$50.

SMITH, Jedidiah. *The Travels of.* Map, 12 plates. Clothbound. Santa Ana, 1934. 1st ed. $100, $75, and $60.

SMITH, Jodie (editor). *History of the Chisum War.* Clothbound. Electra, Tex., no date (1927). 1st ed. $35-$50.

SMITH, Johnston. *Maggie: A Girl of the Streets.* Yellow paperbound. No place, no date (New York, 1893). (By Stephen Crane.) 1st ed. $300-$500 (possibly much more, since no copy has appeared for sale at auction in some years). Another copy, title page and end leaf soiled, covers missing, $145.

SMITH, Joseph, Jr. *The Book of Mormon.* Calfbound. Palmyra, N. Y., 1830. 1st ed., 1st issue, with 2 pp. preface and testimonial leaf at end and without index. $400-$500. Worn, $250-$350. Also, $270 (1964 auction) and $120 (1966 auction). Another copy, stained, rubbed, label lacking, $150. Kirtland, Ohio, 1837. 2d ed. $100-$150-$200. Nauvoo, Ill., 1840, 3d ed. $100-$150. Nauvoo, 1842. 4th Am. ed. $100. Another, worn, $25. New York, 1869. In Deseret (Mormon) alphabet. $100-$150. Plano, Ill., 1874. $25.

SMITH, Joseph, Jr., and others. *Doctrine and Covenants of the Church of the Latter Day Saints.* Calfbound. Kirtland, Ohio, 1835. 1st ed. $150-$200. Also, $140 and $75 (worn). Also,

$90 (1959 auction). Rebound in modern calf, $35 (1962 auction).

SMITH, Joseph, Jr. *Te Buka A Mormona.* Translated by Frank Cutler and others. Clothbound. Salt Lake City, 1904. 1st ed. in Tahitian. $35-$50. Worn, $25.

SMITH, Kate Douglas. *The Story of Patsy. A Reminiscence.* 27 pp., paperbound. San Francisco, 1883. 2d ed. $25. (A rare Kate Douglas Wiggin story. This was listed by the noted Ohio bookseller, Ernest J. Wessen, many years ago, but we have not seen it again.)

SMITH, Michael. *A Geographical View, of the Province of Upper Canada, and Promiscuous Remarks Upon the Government, etc.* 107 pp., paperbound. Hartford, 1813. 1st ed. $100-$150. Another, ex-library copy, worn, $35 (at auction).

SMITH, Moses. *History of the Adventures and Sufferings of.* 2 plates, boards. Brooklyn, 1812. 1st ed. $60. Also, leatherbound, $22.50.

SMITH, Nathan. *A Practical Essay on Typhous Fever.* Half calfbound. New York, 1824. 1st ed. $150. Another, $42 (at auction).

SMITH, Platt. *The Dubuque Claim Case; in the Supreme Court of the United States.* 20 pp., paperbound. Dubuque, 1852. $75.

SMITH, Samuel. *The History of the Colony of Nova-Caesaria, or New Jersey.* Calfbound. Burlington, N. J., 1765. 1st ed., 1st issue, with unpunctuated Roman numerals in date. $150-$200. $120 (1967 auction). Another, rebacked, $75. Another, rebound in modern cloth, $45 (1962 auction).

SMITH, Mrs. Sarah. *A Journal Kept by Mrs. Sarah Foote Smith While Journeying with Her People from Wellington, Ohio, to Footeville, Town of Nepeuskun, Winnebago County, Wis., April 15 to May 10, 1846.* Boards, paper label. No place, no date (Kilbourn, 1905). $35-$50.

SMITH, William (Loughton). *A Comparative View of the Constitutions of the Several States with Each Other, etc.* 34 pp. on fine paper, boards. Philadelphia, 1796. 1st ed. $50-$75.

SMITH, William Rudolph. *Observations on the Wisconsin Territory.* Map. Clothbound; also in boards. Philadelphia, 1838. 1st ed. $150-$200. Also, $100 (1963 auction). Another copy, ex-library, worn, $85. Others noted at $100 and $150 in catalogues. Rebound in cloth, $50 (1966 auction).

SMITH, William Russell. *Reminiscences of a Long Life.* Vol. 1 (all published). 8 portraits. Clothbound. Washington, no date (1889). 1st ed. $50-$75. Rebacked, $32.50.

SOLDIER'S Story of the War (A). 9 plates (some copies without plates). Clothbound. New Orleans, 1874. (By Napier Bartlett.) 1st ed. With plates, $75-$100.

SOMBRERO, The. Quarter-Centennial Number. Yearbook of the Class of 1895, University of Nebraska. White and red clothbound. No place, no date (Lincoln, 1894). 1st ed. Contains Willa Cather's and Dorothy Canfield's prize story "The Fear That Walks at Noonday." $200.

SOME Account of the Work of Stephen J. Field as Legislator, etc. No place, 1895. (By Chauncey F. Black.) 2d ed. $25.

SOME Fruits of Solitude, in Reflections and Maxims, etc. New Port, R. I., 1749. (By William Penn.) (Printed by Benjamin Franklin.) 1st Am. ed. $150 and up.

SONG of Roland (The). Translated by Isabel Butler. 7 hand-colored illustrations by Bruce Rogers. No place, no date (Boston, 1906). One of 220. 1st ed. $250-$350. Also, $180 (1963 auction).

SOULE, Frank, Frank Gihon and James Nisbet. *The Annals of San Francisco.* 6 plates, 2 maps. Half leatherbound. New York, 1855. 1st ed. $75-$100. Another, $65. Another, $50 (1966 auction).

SOUTHERN Business Guide, 1881-82. Illustrated. New York, 1882. $35-$50.

SOWELL, A. J. *Rangers and Pioneers of Texas.* Clothbound. San Antonio, 1884. 1st ed. $200. Another, binding badly worn, $120 (1964 auction).

SPALDING, C. C. *Annals of the City of Kansas.* 7 plates. Clothbound. Kansas City, 1858. 1st ed. $500 and up. $400 (1959 auction). Another, lacking the plates, $100 (1957 auction).

SPANISH Occupation of California (The). (By Miguel Costanso.) Introduced by Douglas S. Watson. Boards. San Francisco, 1934. One of 550. $100. Also, $40 and $50 at auction.

SPECIFICATIONS of Steam Machinery and Building Direc-

tions of Hulls of U. S. Steamers Constructed 1861-1864. (Title on cover.) No place, no date. $25.

SPEED, Thomas. *The Wilderness Road.* Map. Clothbound. Louisville, 1886. 1st ed. $35-$50. Another, $27.50.

SPEER, Emory. *The Banks County Ku-Klux.* 60 pp., paperbound. Atlanta, 1883. 1st ed. $75.

SPENCER, O. M. *Indian Captivity: A True Narrative of the Capture of, etc.* New York, 1836. 2d ed. $35-$50.

SPORTSMAN'S Portfolio of American Field Sports (The). 20 full-page wood engravings, title page vignette, and illustration at end. Oblong paperbound. Boston, 1855. 1st ed. $200. Also, $90 (1957 auction), $112 (1961 auction), and $60 (auction price for a copy listed as "sewn," apparently lacking covers).

SPRAGUE, John T. *The Origin, Progress, and Conclusion of the Florida War.* Folding map, 8 plates. Clothbound. New York, 1848. 1st ed. $75-$100. Also, $65 (1956 auction). Other copies at retail: map torn but repaired, $45; and $20.

SPY (The); A Tale of the Neutral Ground. By the Author of "Precaution." 2 vols., paper-backed boards, paper labels. New York, 1821. (By James Fenimore Cooper.) 1st ed. $5,000 (1964 catalogue). Another copy, $7,600 (1945 auction record). (There are said to be only two copies known in original boards.) Rebound in calf, $300 (at auction).

SQUIER, E. G. and E. H. Davis. *Ancient Monuments of the Mississippi Valley.* 48 plates. Clothbound. New York, 1848. 1st ed., 2d issue. (1st issue was published in Washington in 1848.) $60. Also, $25 (1959 auction). Rebacked copy, $25 (1964 auction).

STANLEY, F. *The Grant That Maxwell Bought.* Clothbound. No place, no date (Denver, 1952). One of 250, signed. $100. Also, $50 (at auction).

STANSBURY, Philip. *A Pedestrian Tour of 2,300 Miles, in North America, etc.* 9 plates. Boards. New York, 1822. 1st ed. $50-$75.

STAPP, William P. *The Prisoners of Perote.* Clothbound and paperbound. Philadelphia, 1845. 1st ed. Paperbound, $300-$400. Another, front cover detached and damaged, $100.

Clothbound, $100 and up. Another, rebound in full calf, $170 (1966 auction).

STARBUCK, Alexander. *History of the American Whale Fishery, etc.* 6 plates. Half leatherbound. Waltham, Mass., 1878. $75. (This first appeared in Washington in 1878 as Part IV, *Report of the U. S. Commissioner of Fish and Fishing,* which is a $50 item.)

STAR City of the West (The): Pueblo and Its Advantages. 24 pp., folded. Pueblo, 1889. $45.

STARKEY, Capt. James. *Reminiscences of Indian Depredations.* 25 pp., paperbound. St. Paul, 1891. 1st ed. $125.

STATE of Indiana Delineated (The). Map (in only a few copies). Boards. New York, (Colton, publisher), 1838. 1st ed (?). $150 (1945 auction). Another copy, without the map, $25 (in a dealer's catalogue some years ago).

STATEMENT of Payments on River Property in the City of Chicago, Belonging to John S. Wright, etc. 24 pp., paperbound. Chicago, 1849. $75.

STATEMENT and Reports Concerning the Uncle Sam and Gold Canon Silver Lodes in Nevada. 2 colored maps. Paperbound. Boston, 1865. (By S. Chapin and J. Veatch.) $30.

STATISTICS of Dane County, with a Business Directory of the Village of Madison. 24 pp., paperbound. Madison, Wis., 1851. $25. Another, $14 (at auction).

STAUFFER, David McNeeley and Mantle Fielding. *American Engravers Upon Copper and Steel.* 3 vols., half clothbound. New York and Philadelphia, 1907-17. Vols. 1 and 2, limited to 350 copies (1907); Vol. 3, limited to 220, signed by Fielding (1917). The 3 vols. complete, $150-$200. Incomplete set, Vols. 1 and 2 only, $100-$125. Vol. 3 only, $50.

STEDMAN, Edmund C. *Songs and Ballads.* Morocco. New York, 1884. One of 100 on Japanese paper. In morocco slip case, $37.50.

STEEDMAN, Charles J. *Bucking the Sage Brush.* 3 portraits, map, 9 Charles M. Russell plates. Clothbound. New York, 1904. 1st ed. $50 and $37.50.

STEELE, James W. *The Klondike.* Map. 80 pp., paperbound.

Chicago, 1897. 1st ed. $35-$50.

STEELE, Zadock. *The Indian Captive.* Leatherbound. Montpelier, Vt., 1818. 1st ed. $75-$150. Also, $110 (1964 auction) and $30 (1965 auction).

STEIN, Gertrude. *Tender Buttons. Objects. Food. Rooms.* Boards, paper label. New York, 1914. 1st ed. $50. Worn, $25.

STEIN, Gertrude. *Three Lives.* Blue clothbound. New York, 1909. 1st ed. $75.

STEINBECK, John. *Cup of Gold.* Clothbound. New York, 1929. 1st ed., 1st issue, with "First published, August, 1929" on copyright page. $100 and up, with a wide range of prices noted: $100 in a dealer's catalogue; $125, inscribed; and, at auction, $110 (1962) and $170 (1963) for fine copies in dust jacket.

STEINBECK, John. *In Dubious Battle.* Boards. New York, no date (1936). 1st ed. One of 99, numbered and signed, boxed. $175. Also, at auction, $110 (1963) and $70 (1962). 1st trade ed. Clothbound. In dust jacket, $20-$40. In dust jacket, signed. $125. Also, $45 (1963 auction).

STEINBECK, John *The Pastures of Heaven.* Clothbound. New York, 1932. 1st ed., 1st issue, with Brewer, Warren & Putnam imprint. In dust jacket, $85-$125. Also, $110 and $50 at auction in 1963. Presentation copy, signed by the author, $175. 2d issue copy, with Ballou imprint, in dust jacket, with a 4 pp. Ballou brochure, "The Neatest Trick of the Year," $55 (1962 auction).

STEINBECK, John. *Saint Katy the Virgin.* Boards. No place, no date (New York, 1936). 1st ed. One of 199, numbered and signed. $150-$300. Also, at auction: $100 (1962) and $220 and $110 (1963).

STEINBECK, John. *Tortilla Flat.* Clothbound. New York, no date (1935). 1st ed. In dust jacket, signed by the author. $50-$75. Also, $47 (1962 auction). Unsigned, $35-$50. Advance issue of 500, paperbound. $65 (1962 auction).

STEPHENS, Alexander H. *Speech in January, 1861, Before the Georgia State Convention.* 12 pp., paperbound. Baltimore, 1864. $25.

STEPHENS, Mrs. Ann S. *Malaeska: The Indian Wife of the White Hunter.* Paperbound (light brown). New York, no date (1860). 1st ed., 1st issue. $200-$250. Title page stained, $165.

STEPHENS, Ann Sophia. *The Portland Sketch Book.* Portland, 1836. 1st ed. Spine worn, $27.50.

STEPHENS, Lorenzo Dow. *Life Sketches of a Jayhawker of '49.* 6 plates. 68 pp., paperbound. No place (San Jose), 1916. 1st ed. One of 300. $50-$75. Also, $55 (1966 auction).

STERLING, E. C. *First Biennial Report of the Territorial Treasurer. For the Years 1867-8.* 14 pp., sewed. Boise City, 1868. Uncut, $75.

STERLING, George. *The Testimony of the Suns.* San Francisco, 1903. 1st ed. $25-$35. San Francisco, 1927. One of 300. Boards. $20-$25.

STERLING, R. and J. Campbell. *Our Own Second Reader: for the Use of Schools and Families.* Clothbound. Greensboro, N. C., no date (1862). $30.

STEVENS, Isaac I. *A Circular Letter to Emigrants Desirous of Locating in Washington Territory.* 21 pp., sewed. Washington, 1858. 1st ed. $65-$75. Also, $53.20 (1958 auction).

STEVENSON, Robert Louis. *An Inland Voyage.* Illustrations by Jean Hugo. Stamford, Conn., 1938. One of 150 in board slipcase. Uncut, $35-$50.

STEWART, William F. *Last of the Filibusters.* 85 pp., paperbound. Sacramento, 1857. $175.

STIFF, Edward. *The Texan Emigrant.* Folding map. Calfbound. Cincinnati, 1840. 1st ed. $125.

STILLWELL, Margaret Bingham. *Gutenberg and the Catholicon of 1460.* New York, 1936. With an original leaf of the Catholicon printed by Gutenberg in 1460. $150-$200.

STITH, William. *The History of the First Discovery and Settlement of Virginia; Being an Essay Toward a General History of This Colony.* Calfbound. Williamsburg, 1747. 1st ed. $200-$400. Also, $336 (1961 auction). Rehinged, $150. Another, back cover missing, label off spine, $100. Rebound in modern leather, title page repaired, etc., $150 (1963 auction). Rehinged, $150. Another copy, back cover missing, label missing from spine, $100.

STOCKTON, Frank R. *The Casting Away of Mrs. Lecks and Mrs. Aleshine.* Clothbound and paperbound. New York, no date (1886). 1st ed., 1st issue, with signatures (divisions of paper) at pp. 9, 25, 49, 57, 73, 81, 97, 105, 121, and 125. Paperbound, $40. Clothbound, half inch across top of covers, $35.

STOCKTON, Frank R. *The Great War Syndicate.* Paperbound. New York, 1889. 1st ed., with Collier imprint. $37.50.

STOCKTON, Frank R. *The Lady, or the Tiger? and Other Stories.* Clothbound. New York, 1884. 1st ed. $40. Also, $22 (1962 auction).

STOCKTON, Frank R. *Rudder Grange.* Red clothbound. New York, 1879. 1st ed., 18 chapters, no ads or reviews of this title. $25.

STOCKTON, Frank R. *Ting-A-Ling.* Clothbound. New York, 1870. 1st ed. $25.

STODDARD, Richard Henry. *Abraham Lincoln: An Horatian Ode.* Paperbound. New York, no date (1865). 1st ed. $35-$50. Covers chipped, $27.50.

STOKES, I. N. Phelps. *The Iconography of Manhattan Island.* 6 vols., half vellum. New York, 1915-28. One of 360 sets. Presentation copy, inscribed by Stokes. $950 (1964 auction). Also bound in cloth and in calf. $750-$1,000 retail price range. Auction records: $420, $380, $375, $310, $300. In 1963 a set of the six volumes bound in 12 leather volumes brought $550 at auction. Also noted: an issue of 42 copies printed on Japan vellum. $750 and up.

STONE, George C. *A Glossary of the Construction, Decoration and Use of Arms and Armour, etc.* Clothbound. Portland, Me., 1934. $75-$100. Also, 35 copies, leatherbound, de luxe issue. $100-$150. New York, 1961. One of 500. Clothbound. $40-$60.

STONE, Herbert Stuart. *First Editions of American Authors.* Clothbound. Cambridge, 1893. One of 50 large paper copies signed by the publishers. $35-$50. Trade ed. $25.

STONG, Phil. *Horses and Americans.* Clothbound. New York, 1939. 1st ed. $25.

STOWE, Harriet Beecher. *Uncle Sam's Emancipation.* Philadelphia, 1853. 1st ed. Backstrip worn, $27.50.

STOWE, Harriet Beecher. *Uncle Tom's Cabin.* 2 vols. Paperbound and clothbound. Boston, 1852. 1st ed., 1st issue, buff paper covers. $1,000 and up. 2d issue, plum colored cloth, no indication of number of thousands on title page, bottom of spine reading "J. P. Jewett & Co." $600-$1,000. Also, $400 (1962 auction). Another copy, bindings spotted, spines faded, $195 (1959 auction). Other defective copies, $30-$60 at auction. Black cloth: A "brilliant copy," $1,200 (1960 auction). Others: recased, $55 (1965 auction); defective, $30 (at auction). Blue cloth, "gift binding": Rubbed copy, $325 (1963 auction). Red cloth, "gift binding": $150 (1964 auction); worn, $80 (1964 auction). Other defective copies, colors of cloth not specified, $20-$50 at auction. Rebound in leather, half leather, etc., $25-$42 at auction. Half leather, original cloth covers bound in, $53.20 (at auction).

STRAHORN, Mrs. Carrie A. *15,000 Miles by Stage.* 5 plates. Clothbound. New York, 1911. 1st ed. $75-$100. Also, $60 (1959 auction). New York, 1915. 2d ed. $35-$50.

STRAHORN, Robert E. *Montana and Yellowstone National Park.* 205 pp., paperbound. Kansas City, 1881. $25 and $35.

STRAHORN, Robert E. *To the Rockies and Beyond, etc.* Maps and plates. 216 pp., paperbound. Omaha, 1878. 1st ed. $75-$100. Omaha, 1875. 2d ed. $75.

STRATTON, R. B. *Captivity of the Oatman Girls, etc.* 231 pp., paperbound. San Francisco, 1857. (2d ed. of STRATTON: *Life Among the Indians,* which see.) $150-$200. Chicago, 1857, reprint of the 2d ed. $75-$100. Rubbed, foxed, $57.50. San Francisco, 1935. Half clothbound. One of 550. $30-$40.

STRATTON, R. B. *Life Among the Indians, etc.* 183 pp., paperbound. San Francisco, 1857. 1st ed. $600 and up. (See STRATTON: *Captivity of the Oatman Girls.*)

STREETER, Floyd Benjamin. *Prarie Trails and Cow Towns.* 12 plates. Clothbound. Boston, no date (1936). 1st ed. $50-$65.

STUART, Granville. *Forty Years on the Frontier.* Plates. 2 vols., clothbound. Cleveland, 1925. 1st ed. $50-$75.

STUBBS, Charles H. *Historic-Genealogy of the Kirk Family,*

etc. Lancaster, 1872. New cloth, $27.50.

STUDER, Jacob H. *The Birds of North America.* Clothbound and leatherbound. 119 colored lithographs after Jasper. Columbus, Ohio, 1878. 1st ed. $50-$75. Worn, $45. New York, 1881. $25-$30. New York, 1895. Leatherbound. $35-$50. New York, 1903. Clothbound. $40-$50.

SUAREZ y Navarro, Juan. *Defensa que el Licenciado Jose G. P. Garay Hizo ante el Juez Primero de lo Civil, Don Gayetano Ibarra, etc.* 64 pp., sewed. Mexico, 1849. $100.

SULLIVAN, James. *The History of the District of Maine.* Folding map. Leatherbound. Boston, 1795. 1st ed. $100-$150. Rebound in new leather, $95.

SULLIVAN, W. John L. *Twelve Years in the Saddle, etc.* 13 plates. Clothbound. Austin, 1909. 1st ed. $35-$50. Another, bookplate, $30.

SUMMERFIELD, Charles. *The Rangers and Regulators of the Tanaha.* Clothbound. New York, no date (1856). (By A. W. Arrington.) 1st ed. $25-$35. Worn, $15-$20.

SUN Pictures of Rocky Mountain Scenery, etc. New York, 1870. $35-$50.

SUNDERLAND, LaRoy. *Mormonism Exposed and Refuted.* 54 pp., paperbound. New York, 1838. 1st ed. $35-$50.

SUNDRY Documents Referring to the Niagara and Detroit River Railroad. 8 pp., paperbound. No place, no date (Albany?, 1845). (By W. H. Merritt.) Waterstained, $35.

SUTHERLAND, Thomas A. *Howard's Campaign Against the Nez Perce Indians.* 48 pp., paperbound. Portland, Ore., 1878. 1st ed. $450.

SUTRO, Adolph. *Mineral Resources of the U. S.* Folding map, plates. Clothbound. Baltimore, 1868. $40. Inscribed by author, $30.

SWAN, Alonzo M. *Canton: Its Pioneers and History.* Clothbound. Canton, Ill., 1871. 1st ed. $50-$75. Back leaves lightly stained, $40.

SWAN, Alonzo M. *Life, Trial, Conviction, Confession and Execution of John Osborn, the Murderer of Mrs. Adelia Mathews, etc.* 85 pp., paperbound. Peoria, 1872. $100. Another copy, leatherbound, original wrappers bound in, $75.

SWAN, James G. *The Northwest Coast.* Map, plates. Clothbound. New York, 1857. Author's presentation copy, $25.

SWASEY, William F. *The Early Days and Men of California.* Portrait, 2 plates. Clothbound. Oakland, 1891. 1st ed. $75-$100. Also, $60 (1966 auction). Worn, $50, $40, and $35. Rebound in morocco, $40 (at auction).

SWEET, Willis. *The Carbonate Camps, Leadville and Ten-Mile, of Colorado.* Map. 83 pp., paperbound. Kansas City, 1879. 1st ed. $125.

SWISHER, James. *How I Know.* Clothbound. Cincinnati, 1881. 1st ed. $35-$50.

SYDENHAM, Thomas. *The Works of Thomas Sydenham, M. D.* Leatherbound. Philadelphia, 1809. 1st Am. ed. Rebacked, $35.

SZYK, Arthur (artist). *Ink and Blood: A Book of Drawings.* Text by Struthers Burt. Leatherbound. New York, 1946. One of 1,000, signed by Szyk. $100-$125.

TABB, John Banister. *Lyrics.* Boards. Boston, 1897. 1st ed. One of five on China paper. $60. One of 50 on handmade paper. $25. One of 500. $10-$15.

TABLES of Allowances, etc. (For Navy vessels.) Washington, 1844. Waterstained, $25.

TABLES, Showing in Three Different Views, the Comparative Value of the Currency of the States of New-Hampshire, etc. 40 pp., sewed. Portsmouth, 1796. Uncut, $45.

TAFT, Robert. *Photography and the American Scene.* Clothbound. New York, 1942. 1st ed. $30-$40. Worn, $15-$20.

TAILFER, Patrick. *A True and Historical Narrative of the Colony of Georgia, etc.* 176 pp., boards. Charles Town, 1741. 1st ed. Full leather binding, $250. Another issue, Charles Town: "Sold at London, 1741" (probably printed at London). 3d printing. $140 (1963 auction).

TALBOT, Eugene S. *Irregularities of the Teeth, etc.* Clothbound. Philadelphia, 1888. 1st ed. $26.

TALLENT, Annie. *The Black Hills; or The Last Hunting Grounds of the Dakotahs, etc.* 50 plates. Clothbound or half leather-bound. St. Louis, 1899. 1st ed. $75-$100.

TAMERLANE and Other Poems. By a Bostonian. Paperbound. Boston, 1827. (By Edgar Allan Poe.) 1st ed. Only 500 were printed. Last known price, $25,000. If another copy were to turn up, the price doubtless would go much higher. (Do not be fooled by facsimile copies, which are not uncommon.)

TANNER, H. S. *A Brief Description of the Canals and Rail-roads of the United States, etc.* 2 plates, map. 63 pp. Phila-delphia, 1834. 2d ed. $35-$50. New York, 1840. Enlarged ed. *(A Description, etc.)*, 3 maps, 2 diagrams, 272 pp., $35-$50.

TARASCON, Louis. *An Address to the Citizens of Philadelphia, on the Great Advantages Which Arise from the Trade of the Western Country.* 13 pp., paperbound. Philadelphia, 1806. $150.

TARKINGTON, Booth. *The Gentleman from Indiana.* Green clothbound, top stained green. New York, 1899. 1st ed., 1st issue, with "eye" as last word in line 12, page 245, and with line 16 reading "so pretty." $35.

TARKINGTON, Booth. *Monsieur Beaucaire.* Red clothbound. New York, 1900. 1st ed., 1st issue, with publisher's seal on page after end of text exactly one half inch in diameter. $30-$50. Another copy, slight cover stain, $25. Autographed copies, $35 and $40 (at auction).

TARKINGTON, Booth. *Seventeen.* Clothbound or leatherbound. Indianapolis, no date (1916). 1st ed., 1st issue, with letters "B-Q" beneath copyright notice. $25-$35-$40. Inscribed copy at auction, $42.

TAYLOR, Bayard. *Eldorado, or, Adventures in the Path of Empire, etc.* 8 lithograph views. 2 vols., clothbound. New York, 1850. 1st ed., with list of illustrations in Vol. 2 giving Mazatlan at page 8 instead of page 80. $125. Another, $100. Also, $65 (1964 auction). Another, bindings faded, $47 (at auction). New York, 1850. 2d ed. 2 vols. With Mazatlan reference corrected, $25. New York, 1850. 3d ed. One volume, no plates. $5-$10.

TAYLOR, F. *A Sketch of the Military Bounty Tract of Illinois.* 12 pp., boards and calf. Philadelphia, 1839. 1st ed. $125.

TAYLOR, John. *An Argument Respecting the Constitutionality of the Carriage Tax, etc.* 34 pp., paperbound. Richmond, 1795. $100.

TAYLOR, Joseph Henry. *Sketches of Frontier and Indian Life, etc.* 12 plates. Half leather and boards. Pottstown, Pa., 1889. 1st ed. $150-$200. Another, front cover detached, $175.

TAYLOR, Oliver I. *Directory of the City of Wheeling and Ohio County, etc.* 2 plates. Wheeling, 1851. 1st ed. $35-$50.

TEASDALE, Sara. *Sonnets to Duse and Other Poems.* Boards, paper labels. Boston, 1907. 1st ed. $75-$100. Another, worn, $35.

TEN Years Almanac, 1755 to 1764 (The). Sewed. Portsmouth, N. H., 1765. $400.

THACKERAY, William Makepeace. *The Great Hoggarty Diamond.* Clothbound. New York, no date (1848). 1st ed., 1st issue, with "82 Cliff Street" address and six-page Harper catalogue at end. Rebacked, foxed, $35.

THOMAS, David. *Travels Through the Western Country in the Summer of 1816.* Folding map, 2 errata notices. Boards or leatherbound. Auburn, N.Y., 1819. 1st ed. $150. Another, spine chipped, $65. Another, rebound in cloth, soiled and frayed, $95. Another, map torn, $72.80 (1962 auction). Others at auction, $35 and $40.

THOMAS, Joseph B. *Hounds and Hunting Through the Ages.* Clothbound. New York, 1928. 1st ed. One of 750. $35-$50. New York, 1929. 2d ed. One of 250. $35-$50.

THOMPSON, Albert W. *The Story of Early Clayton, N. M.* Clayton, 1933. 1st ed. $35-$50.

THOMPSON, David. *History of the Late War, Between Great Britain and the U.S.A.* Boards or leatherbound. Niagara, U. C. (Upper Canada), 1832. 1st ed. $75-$100. Another, worn, $35. Rebound in half morocco, $30 (at auction).

THOMPSON, David. *David Thompson's Narrative of His Explorations in Western America: 1784-1812.* Edited by J. B. Tyrrell. 23 maps and plates. Toronto, 1916. Champlain Society. 1st ed. One of 550. $290. Another, $150.

THOMPSON, Maurice. *Alice of Old Vincennes.* Clothbound.

Indianapolis, no date (1900). 1st ed., 1st issue, with no page of "Acknowledgements" at end of text. $30 and $50. Another, hinges weak, $20.

THOMPSON, Maurice. *The Story of Louisiana.* Boston, no date (1888). 1st ed. $30.

THOMPSON, William. *To the Committee on Election. Ought the Kanesville Vote in August, 1848, to Have Been Allowed?* 19 pp., calfbound. No place (Iowa City?), 1850. $150.

THOREAU, Henry David. *The Maine Woods.* Clothbound. Boston, 1864. 1st ed., 1st issue, with ad leaves at back dated January. $75-$125. Also, $80 (1960 auction). Others, $55 (1964 auction), $40 (1963 auction).

THOREAU, Henry David. *Walden; or, Life in the Woods.* Brown cloth. Boston, 1854. 1st ed., 1st issue, with ads dated April. $300-$500. Auction records range from $90 (1959) to $225 (1960 and 1961); for worn copies, from $25 to $90. Another copy, rebound in modern morocco, $40 (at auction). Another, ads dated May, $350 (1962 auction). (Note: Some bibliographers do not stress the importance of the dating of the ads.) Boston, 1909. 2 vols., half vellum. One of 488. $50-$60. Also, $25 (at auction). Chicago, 1930. Half clothbound. Illustrated by Ruzicka. $50. Also, $32 (at auction).

THOREAU, Henry David. *A Week on the Concord and Merrimack Rivers.* Tan or brown clothbound. Boston and Cambridge, 1849. 1st ed. $500-$750. Also, $600 (1960 auction). Signed copy, spine repaired, $550 (1960 auction). Review copy, penciled notes on end papers, binding frayed, $600. Worn copies, $100-$200. Also, $200 (1961 auction).

THOROUGHBRED Broodmare Records, 1935-1939. No place (Lexington, Ky.), June, 1940. One of 250 bound in morocco by Monastery Hill Bindery. $350.

THOUGHTS on Taxation, in a Letter to a Friend. 22 pp. New York, 1784. (By Timothy Davis.) Lower part of title page missing, $45.

THOUSAND Miles in a Canoe from Denver to Leavenworth (A). Paperbound. Bushnell, 1880. (By W. A. Spencer.) 1st ed. $150.

THRALL, Rev. S. C. *The President's Death: A Sermon Delivered at Christ Church.* 12 pp., paperbound. New Orleans, 1865. $45.

THRILLING Narrative of Dr. John Doy of Kansas (The). 132 pp., paperbound. Boston, 1860. Lacking back cover, $27.50. (1st ed., New York, 1860. *The Narrative of, etc.* $45 [1966 auction].)

THWAITES, Reuben G. (editor). *Original Journals of the Lewis and Clark Expedition, 1804-1806.* 8 vols., clothbound (including atlas). New York, 1904-05. 1st ed. $600 and up. Also, $300 (at auction). Large paper ed., same date. 15 vols. (7 vols. in 14, plus atlas vol.), clothbound. $600-$800. Also, $470 (1959 auction), $300 (1960 auction), and $400 (1964 auction). One of 50 on Japan paper. $1,200 (1966 auction). New York, 1959. 8 vols., clothbound. Facsimile of 1904-1905 ed. $150. Also, $32.40 and $89.60 (at auction).

TOPOGRAPHICAL Description of the State of Ohio, Indiana Territory, and Louisiana (A). 5 plates. Calfbound. Boston, 1812. (By Jervis Cutler.) 1st ed. $325 and $225. Also, $200, $220, and $225 at auction. Copies with various defects, $100, $135, and $160.

TORY, Geoffroy. *Champ Fleury.* Translated by George B. Ives. Vellum and boards. New York, 1927. 1st ed. Printed by Bruce Rogers. One of seven on larger paper, of an edition of 397. $150. One of the 390 regular copies, boxed. $75-$100. Also, $40 and $50 at auction.

TOTTEN, B. J. *Naval Text-Book.* Plates. Boston, 1841. $25.

TOUR Through Part of Virginia in the Summer of 1808 (A). New York, 1809. (By John E. Caldwell.) 1st ed. $50-$100.

TOWER, Col. R. *An Appeal to the People of New York in Favor of the Construction of the Chenango Canal, etc.* 32 pp., sewed. Utica, 1830. $35.

TOWLE, Mrs. C. W. *Stories for the American Freemason's Fireside.* Clothbound. Cincinnati, 1868. (By Catharine Webb Barber Towles.) 1st ed. $25.

TOWN and Countryman's Almanack, . . . 1788, etc. Philadelphia, no date (1787). $50. Another, two leaves of ads missing at end, $25.

TOWNSEND, George A. *The Real Life of Abraham Lincoln.* 15 pp., paperbound. New York, 1867. 1st ed. $35-$50.

TOWNSEND, John K. *Narrative of a Journey Across the Rocky Mountains, etc.* Clothbound. Philadelphia, 1839. 1st ed. $100-$125. Also, $50 (1959 auction). Worn copies, $50-$75. Rebound in half morocco, $50 (1963 auction). Rebound in new cloth, $35 (1964 auction).

TOWNSHIP Maps of the Cherokee Nation. 130 maps on linen. Published by Indian Territory Map Co. Muskogee, Okla., no date. $150. Damaged set, $75.

TRACY, J. L. *Guide to the Great West.* 2 maps. Clothbound. St. Louis, 1870. 1st ed. $50. Foxed, back faded, $25.

TRAVELS on the Western Slope of the Mexican Cordillera, etc. Clothbound. San Francisco, 1857. (By Marvin T. Wheat.) 1st ed. $75-$100.

TRAVELLER'S Directory and Emigrant's Guide, etc. (The). Boards. Buffalo, 1832. (By Oliver G. Steele.) 1st ed. $150. Other Buffalo editions, 1834, 1836, 1839, 1846, and 1847, each $25-$35.

TREADWELL, Edward F. *The Cattle King.* 4 plates. Clothbound. New York, 1931. 1st ed. $25-$35. Boston, 1950. Clothbound. $18.

TREATISE on Marriage. 20 pp., sewed. No place, no date. $30.

TRIAL of Edward Tinker, Mariner, for the Willful Murder of a Youth Called Edward, at Carteret Superior Court. 95 pp., sewed. Newbern, 1811. $45.

TRIBUNE Tracts No. 6. Life of Abraham Lincoln. 32 pp., sewed. New York, 1860. (By John Locke Scripps.) $35-$50. (The first appearance of this book was in an undated Chicago edition of 1860, 32 pp., in double columns of type, under the caption title *Life of Abraham Lincoln.* It is a rare item, worth $1,000 and up.)

TRIGGS, J. H. *History and Directory of Laramie City, Wyoming Territory.* 91 pp., paperbound. Laramie, 1875. 1st ed. $300-$400. Also, at auction: $190 (1959), $150 (1963), and $200 (1965).

TRIGGS, J. H. *History of Cheyenne and Northern Wyoming, etc.* Folding map. 144 pp., paperbound. Omaha, 1876. 1st ed. $350-$500. Also, at auction: $220 (1959), $225 (1963), and $275 (1966).

TRIPLETT, Frank. *The Life, Times and Treacherous Death of Jesse James.* Pictorial clothbound. Chicago, 1882. 1st ed. $150-$250. Leatherbound, end papers chipped, covers worn, $125.

TROWBRIDGE, John Townsend. *Jack Hazard and His Fortunes.* Clothbound. Boston, 1871. 1st ed. $50.

TRUMAN, Maj. Ben. C. *Life, Adventures and Capture of Tiburcio Vasquez.* Frontispiece map. 44 pp., pictorial paperbound. Los Angeles, 1874. 1st ed. $100 and up. Los Angeles, 1941. Cloth and leather. One of 100. $35-$50.

TUCKER, E. *History of Randolph County, Indiana.* Chicago, 1882. $40. Shaken, binding shabby, $32.50.

TURNER, Orsamus. *History of the Pioneer Settlement of Phelps and Gorham's Purchase.* Boards and leather. Rochester, 1851. 1st ed. $35-$50.

TURNLEY, Parmenas T. *Reminiscences of. From the Cradle to Three-Score and Ten. By Himself.* 6 plates. Clothbound. Chicago, no date (1892). 1st ed. $90 and $125. Also, $60 (1959 auction). Others, worn and otherwise defective, $37.50 and $42.50. Covers worn, some pages dampstained, $37.50.

TURRILL, H. B. *Historical Reminiscences of the City of Des Moines.* Folding view, 4 plates. Clothbound. Des Moines, 1857. 1st ed. $65. Another copy, foxed, back frayed, title page repaired, $45.

TWAIN, Mark. *Adventures of Huckleberry Finn. (Tom Sawyer's Comrade.).* Blue or green clothbound. New York, 1885. (By Samuel Langhorne Clemens.) 1st ed., 1st issue, with "was" for "saw" in line 23, page 57; with "Him and another man" given in list of illustrations as being on page 88, and with page 283 on a stub. $1,500 (1960 auction). (Note: This copy, in blue binding, was called "Perhaps the finest copy known." Another copy, also in blue, brought $750 at auction in 1963. Another, similarly described but with page 283 not on a stub, brought $325 at auction in 1964. Average copies retail in the $150-$300 range, with defective copies bringing somewhat less. Green binding is commoner than the blue.

TWAIN, Mark. *Adventures of Huckleberry Finn.* (Prospectus for.) Contains samples of text and binding styles. New York,

1885. (By Samuel Langhorne Clemens.) 1st ed. $150-$250.

TWAIN, Mark. *The Adventures of Tom Sawyer.* Blue clothbound. Hartford, 1876. (By Samuel Langhorne Clemens.) 1st ed., 1st issue, printed on calendered paper, with versos of frontispiece, half title and preface blank. Up to $2,000. Auction records: $1,500 (1960) and $1,400 (1962)—the latter for a copy the spine of which was slightly rubbed. 2d issue, without the blank leaf before the frontispiece, same date. $150-$200. (Note: The book was also issued in leather binding.) Repaired and rebound copies of the clothbound and leatherbound first issues have ranged in recent years from $100 up.

TWAIN, Mark. *The Celebrated Jumping Frog of Calaveras County, and Other Sketches.* Edited by John Paul. Clothbound, various colors. New York, 1867. (By Samuel Langhorne Clemens.) 1st ed., 1st issue, with perfect "i" in "this" in last line on page 198; with page of yellow tinted ads preceding title page, and with the frog on the front cover in the lower left corner. $500-$600. Also, $275 and $400 at auction. Covers spotted and soiled, $170 (1963 auction). Another, frog in center of cover, soiled, $120 (1962 auction). 2d issue, ad leaf missing. $50. Worn, $20.

TWAIN, Mark. *A Connecticut Yankee in King Arthur's Court.* Green clothbound. New York, 1889. (By Samuel Langhorne Clemens.) 1st ed. $75-$100. Worn, $25 and up.

TWAIN, Mark. *The Gilded Age.* Frontispiece, folded plate, 19 plates. Black clothbound. Hartford, 1873. (By Samuel Langhorne Clemens, in collaboration with Charles Dudley Warner.) 1st ed., 1st issue, without illustration "Philip leaves Laura" on page 403. $35-$50. Also, a prospectus for the book was issued prior to publication in 1873, containing preliminary pages and 1st ed. copy without the usual advertising leaves at the back, with spine chipped and hinges cracked, brought $230 at auction in 1963.)

TWAIN, Mark. *The Innocents Abroad.* Black clothbound. Hartford, 1869. (By Samuel Langhorne Clemens.) 1st ed., 1st issue, without page references on pages xvii and xviii and lacking illustration on page 129. $75.

TWAIN, Mark. *Life on the Mississippi.* Brown clothbound. Boston, 1883. (By Samuel Langhorne Clemens.) 1st ed., 1st issue, with author in flames on page 441 and with caption on page 443 reading "The St. Louis Hotel." $100-$200. Also, $180 (1960 auction price for an exceptionally fine copy). Worn copies, much less. Also issued in leather. Fine copies, $100 and up. Worn, much less. Later issues, same date, $50-$100 for fine copies.

TWAIN, Mark. *The Prince and the Pauper.* Clothbound. Boston, 1882. (By Samuel Langhorne Clemens.) 1st Am. ed., 1st issue, with imprint of "Franklin Press" at foot of copyright page. One of "6 or 8" (?) copies on China paper, with white linen binding. $600 and up. 1st regular issue, green cloth. $150-$250. Defective copies, $50-$100. Also issued in leather. Montreal, 1881. Blue cloth. 1st ed. (?). $50-$75.

TWAIN, Mark. *Roughing It.* Black clothbound. Hartford, 1872. (By Samuel Langhorne Clemens.) 1st ed., 1st issue, with no words missing in lines 20 and 21 of page 242. $50-$100. Worn copies, $25-$50. Also issued in leather. Later issue, same date. $40.

TWAIN, Mark. *Tom Sawyer Abroad.* Tan clothbound. New York, 1894. (By Samuel Langhorne Clemens.) 1st ed. $100-$150. Also, $130 (1960 auction). Worn and dull, $50, $75, $100.

TWAIN, Mark. *Tom Sawyer Abroad, Tom Sawyer, Detective, and Other Stories.* Illustrated by Dan Beard. Red clothbound. New York, 1896. (By Samuel Langhorne Clemens.) 1st ed. $75-$100. Backstrip soiled, $50.

TWAIN, Mark. *The Tragedy of Pudd'nhead Wilson.* Red clothbound. Hartford, 1894. (By Samuel Langhorne Clemens.) 1st ed. $50-$75. Another, $35. Worn, $25. Also issued in leather.

TWAIN, Mark. *A Tramp Abroad.* Black clothbound. Hartford, 1880. (By Samuel Langhorne Clemens.) 1st ed., 1st state, with frontispiece entitled "Moses," not "Titian's Moses." $45-$60. Worn, $15-$25. Also issued in leather.

TWITCHELL, Ralph Emerson. *Old Santa Fe.* No place, no date (Santa Fe, 1925). 1st ed. $35-$50.

TWO Years Before the Mast. A Personal Narrative of Life at Sea. (Harpers' Family Library No. CVI.) Gray, black, or tan clothbound. New York, 1840. (By Richard Henry Dana,

Jr.) 1st ed., 1st issue, with perfect "i" in the word "in", first line of copyright notice. $500-$1,000. Fine copies at auction: Gray cloth, $750 (1960); tan cloth, $100, $130, and $175 (in the 1955-60 period) and $375 (1961); black cloth, $160 (1965). (Note: Few copies in the gray cloth have appeared for sale, and they would appear to be scarce, although copies in tan muslin binding have appeared to be most favored by collectors.) Worn copies in any of the three bindings are worth $100 and upward at retail; even a very poor, badly worn copy in tan cloth having brought $55 at auction in 1964. 2d issue, 1840, black cloth. $100 and up at retail; worn, $25-$100. Chicago, 1930. Illustrated by Edward A. Wilson. Clothbound. One of 1,000. $35. New York, 1936. Grabhorn Press. Boards. $25-$50.

TYLER, Daniel. *A Concise History of the Mormon Battalion in the Mexican War.* Leatherbound. No place (Salt Lake City), 1881 (actually 1882). 1st ed. $150-$175. Recent auction prices have ranged from $40 to $85.

TYSON, James. *Diary of a Physician in California.* 92 pp., paperbound. New York, 1850. 1st ed. $150-$200. Half morocco, original paper covers bound in, $85 (1960 auction). Worn, $90. Another, $40. Another, disbound, $98 (1964 auction).

UDELL, John. *Incidents of Travel to California, Across the Great Plains.* Portrait, errata leaf. Clothbound. Jefferson, Ohio, 1856. 1st ed. $100-$125. Another, leaf torn, foxed, $65. Copies lacking portrait, $35, $50, and $65.

UNCLE Abe's Republican Songster. Paperbound. San Francisco, 1860. $27.50.

UNIFORM and Dress of the Army of the Confederate States. Boards. 5 pp., plus 15 plates and errata slip. Richmond, 1861. 1st ed., 1st issue, black and white plates. $125. 2d issue, four plates colored, plus colored strip showing field caps. $300.

UNIVERSAL Asylum and Columbian Magazine (The). Vol. 1. Philadelphia, 1792. $35.

UPHAM, Samuel C. *Notes From Sunland, on the Manatee River, Gulf Coast of South Florida.* Frontispiece. 83 pp., sewed. Braidentown, 1881. 1st ed. $75. Worn, $37.50. Also, $30 and $40 at auction.

VAIL, Alfred. *Description of the American Electro Magnetic Telegraph.* Unbound. Washington, 1845. 1st ed. $27.50.

VALENTINER, Wilhelm R. *Rembrandt Paintings in America.* Half morocco. New York, 1931. 1st ed. One of 200, signed. $32.50 and $25.

VANDERBILT, William K. *To Galapagos on the Ara, 1926.* No place (New York), 1927. One of 500. $27.50.

VAN DE WATER, Frederic F. *Glory-Hunter: A Life of Gen. Custer.* 2 maps, 13 plates. Clothbound. Indianapolis, no date (1934). 1st ed. $37.50. Another, $25.

VAN DYKE, T. S. *The Advantages of the Colony of El Cajon, San Diego County, and the Superiority of Its Fruit Lands.* 32 pp., paperbound. San Diego, 1883. $45.

VAN WYCK, Frederick. *Keskachauge, or the First White Settlement on Long Island.* 6 maps, 55 plates. Clothbound. New York, 1924. 1st ed. $35.

VAN ZANDT, Nicholas Biddle. *A Full Description of the Soil, Water, Timber, and Prairies of Each Lot, or Quarter Section of the Military Lands Between the Mississippi and Illinois River.* 127 pp., folding map. Boards and calf. Washington City, 1818. 1st ed. Without the separately issued map, $250. With map, $1,250. Also, $420 (1959 auction).

VAUGHN, Robert. *Then and Now, or 36 Years in the Rockies.* Clothbound. Minneapolis, 1900. 1st ed. $32.50 and $40. Another copy, worn, $25. Also, $50 (1966 auction).

VEBLEN, Thorstein. *The Theory of the Leisure Class.* Green clothbound. New York, 1899. 1st ed. $27.50. Another copy, presentation copy with author's signed inscription, $75.

VELASCO, Francisco. *Sonora: Its Extent, Population, Natural Productions, Indian Tribes, Mines, Mineral Lands, etc.* Translated from the Spanish by Wm. F. Nye. San Francisco, 1861. 1st Am. ed. $30.

VENABLE, W. H. *Beginnings of Literary Culture in the Ohio Valley.* Cincinnati, 1891. 1st ed. $30.

VILLAGE Merchant, (The): A Poem. 16 pp. Philadelphia, 1794. (By Philip Freneau.) 1st ed. Bound in modern calf. $750.

VILLON, Francois, *The Complete Works of.* 2 vols., clothbound.

New York, 1928. One of 960. $35 and $50.

VINDICATION of the Recent and Prevailing Policy of Georgia in Its Internal Affairs, etc. (A). Athens, 1827. (By Augustin S. Clayton.) 1st ed. $85.

VIRGINIA Illustrated. Clothbound. New York, 1857. (By David Hunter Strother.) 1st ed. $45.

VISSCHER, Wm. Lightfoot. *Black Mammy.* Cheyenne, 1885. 1st ed. $25.

VOLNEY'S Answer to Doctor Priestley, on His Pamphlet Entitled, Observations Upon the Increase of Infidelity, etc. 15 pp., paperbound. Philadelphia, 1797. (By Constantin Francis Chasseboeuf Boisgirais, Comte de Volney.) 1st ed. Foxing, minor marginal defects in first and last leaves, $60.

VOLTAIRE, Jean Francois Marie Arouet de. *Candide.* Translated by Richard Aldington, illustrated by Rockwell Kent and colored by hand. Clothbound, leather spine. New York, 1928. One of 95. $150-$200.

VOTES and Proceedings of the House of Representatives of the Province of Pennsylvania. Beginning the Fourth Day of December, 1682. Vol. I. Leatherbound. Philadelphia, 1752. Franklin imprint. $50.

VOTES and Proceedings of the House of Representatives of the Province of Pennsylvania. Beginning the Fourteenth Day of October, 1707. Vol. II. Leatherbound. Philadelphia, 1753. Franklin imprint. $30 and $40.

WAGNER, Henry R. *The Plains and the Rockies.* Boards and cloth. San Francisco, 1920. 1st ed. (suppressed). With 6-page pamphlet of corrections. $100-$150. Also, $40 and $60 (at auction). San Francisco, 1921. 1st published ed. Boards. $25-$50. San Francisco, 1937. Clothbound. Grabhorn Press. Revised by C. L. Camp. One of 600. $50-$75. Columbus, 1953. Clothbound. $45-$50. Also, de luxe ed. Boards. One of 50. $100.

WAGNER, Henry R. *The Spanish Southwest, 1542-1794.* Half morocco. Berkeley, 1924. One of 100. $300. Also, $190 (1960 auction). Albuquerque, 1937. 2 vols., half vellum, $150.

WAGSTAFF, David, H. P. Sheldon, Lawrence B. Smith and others. *Upland Game Bird Shooting in America.* New York,

1930. One of 850. In dust jacket, $50-$75.

WAKEFIELD, John A. *History of the War Between the U.S. and the Sac and Fox Nations of Indians, etc.* Boards or clothbound. Jacksonville, Ill., 1834. 1st ed. $250-$350. Another, $285. Another, $200 (worn). Other copies, rebacked or worn, $80-$150. Rebound in cloth, stained, $80 (1959 auction).

WALGAMOTT, C. S. *Reminiscences of Early Days.* Plates. 2 vols., clothbound. No place, no date (Twin Falls, 1926-27). 1st ed. $85.

WALL, W. G. *Wall's Hudson River Portfolio.* 21 color plates. Oblong. New York, no date (around 1824-26.) 1st ed. $2,500. New York, 1828, 2d ed. $600.

WALLACE, Ed. R. *Parson Hanks.* Arlington, Tex., no date (1906?). 1st ed. $40.

WALLACE, J. H. *Wallace's American Stud-Book.* Vol. I. New York, 1867. $25.

WALLACE, Lew. *Ben-Hur.* Light blue floral clothbound. New York, 1880. 1st ed., 1st issue, with dated title page, six-word dedication, $150-$200. Another copy, newspaper clippings pasted in, backstrip frayed, $100. Another, binding rubbed, soiled, $74. Others, with various defects, $40-$100.

WALTERS, Lorenzo D. *Tombstone's Yesterdays.* Portrait. Clothbound. Tucson, 1928. 1st ed. $80 and $60. Also, $55 (1965 auction).

WALTON, Isaac and Charles Cotton. *The Complete Angler.* Light tan cloth, horizontal red stripes. New York, 1847. 1st ed. of this to be edited, published and printed in America. $100. Foxed, $37.50. Other copies with defects, $15-$25. (Another edition: See WALTON, Izaak. *The Compleat Angler.*)

WALTON, Izaak (Isaac). *The Compleat Angler.* Boards. No place (Boston), 1909. Limited ed. (one of 440, 540, or 450—?) designed by Bruce Rogers. $37.50. (Another edition: See WALTON, Isaac and Charles Cotton. *The Complete Angler.*)

WALTON, W. M. *Life and Adventures of Ben Thompson, the Famous Texan.* 15 plates. 229 pp., paperbound. Austin, 1884. Repaired, in morocco slipcase, $300. Another, last 2 pages in facsimile, $175. Another, $150.

WANDERER in Washington. Washington, 1827. (By George Watterson.) 1st ed. $50.

WAR in Florida (The). By a Late Staff Officer. Folding map, 2 plates. Green clothbound. Baltimore, 1836. (By Woodburn Potter.) 1st ed. $100-$150. Also, $50 (1963 auction) and $100 (1967 auction). Repaired and washed, $16 (1957 auction).

WARE, Joseph E. *Emigrant's Guide to California.* Map. 56 pp. St. Louis, no date (1849). 1st ed. $1,000 and up.

WARREN, John. *The Conchologist.* 34 plates, 17 colored. Morocco. Boston, 1834. 1st ed. $75. Another, rubbed, $50.

WASHINGTON, Maj. George. *The Journal of: Sent by the Hon. Robert Dinwiddie . . . to the Commandant of the French Forces on the Ohio.* 28 pp. Williamsburg, Va., 1754. 1st ed. $25,000. (Auction price in 1955; a few years earlier one bookseller listed a copy at $160.)

WATKINS, Lucy. *The History and Adventures of Little James and Mary.* 15 pp., paperbound. Philadelphia, no date (1810). Some pages repaired, $25.

WATSON, R. *Christian Panoply: Containing an Apology for the Bible, etc.* Shepherd's Town, 1797. 1st ed. $250.

WAYLAND, John W. *Historic Homes of Northern Virginia and the Eastern Panhandle of Western Virginia.* Staunton, 1937. 1st ed. $50-$60. Another, $45.

WAYNE and Holmes Counties, Ohio, Commemorative Biographical Record of. Chicago, 1889. $25.

WEBBER, C. W. *Wild Scenes and Song Birds.* 20 colored plates. Morocco. New York, 1854. $75-$100. Also, $55 (1964 auction). New York, 1855. Clothbound. $37.50.

WEBSTER, Noah. *A Brief History of Epidemic and Pestilential Diseases, etc.* 2 vols., leatherbound. Hartford, 1799. 1st ed. $200-$400. Also, $275, $225. Rebacked, $275 (1962 auction). Disbound, $120 (1964 auction).

WEBSTER, Noah. *An American Dictionary of the English Language.* 2 vols., light brown boards, linen backs, paper labels. New York, 1828. 1st ed. With two-page ad leaf laid in. $500 and up. (The ad leaf is not present in all copies, but those copies with it are more valuable than those without.) A presentation copy, with a letter of 4 pages in Webster's hand brought $1,200 at auction in 1963. Also, rebound in calf, $240 (1964 auction).

WEBSTER, Noah. *History of Animals.* Leatherbound. New-Haven, 1812. 1st ed. $25. Worn, $15.

WEEMS, M. L. *A History of the Life and Death, etc., of Gen. George Washington.* Philadelphia, no date (1800?). Margins shaved, $125. (This is one of a great many editions, under various titles, based on Parson Weems' original work, *The Life and Memorable Actions of George Washington,* Baltimore, 1800?, an extremely rare book of which only two copies are known. Most of the editions to about 1810 are scarce and are valued in the $25-$100 range.)

WEIZMANN, Chaim. *Trial and Error.* 2 vols., clothbound. New York, no date (1949). 1st ed. One of 500, signed, and boxed. $100 and $75. Also, $45 (1964 auction).

WELLS, H. G. *The Door in the Wall.* Plates. Clothbound. New York, 1911. 1st ed. One of 300. $25.

WENDTE, Chas. H. and H. S. Perkins. *The Sunny Side: A Book of Religious Songs, etc.* New York, no date (1875). 1st ed. $60.

WEST, Moses. *A Treatise Concerning Marriage.* 39 pp., sewed. Philadelphia, no date (1738). $30.

WEST Wind: The Life Story of Joseph Reddeford Walker. Map. Los Angeles, 1934. (By Douglas Watson.) 1st ed. One of 100. $120 and $125.

WESTCOTT, Edward Noyes. *David Harum.* Yellow clothbound. New York, 1898. 1st ed., with perfect "J" in "Julius" on page 40. $40-$75. Also, $40 (1960 auction). Worn, $12.50 and up. New York, no date (1900). 1st illustrated ed. One of 750. $25.

WESTERN Reserve Register for 1852 (The). Hudson, Ohio, 1852. 1st issue. $25.

WESTERN Tourist (The), or Emigrant's Guide Through the States of Ohio, Michigan, Indiana, Illinois and Missouri, etc. New York, 1845. (By J. Calvin Smith, published by J. H. Colton.) $35-$50. (Numerous editions under similar titles in this period; all are mildly scarce and in this price range if in fine condition.)

WESTERNERS Brand Books. Chicago, New York, Los Angeles, and Denver, various dates. Most of these range at retail from $35 to $50. (For more detailed listings, see More Gold in Your Attic.)

WETHERBEE, J., Jr. A Brief Sketch of Colorado Territory and the Gold Mines of That Region. 24 pp., paperbound. Boston, 1863.1st ed. $350. Another, back cover missing, $200.

WETMORE, Alphonso. Gazetteer of the State of Missouri. Folding map. Clothbound, leather spine. St. Louis, 1837. 1st ed. $75 and $80. Another, ex-library, rubbed, stained, map repaired, blank end leaf missing, $27.50. Another, dampstained, $35. Another, worn and stained, $47.50. Also, $40 (1966 auction).

WHALING Directory of the United States in 1869. Colored flags. New Bedford, 1869. $27.50.

WHARTON, Edith. Ethan Frome. Clothbound. New York, 1911. 1st ed., 1st issue, with perfect type in last line of page 135. $150. Also, $130, $80, $75 and $55 at auction. Worn copies, $35 and up at retail.

WHEAT, Carl. Books of the California Gold Rush. Boards. San Francisco, 1949. 1st ed. One of 500. Grabhorn Press. $40-$50.

WHEAT, Carl. The Maps of the California Gold Region, 1848-1857. 26 maps. Clothbound. San Francisco, 1942. 1st ed. One of 300. Grabhorn Press. $300-$500.

WHILLDIN, M. A Description of Western Texas. 120 pp., paperbound. Galveston, 1876. 1st ed. $75.

WHITAKER, Arthur Preston (editor). Documents Relating to the Commercial Policy of Spain in the Floridas. 7 maps and plates. DeLand, 1931. 1st ed. $50-$60. Another, $35.

WHITE, Philo. Agricultural Statistics of Racine County (Wisconsin). 16 pp., paperbound. Racine, 1852. Presentation copy from the author, $75.

WHITEHEAD, Charles E. Wild Sports in the South, etc. Clothbound. New York, 1860. 1st ed. $40-$50.

WHITELY, Ike. Rural Life in Texas. 82 pp., paperbound. Atlanta, 1891. 1st ed. $50. Worn, edges torn, $25 and $35.

WHITFIELD, George. *A Letter from the Reverend Mr. Whitfield, to the Religious Societies Lately Formed in England and Wales.* 19 pp. Philadelphia, no date (1739). Half calf, $75.

WHITMAN, Walt. *As a Strong Bird on Pinions Free and Other Poems.* Green clothbound. Washington, 1872. 1st ed. $100. Also, $50 and $55 at auction.

WHITMAN, Walt. *Complete Poems & Prose of: 1855-1888.* Half clothbound, paper label: No place, no date (Philadelphia, 1888). One of 600, with Whitman's signature on title page of "Leaves of Grass." $100-$150. Also, $80 at auction (an unopened copy). Others, worn, $60 and $42.50.

WHITMAN, Walt. *Good-Bye, My Fancy.* Clothbound. Philadelphia, 1891. 1st ed. Large paper. $35-$50. Worn, $25.

WHITMAN, Walt. *Leaves of Grass.* Clothbound. Brooklyn, 1856. 2d ed., green cloth, gold stamped, 342 pp. plus 39 pp. of quoted comment. $150-$200. Also, $100, $120, and $140 at auction. Boston, 1860-61. 3d ed., 1st issue, with line printed by "George C. Rand and Avery" on copyright page, tinted frontispiece, rough, brick-colored cloth, 456 pp., $100. Also, spurious issue, same date, without the Rand and Avery imprint, $25-$30. New York, 1867. 4th ed. Boards. $100. Washington, 1871. 1st ed. Paperbound. $90. Also, half morocco, $85 (at auction). Washington, 1872. Clothbound. $25-$35. Philadelphia, 1891. One of 100. $60-$100. Camden, N. J., 1876. Author's Ed. Boards. $75. New York, 1930. One of 400. Grabhorn Press. Leatherbacked wood boards. $300. Also, $110 to $210 at auction. New York, 1942. Limited Editions Club ed., with Weston photographs. 2 vols. $75-$150. (See also *LEAVES of Grass.*)

WHITMAN, Walt. *Walt Whitman's Drum-Taps.* Clothbound. New York, 1865. 1st ed., 1st issue. 72 pp. $75-$100. New York, 1865-1866. 2d issue, with 24 more pages and separate title page, "Sequel, etc." $75. Also, $32 and $55 at auction.

WHITMER, David. *An Address to All Believers in Christ.* 77 pp., paperbound. Richmond, Mo., 1887. $55 and $27.50.

WHITNEY, Henry C. *Life on the Circuit With Lincoln.* 67 plates. Clothbound. Boston, no date (1892). 1st ed. $35-$50. At auction: $25 and (shaken) $20.

WHITTIER, John Greenleaf. *The Captain's Well.* Illustrated by Howard Pyle. 4 pp., leaflet, imitation alligator leather binding, supplement to New York Ledger, January 11, 1890. 1st ed. Worn at folds, $30.

WHITTIER, John Greenleaf. *Mogg Megone, a Poem.* Clothbound. Boston, 1836. 1st ed. In half morocco slipcase, $75. Another, covers stained, $25 (at auction).

WHITTIER, John Greenleaf. *Moll Pitcher.* Paperbound. Boston, 1832. 1st ed. $500. Another, rebound in cloth, title page repaired, $100 (1960 auction).

WHITTIER, John Greenleaf and others. *Poems of the "Old South,"* etc. Boston, 1879. Signed by contributors. Mint, in dust jacket, $42.50.

WHITTIER, John Greenleaf. *Snow-Bound.* Green, blue, or terra cotta cloth. Boston, 1866. 1st ed., 1st issue, with last page of text numbered "52" below printer's slug. $200-$250. Also, $160 (1961 auction). Another, bookplate, $125. Another, spine chipped, $55 (at auction). Large paper ed., white cloth binding. One of 50. $70.

WHOLE Booke of Psalms (The). No place (Cambridge), 1640. (Translated by Richard Mather, John Eliot and Thomas Weld and printed by Stephen Daye.) $151,000 (auction price).

WHO'S Who In America. Clothbound. Chicago, 1899. 1st ed. $25.

WICKERSHAM, James. *Is it Mt. Tacoma or Rainier. What Do History and Tradition Say?* 16 pp., paperbound. Tacoma, 1893. $35.

WIELAND; or The Transformation. Leatherbound. New York, 1798. (By Charles Brockden Brown.) 1st ed. $120 and up. Also, $70 (1960 auction).

WIERZBICKI, F. P. *California As It Is and As It May Be.* Paperbound (?). San Francisco, 1849. 1st ed., 60 pp., errata leaf. Rebound in half morocco, edges trimmed, title page repaired, $5,750 (1966 auction). San Francisco, 1849. 2d ed., 76 pp., errata leaf. $1,000 and up. San Francisco, 1933. Grabhorn Press. $35-$50.

WILBARGER, J. W. *Indian Depredations in Texas.* 38 plates

(37 listed). Pictorial clothbound. Austin, 1899. 1st ed. $75. Rebound in new buckram, $65.

WILBUR, Homer (editor). *Meliboeus-Hipponax. The Biglow Papers.* Clothbound or boards. Cambridge, 1848. (By James Russell Lowell.) 1st ed. $50. Another, $37.50.

WILDE, Oscar. *The Fisherman and His Soul.* Boards. No place, no date (San Francisco, 1939). One of 200. Grabhorn Press. $50.

WILKES, Charles. *Synopsis of the Cruise of the U. S. Exploring Expedition During the Years 1835-42.* Folding map. 56 pp., paperbound. Washington, 1842. 1st ed. $100-$125. Also, $65 (at auction). Rebound in half morocco, $50.

WILKES, George. *The History of Oregon, Geographical and Political.* Folding map. Half leather and boards. New York, 1845. 1st ed. $500-$750. Also, $300, $375, and $450 at auction in 1959-1964 period. Earlier catalogue prices, $450 and $475.

WILKINSON, James. *Memoirs of My Own Times.* 9 folding tables, 3 folding facsimiles. 3 vols., boards and half calf. Philadelphia, 1816. 1st ed. $135. Worn, $65 and $75. Atlas (to accompany the *Memoirs,* but sold separately). Philadelphia, 1816. 8 pp., boards, with 19 maps and plans. $40-$50. Worn, $30.

WILLCOX, R. N. *Reminiscences of California Life.* Clothbound. Avery, Ohio, 1897. 1st ed. $37.50 and $45.

WILLIAMS, Mrs. Ellen. *Three Years and a Half in the Army, etc.* New York, no date (1885). 1st ed. $60. Another, $45. Another, worn, $30.

WILLIAMS, Jesse. *A Description of the United States Lands of Iowa.* Folding map in color. Boards. New York, 1840. 1st ed. $200. Also, $170 (1966 auction). Another, lacking map, $67.50.

WILLIAMS, John. *The Redeemed Captive, Returning to Zion.* 104 pp., calfbound. Boston, 1707. 1st ed. $10,000 (1967 auction). 6 perfect copies known. Boston, 1795. "6th ed." Boards. With title inked in on cover, $32.50. (See *REDEEMED Captive.*)

WILLIAMS, John G. *The Adventures of a Seventeen-Year-Old Lad, etc.* Boston, 1894. 1st ed. $35 and $25.

WILLIAMS, John Lee. *The Territory of Florida.* Folding map, portrait, 2 plates. Clothbound. New York, 1837. 1st ed. $100-

$125. Another, $75 (worn). Also, at auction, $90 (1967) and $84 (1960). New York, 1839. $45.

WILLIAMS, John Lee. *A View of West Florida.* Folding map. Boards and leather. Philadelphia, 1827. 1st ed. $100-$150. Another, $85 (worn). Also, $100 (1967 auction). Another, lacking the map, $20 at auction.

WILLIAMS, John R. *Biographical Sketch of the Life of William G. Greene, of Menard County, Ill.* No place, 1874. $35.

WILLIAMS, Tennessee. *One Arm and Other Stories.* Boards, vellum spine. No place, no date (Norfolk, Conn., 1948). 1st ed. One of 50, signed, boxed. $150-$200. Also, at auction, $120 (1963) and $70 (1963).

WILLIAMS, Thomas J. C. *A History of Washington County* (Maryland). 2 vols. No place (Hagerstown), 1906. 1st ed. $50.

WILLIS, Byrd C. and Richard H. Willis. *A Sketch of the Willis Family of Virginia, etc.* Richmond, no date (1898). $27.50.

WILSON, Elijah N. *Among the Shoshones.* 8 plates. Clothbound. Salt Lake, 1910. 1st ed., 222 pp. (suppressed ed.). $75-$100. 2d ed., same place and date, 247 pp. $50 and $75.

WILSON, Woodrow. *Goerge Washington.* Clothbound. New York, 1897. 1st ed. $35-$50. Worn, $25.

WINSHIP, George Parker. *The First American Bible.* With leaf from John Eliot's Indian Bible. Clothbound. Boston, 1929. One of 157. Merrymount Press. $75 and $50.

WINSHIP, George Parker (editor). *The Journey of Francisco Vazquez de Coronado, 1540-1542.* Clothbound. San Francisco, 1933. One of 550. $75, $45, and $35.

WINTHROP, John. *A Journal of the Transactions and Occurrences in the Settlement of Massachusetts.* Leatherbound. Hartford, 1790. 1st ed. $65 and $40. Also, at auction, $32.50 (1960).

WISTAR, Casper. *A System of Anatomy for the Use of Students of Medicine.* 2 vols., boards. Philadelphia, 1811-1814. 1st ed. $75.

WISTAR, Isaac Jones. *Autobiography.* Folding map, portrait, plates. 2 vols., boards. Philadelphia, 1914. 1st ed. One of 250. $200-$250.

WISTER, Owen. *The Virginian.* Clothbound. New York, 1902. 1st ed. $75-$100. Signed, $80. Worn, $50. Also, at auction, $30 and $75.

WITHERS, Alexander S. *Chronicles of Border Warfare.* Leatherbound. Clarksburg, Va., 1831. 1st ed. $100-$150. Also, $85 (1964 auction) and $50 (1962 auction). Worn, $40, $50, $100. Rebound in modern cloth, $30 (at auction). Cincinnati, 1895. Clothbound. $25.

WITHERSPOON, John. *A Series of Letters on Education.* New York, 1797. 1st ed. Binding split and rubbed, $125.

WOLCOTT, Samuel. *Memorial of Henry Wolcott, and of Some of His Descendants.* New York, 1881. New cloth, $25.

WOLFE, Thomas. *Look Homeward, Angel.* Clothbound. New York, 1929. 1st ed., 1st issue, with seal of Scribner Press on copyright page. In first state dust jacket with Wolfe's picture on back, $125-$200. Also, at auction, $80, $110, and $125. In later dust jacket, $100-$150. In worn dust jacket, $75-$100. Others, lacking dust jacket, $50-$60. Worn copies, $25 and up.

WONDERFUL Discovery of a Hermit Who Lived Upwards of 200 Years. 12 pp. Springfield, 1786. (By John Buckland and John Fielding.) $87.50.

WONDERFUL Providence (A), In Many Incidents At Sea, etc. 24 pp., paperbound. *Buffalo,* 1848. $37.50.

WOOD, Arnold. *John Wood of Attercliffe, Yorkshire, England, and Falls, Bucks County, Pennsylvania, etc.* New York, 1903. One of 50. $32.50.

WOOD, William. *New England's Prospect, etc.* Boston, 1764. $25.

WOODS, George. *Governor's Message to the Legislative Assembly of the Territory of Utah.* 16 pp., sewed. Salt Lake, 1874. $35.

WOOTON, Dudley G. (editor). *A Comprehensive History of Texas, 1865 to 1897.* 23 plates. 2 vols., leatherbound. Dallas, 1898. 1st ed. $100-$150. Worn, $50. Also, $80 (1964 auction).

WRIGHT, Harold Bell. *The Shepherd of the Hills.* Clothbound. Chicago, 1897. 1st ed. Presentation issue, with leaf bearing Wright's signature and an inscription by the author on an end paper, $35.

WRIGHT, Robert M. *Dodge City, the Cowboy Capital.* Colored frontispiece, 40 plates. Clothbound. No place, no date (Wichita, 1913). 1st ed., 344 pp. $100. Also, $55 (1959 auction). 2d ed., same place and date, 342 pp., black and white portrait. $15-$25.

WRISTON, Jennie A. *A Pioneer's Odyssey.* No place (Menasha, Wis.), 1943. $25.

WYLIE, Elinor. *Nets to Catch the Wind.* Brown clothbound. New York, 1921. 1st ed., 1st printing, with no watermark in paper, $45.

YELLOW BIRD. The Life and Adventures of Joaquin Murieta. 91 pp., paperbound. San Francisco, 1854. (By John R. Ridge.) 1st ed. $10,000 at auction. (One of two or three known copies.)

YEMASSEE (The): A Romance of Carolina. 2 vols., clothbound, paper labels. New York, 1835. (By William Gilmore Simms.) 1st ed., 1st issue, with copyright notice pasted in in Vol. 1. $400-$600. Also, $525 (1960 auction). Other copies at auction: $190 (1964) and spines chipped, $230 (1960).

YOUNG, Ansel. *The Western Reserve Almanac for the Year 1844.* 32 pp., paperbound. Cleveland, no date (1843). $25.

YOUNG, Edward. *Resignation: In Two Parts.* 30 leaves. Worcester, Mass., 1799. 2d Worcester ed. Foxed, $25.

YOUNG, Frank C. *Across the Plains in '65.* Folding map. Clothbound. Denver, 1905. 1st ed. One of 200. $125.

YOUNG, John. *An Address to the Senior Class, Delivered at the Commencement in Centre College, September 22, 1831.* 15 pp., sewed. Danville, Ky., 1831. $25.

YOUNG, John R. *Memoirs.* 4 portraits. Clothbound. Salt Lake City, 1920. 1st ed. $75. Also, $55 (1960 auction).

ZUBLY, John J. *The Law of Liberty.* Boards. Philadelphia, 1775. 1st ed. $50-$75. Rebound in modern leather, $20 (auction price).

ZUCKER, E. *The Chinese Theatre.* Boston, 1925. Limited ed. $25.

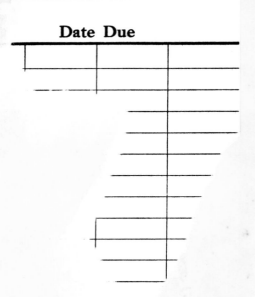

Date Due